**The Combat Chronicles of
George W. Smith**

The Siege at Hue

"Smith has put together a harrowing eyewitness account of the largest single engagement of the Vietnam War. Smith has written a disturbing and informative book that would be a welcome addition to any military library."
—*The Hartford Courant* (CT)

"Smith was present [at Hue] and provides a sense of intimate knowledge as he outlines the desperate nature of urban conflict. The dramatic presentation of the siege makes the book worthy."
—*Library Journal*

"A riveting, first-person account of the pivotal 25-day 1968 Battle of Hue."
—*The VVA Veteran*

"*The Siege at Hue* belongs in all Vietnam War collections."
—*Vietnam*

Carlson's Raid

A Military History Book-of-the-Month Club Selection

"Well-researched and objective."
—*World War II History*

"Gripping."
—*The Hartford Courant*

Books by George W. Smith

Carlson's Raid

The Do-or-Die Men

The Siege at Hue

THE
The 1st Marine Raider Battalion at Guadalcanal
DO-OR-DIE MEN

GEORGE W. SMITH

POCKET BOOKS

New York   London   Toronto   Sydney   Singapore

An *Original* Publication of POCKET BOOKS

 POCKET BOOKS, a division of Simon & Schuster, Inc.
1230 Avenue of the Americas, New York, NY 10020

ISBN: 0-7434-7005-2

First Pocket Books paperback edition September 2003

10   9   8   7   6   5   4   3   2   1

POCKET and colophon are registered trademarks of Simon & Schuster, Inc.

Cover design by Patrick Kang
Front cover photo by William C. Shrout/TimePix

Manufactured in the United States of America

For information regarding special discounts for bulk purchases, please contact Simon & Schuster Special Sales at 1-800-456-6798 or business@simonandschuster.com.

ACKNOWLEDGMENTS

Any attempt at constructing a faithful accounting of events some sixty years after the fact must of necessity rely heavily on the written and oral testimony of those who were there as well as the conclusions drawn by competent historians who have wrestled with the same subject over the years. Many of the books I consulted before attempting such a daunting challenge are listed in the Bibliography. There are some that deserve special recognition, however.

Richard B. Frank's classic *Guadalcanal* is probably the most thoroughly researched volume on the subject and generally recognized as the best. When other sources disagreed on the "facts" or the chronology, I usually went with Frank's accounting. There are two other books I found equally helpful, Richard Tregaskis' timeless *Guadalcanal Diary* and Jon Hoffman's excellent biography of Merritt Edson, *Once a Legend*. The former, written by a civilian, offered a brilliant first-person account of what it must have been like to participate in America's first offensive action of World War II and the latter contained the best summary of Merritt Edson's early life before he achieved widespread fame as leader of the 1st Marine Raider Battalion.

Other books that offered unique perspectives on the activities of the 1st Raiders in its first year of existence, and from which I quoted liberally, include Joe Alexander's *Edson's Raiders*, Alexander A. Vandegrift's *Once a Marine*, Merrill Twining's *No Bended Knee* and Samuel

B. Griffith's *The Battle for Guadalcanal*. All but Alexander had personal experiences on the ground during the Guadalcanal campaign.

Rather than bog the reader down with a flood of footnotes, which would only interfere with the flow of the story, most of the sources of the quoted material are identified within the text. Those not immediately identified either came from sources listed in the bibliography or came from the dozens of magazine and newspaper articles I consulted, to include the recollections of eyewitnesses that have been printed in publications like *Guadalcanal Echoes,* the 1st Raider Battalion's *Dope Sheet* or the Raider Association's *Raider Patch.* (See Notes.)

Other great sources include dispatches printed by the *New York Times* and the after-action reporting of the 1st Marine Division historian Lt. Herb Merillat.

At the outset, I want to express my appreciation for the cooperation of many surviving veterans, some of whom I had the pleasure of meeting at the Raider Reunion in Washington, D.C. in the summer of 2001.

I also want to give special thanks to veterans John Sweeney and Frank Guidone, who each provided me with a wealth of written and verbal information on the 1st Raiders. Each had a unique, personal perspective of his service with this historic outfit, Sweeney from the viewpoint of an officer and Guidone as an enlisted man. Though they had told their stories to many writers over the years, both men never wavered in their enthusiasm and encouragement. Neither would let me give up on this project.

It was my intention to write an easy-to-read history lesson of this unique unit that played such a prominent role in one of the most critical battles in the first few months of World War II. Like my previous book about the 2nd Raider Battalion (*Carlson's Raid*), I have tried to capture what it must have been like living through one of the darkest periods in American history and what it took to survive—and then triumph.

I've also attempted to keep this book simple and interesting so that it would appeal to both the military and nonmilitary reader. I've tried doubly hard to get the facts straight and the chronology correct. Any mistakes that may have been made in the process are entirely mine.

This book is certainly not a definitive account of the 1st Raider Battalion or of Merritt Edson or, for that matter, of the battle for Guadalcanal. It is, I hope, part of the whole story.

CONTENTS

INTRODUCTION

No campaign in World War II was undertaken with as many shortcomings as the invasion of Tulagi and Guadalcanal in the summer of 1942.

Rushed into action with a minimum of preparation, virtually no enemy intelligence, and using equipment left over from World War I, the grass-green infantrymen of the 1st Marine Division and its attached units were forced to endure almost four months of constant shelling, bombing and ground attacks before the issue of who would ultimately prevail—the Japanese or the Americans—was finally decided.

Conceived, planned, and launched on a crash basis, Operation Watchtower, as the Guadalcanal campaign was called, defied all the odds and somehow managed to succeed, beating the more experienced Japanese at their own game.

"One reason the struggles in the Pacific constantly teetered on the brink of disaster is that they were shoestring operations," wrote historian William Manchester, who was a twenty-year-old sergeant with the 5th Marines on Guadalcanal. "The Navy let the Marines on the Canal down because Washington was letting the Navy down, devoting nearly all its resources to Eisenhower's coming invasion of North Africa. We knew that our theater was a casualty of discrimination, not because Tokyo Rose told us—though she did, again and again—but because our own government, appealing to its national constituency, which was almost entirely comprised of former Europeans and their descendants, boasted of it."[1]

(Tokyo Rose was an American citizen of Japanese descent who broadcast Japanese propaganda to American troops in the Pacific. Following the war, she was tried for treason and served six years in prison. She received a Presidential pardon in 1977.)

These untested leathernecks learned on the job in one of the most inhospitable and unknown environments on the planet. "If Admiral [Richmond Kelly] Turner's task force had been embarked on a voyage to the moon, the junior officers and bluejackets would have been only a little more ignorant of their destination than they were of Guadalcanal,"[2] historian Samuel Eliot Morison wrote.

According to Frank, "no campaign in World War II saw such sustained violence in all three dimensions—sea, land, and air—where the issue hung in doubt so long.[3]

"Guadalcanal is not a name but an emotion," Morison wrote, "recalling desperate fights in the air, furious night naval battles, frantic work at supply or construction, savage fighting in the sodden jungle, nights broken by screaming bombs and deafening explosions of naval shells . . . It was a desperate campaign for control of an island that neither side really wanted, but which neither could afford to abandon to the enemy."

Morison, the preeminent historian of the campaign, believed that Japan's only interest in Guadalcanal was to protect the eastern flank of its advance on Port Moresby on New Guinea.

"The Allies reacted quickly, realizing that if they could not hold Guadalcanal they might never be able to climb the Solomons ladder to Rabaul," he wrote. "The Japanese strategists, notoriously inflexible, required almost a month to see the point. They continued to push the Port Moresby business, and reinforced their Guadalcanal garrison by driblets, hoping that a few hundred more troops and a few more air strikes and bombardment missions would wipe out the Marines. When they finally 'threw the book' at Guadalcanal, it was too late; if they had done so in August or the first week of September, they could hardly have failed to clean up."[4]

The Battle of Guadacanal was a wellspring of extraordinary acts of unit and individual heroism—on both sides. Heroism under fire was the order of the day, every day, from the landings on August 7 until the island was officially declared secure six months later.

There is no doubt that the speed of America's decision to assault Guadalcanal only two months after the victory at Midway caught the Japanese by surprise. It is also quite probable that the enemy just might have overextended themselves and were vulnerable to a quick, decisive strike at their flank. The surprise of the assault gave the Marines just enough time to consolidate and expand their toehold around Henderson Field before the Japanese could react.

Fortunately for the Marines, the Japanese, who had much more combat experience and far better equipment, failed to develop a sound battle plan to retake the airfield. They adhered to a fatal policy of piecemeal commitment, consistently underestimating Marine strength and their capacity to fight. And, they did a poor job of understanding the logistics necessary to support their own soldiers once ashore. After each defeat, the Japanese fell back into the jungle, often with no food, water, medicine, or weapons. They quickly came up with a new name for Guadalcanal. They called it "Starvation Island."

Japanese General Kiyotake Kawaguchi put it even better when he wrote in his memoirs that "Guadalcanal is no longer merely a name of an island in Japanese military history. It is the name of the graveyard of the Japanese Army."[5]

"Many of the Japanese soldiers and officers believed their own propaganda—that Americans were unable to bear hardship and worshiped only material luxuries which could be seen in American movies," wrote William H. Whyte, an intelligence officer with the 1st Marines. "American tactics, their manuals explained, disdained the spiritual element exemplified by Japanese doctrine and relied on material to carry the day. The Yankees, they believed, feared cold steel. Americans themselves, it needs to be said, worried if their own fighting men would be a match for these proud and fanatical warriors from Japan. Guadalcanal would change that.

"By all accounts, Japanese soldiers were supposed to be brilliant tacticians, merciless night fighters, capable sharpshooters. Guadalcanal would change that too. They were, we would find, none of these things. They attacked foolishly, closely bunched together, making themselves bull's-eyes for our own sharpshooters. They frequently got lost at night and had a terrible time coordinating night attacks . . . When things went right, they frequently failed to follow up their successes, losing the advantage time and time again. And when things went wrong, as they frequently did, their commanding officers, in the best Bushido warrior tradition, would commit suicide."[6]

Much of the credit for the American victory belongs to Maj. Gen. Alexander A. Vandegrift, the commander of the 1st Marine Division. Vandegrift, who would earn the Congressional Medal of Honor for his leadership, and his staff always managed to stay one step ahead of the Japanese, thwarting every attempt to recapture Henderson Field during the first three months of the campaign. He had just enough confidence to win the day.

"I knew only too well that if someone at Marine Corps Schools had answered a problem of this nature with the forces now at my disposal he would have failed the course," he wrote shortly after landing. "We didn't have much of anything, we didn't know what we were going to hit, but we did know enough, in my opinion, to justify what military writers like to call 'a calculated risk.' "[7]

Even when the issue was in serious doubt—and that was the case several times—Vandegrift, like the Marines under him, stood resolute. Guadalcanal, he told his deputies, would not become another Wake Island or Bataan.

America's greatest asset during these dark opening days of the war in the Pacific was the individual courage of its Marines, sailors and airmen, who, despite inferior equipment and constant harassment, met every challenge the Japanese threw at them. For the most part, they were just kids with the cocky swagger of youth. They had nicknames like "Black Jack," "Red," "Tex," and "Spike." Volunteers all, they had a toughness beyond their years.

The price of victory did not come cheap. The fierce fighting left thousands of corpses littering the jungle, while the waters around Guadalcanal claimed fliers by the hundreds and sailors by the thousands. The twenty-mile strait between Tulagi and Guadalcanal became a watery graveyard for some forty U.S. and Japanese ships and hundreds of aircraft from both sides. Called Sealark Channel, it took only a few days to earn the nickname of "Ironbottom Sound."

Best estimates put American casualties at 7,100 killed (1,207 Marines, 562 Army troops, 4,911 Naval personnel and 420 airmen).[8] It is believed that more than 30,000 Japanese soldiers, sailors and airmen perished during the battle, the majority from disease and famine.

The American triumph at Guadalcanal was the literal turning point of the war in the Pacific. While the sea and air victory at Midway in early June of 1942 stopped Japanese expansion in the central Pacific, the defeat at Guadalcanal redirected Japan's strategic initiatives from the offensive to the defensive. It also relieved the threat the Japanese posed to Australia, New Zealand and other islands in the South Pacific.

Sixteen Medals of Honor were awarded for bravery during the Guadalcanal campaign, four to Navy personnel, one to a Coast Guardsman, five to pilots and six to Marines on the ground. A total of 166 Navy Crosses were awarded. Many of these recipients were recommended for the Medal of Honor.

No outfit was more heroic than the 1st Marine Raider Battalion. No individual was more courageous than its commander, Col. Merritt A. Edson. Edson and his beaten-down composite battalion of just over 800 men won everlasting glory during the nights of September 12 and September 13, beating back a force of about 2,500 Japanese infantrymen on a ridge a mile south of Henderson Field to keep the enemy from overrunning the airfield and retaking Guadalcanal. Though there were other battles of equal fury on Guadalcanal, the victory at "Bloody Ridge," later renamed "Edson's Ridge," gave the Marines the confidence and breathing room they needed to hang on to this critical piece of terrain.

Of all the many dark days early in the fighting at Guadalcanal, the period just before the desperate two-day battle of "Edson's Ridge" in mid-September may have been the darkest. Many years later, it moved historian Matthew Stevenson to write that "if Guadalcanal was Gettysburg in the Pacific, this was Little Round Top."[9]

Lady Luck shined on the Raiders several times during

their ten weeks of action, first at Tulagi, where they were the first offensive unit to kill and be killed in the Pacific war, and then at Guadalcanal, where they became the 1st Marine Division's "fire brigade." Vandegrift came to call the Raiders his "do-or-die" men.

Several times fate interceded to spare the Raiders from disaster. When ships finally arrived to take them off Guadalcanal on October 13, less than half of the original force of 875 men were still on the island. Many of the survivors, weakened by malaria and other tropical illnesses, had to be assisted in boarding the transports. The rest of the battalion had either been killed or previously evacuated with wounds or debilitating diseases.

In ten weeks of almost continuous action, this small group of brave Marines had earned two Congressional Medals of Honor and 37 Navy Crosses. Another dozen Navy corpsmen and two Navy doctors assigned to the Raiders would also receive the Navy Cross during this period.

Heroes all, this book is dedicated to these steadfast Marines of the 1st Raider Battalion.

THE DO-OR-DIE MEN

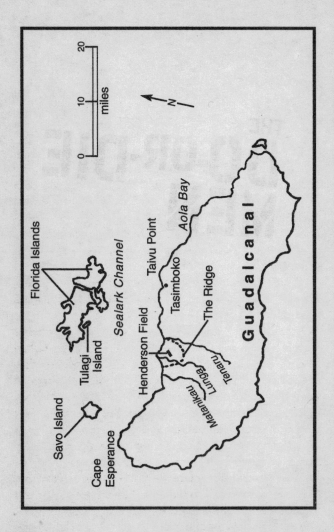

1

Background

When Adm. Chester W. Nimitz assumed command of the Pacific Fleet on December 31, 1941, a little more than three weeks after the disaster at Pearl Harbor, his orders from his boss, Adm. Ernest J. King, were to cover and hold the Hawaii-Midway line, maintain communications with the West Coast and try to protect the sea lanes to Australia.

There was no talk of any offensive action. That probably wouldn't happen until at least January of 1943, Nimitz was told.

America's first offensive priority would be directed at stopping Germany. President Franklin D. Roosevelt had reached an agreement with British Prime Minister Winston Churchill that the defeat of Adolf Hitler's regime was paramount to democracy's survival. Having overrun much of Europe, the Germans seemed poised to overwhelm England and Russia and move into the oil-rich Middle East. America had decided that every ship, every bomb, every ounce of war material and every unit not urgently needed elsewhere would go toward bolstering the Soviet armies and to build up Allied forces in Britain for a possible assault on continental Europe late in 1942. The Pacific would have to wait.

Admiral King, who was possessed with a ruthless determination, had no intention of sitting and watching Japan's aggressions go unchecked in the Pacific. He would not be a party to any "holding action." Just a year short of mandatory retirement in 1942, King had served his country well for forty-one years. He was a legendary figure in the Navy both on and off duty. Intelligent and dedicated, King was a visible and colorful force in the politically charged arena of Washington politics. Asked how he got his appointment as Commander in Chief of the Navy, one of his aides told a reporter: "Well, I guess when the going gets tough, they send for the sons of bitches."[1]

King was a hard-driving taskmaster who once told a subordinate: "You ought to be very suspicious of anyone who won't take a drink or doesn't like women." King, the father of seven, was deficient in neither category.[2]

"He's so tough he shaves with a blowtorch," President Roosevelt said of his Navy chief more than once.[3]

King knew very well he had to keep his fiery temper under control. To object too strongly could cost him his career. So, he gave lip service to the "Europe first" strategy and bit his tongue while working tirelessly behind the scenes, lobbying anyone who would listen for men and equipment to slow down the Japanese expansion.

Token naval forces were sent to such backwater Pacific outposts as Canton Island and Christmas Island south of Hawaii and Samoa, Fiji and New Caledonia to the southwest. This last island, a French possession, was to be the principal advance base in the South Pacific. It had a great harbor near its capital city of Noumea.

The Japanese had established a similar ring of bases during their expansion after the outbreak of war. The most formidable base in the southwestern Pacific was at Rabaul on the island of New Britain. To the north was the bastion of Truk, Japan's equivalent to Pearl Harbor. Both had excellent harbors and adjacent airfields.

The Japanese advances had caused serious alarm in Australia where they were woefully unprepared for war. Four of the country's best divisions were deployed elsewhere, three in the Middle East and one in Malaya, all fighting under British control. Australian Prime Minister John Curtin demanded the return of at least two divisions from the Middle East to defend their homeland.

To insure allied harmony, Roosevelt decided on February 15, 1942 that the United States would assume responsibility for the defense of both Australia and New Zealand, promising to send two Army divisions (41st and 32nd) to the former and another (37th) to the latter. Admiral King also convinced FDR to send the carrier *Lexington* and its supporting ships to the South Pacific under the command of Rear Adm. Herbert Leary.[4]

Admiral King had a powerful ally in his quest to strike back at the Japanese. The American people were still seething with anger over the unprovoked attack at Pearl Harbor and they wanted revenge. Roosevelt, one of the most astute politicians in American history, knew he had to listen to the people. He loathed the Japanese for their treachery at Pearl Harbor. Nobody wanted payback more than he did.

With Roosevelt's tacit approval, King moved aggressively to set up a line of bases in the South Pacific from which he could initiate future advances through the New Hebrides, Solomons and Bismarck Archipelago. Orders were given to Nimitz to formulate operational plans to assume the offensive against Japan. King made it clear, no matter what the consequences, that he absolutely refused to sit back and do nothing to counter Japanese aggression.

At a meeting of the Joint Chiefs of Staff on March 5, one chaired by Roosevelt, King again lobbied hard for offensive action in the Pacific. He reiterated his intentions of holding Hawaii and supporting Australia but he also offered a plan to drive northward from the New Hebrides to take the fight to the Japanese. FDR listened intently. King could tell by the end of the meeting that he had completely won over the commander in chief.

Army Chief of Staff George Marshall and Secretary of War Henry L. Stimson continued to argue for a commitment to an early attack in Europe from England but the strength of their convictions began to wane. The fact that King was outnumbered didn't seem to faze him. On the contrary, the challenge seemed to embolden him. He told Marshall and Stimson he refused to remain on the defensive in the Pacific and if necessary he was prepared to use only Navy and Marine Corps forces for the job.

By mid-March, King had proposed that a series of "strong points" be established in the South Pacific, as a prelude to a step-by-step advance up the Solomon Islands. King did not yet realize it but his finger was pointing at Guadalcanal as the first step.

The bad news in the Pacific reached its nadir on April 9 when word of the surrender of Bataan in the Philippines was announced. Some 76,000 Filipinos and Americans were taken prisoner in the largest capitulation of military forces in the nation's history. The news cast a gloom over the entire country.

Nine days later came the first good news from the Pacific when word was flashed that American aircraft had bombed Japan. Lt. Col. Jimmy Doolittle, an Army pilot, led a flight of sixteen B-25s off the deck of the USS *Hornet* on a daylight bombing raid and then flew off to airfields in China. Thirteen of the planes, each carrying four five-hundred-pound bombs, made runs over Tokyo while the other three, armed with incendiary bombs, flew over Kobe, Nagoya and Osaka.

The raid had Roosevelt's fingerprints all over it. He had been lobbying for some kind of retaliatory action ever since Pearl Harbor.

The raid turned out to be more symbolic than destructive, but the psychological harm to Japan was enormous. It proved to the world that the Japanese homeland was not invulnerable and forced the enemy to divert more of its military resources to the home islands to ensure it wouldn't happen again.

The Doolittle Raid had been a risky venture right from the beginning. It was supposed to be a night raid and all planes were scheduled to land at predetermined airfields deep in China behind Japanese lines. The carrier task force under Adm. Bill Halsey had been spotted some seven hundred miles east of Japan and had been forced to take off early, which put them over their targets about noon. Amazingly, none of the planes were shot down over Japan.

Flying on to China and running low on fuel, the task force ran into a heavy rain squall just as night fell. Eleven of the sixteen crews had to bail out, another four crash-landed, and the remaining crew became disoriented and wound up landing in Russian-held territory near Vladivostok. Two of the crews (a total of eight men) were captured when they were forced to crash-land or bail out over China.

All but nine of the eighty aviators on the raid survived. Four drowned and another was killed in a parachute mishap. Of the eight crewmen captured in China, three were executed by a Japanese firing squad after a sham war-crimes trial and another died in captivity. The executions of the airmen, who were accused of intentionally shooting up a schoolyard, infuriated Americans, who had another rallying cry to go along with "Remember Pearl Harbor" and "Remember Wake Island."

The Japanese, who were unable to determine the size or direction of the attack, were humiliated. Adm. Isoroku Yamamoto was left with the embarrassing chore of explaining what happened to the Emperor and then promising that it would never happen again.

"Even though there wasn't much damage, it's a disgrace that the skies over the imperial capital should have been defiled without a single enemy plane shot down," Yamamoto wrote. "It provides a regrettably graphic illustration of the saying that a bungling attack is better than the most skillful defense."[5]

Roosevelt was delighted with the bombing raid. When asked by the media where the planes had come from, Roosevelt smiled broadly, leaned back in his chair in the oval office and said, "They came from a secret base in Shangri-La," referring to the mythical land in James Hilton's *Lost Horizon*.[6]

A month later in a White House ceremony, Roosevelt presented the Congressional Medal of Honor to a reluctant Doolittle, who had been promoted two ranks to brigadier general. Doolittle felt he had done nothing more than anyone else in the squadron and thus did not deserve to be singled out for such an individual honor.

Doolittle's raid turned out to be more than just a psychological success. It altered the course of the war in the Pacific and helped hasten Japan's capitulation. Within days, Yamamoto, who had promised his Emperor he would defend the homeland, convinced the military leaders to delay planned thrusts southward to capture Samoa, Fiji and New Caledonia, which would have cut off the shipping lanes between the United States and Australia, and concentrate on a strike eastward against Midway in the central Pacific. The Americans, he told the militarists, must not be allowed to hold any territory from which they could ever again launch more air attacks on the Japanese homeland.

Japan's military leaders, deeply embarrassed by the Doolittle Raid, quickly approved Yamamoto's eastward plan of attack and set the date for the first week in June.

America's resounding triumph at Midway, which included the sinking of four enemy carriers and the loss of hundreds of experienced flyers, would be the beginning of the end for the Japanese military machine.

Gen. Douglas MacArthur, who had escaped to Australia from the Philippines in March, had been named Supreme Commander of allied forces in the Southwest Pacific area, which encompassed Australia, New Zealand, New Guinea, the Solomons, the Bismarcks and the Philippines. Admiral Nimitz was commander in chief of everything else in the Pacific that was not under MacArthur's domain.

MacArthur, who was just as outspoken as King, made it known that his first priority was the capture of the huge Japanese air and naval base at Rabaul on New Britain Island and that his ultimate goal was a return to the Philippines. Nimitz did not agree, proposing instead a series of hit-and-run raids against Tulagi and other island bases in the Solomons.

Both camps wrestled with the thorny issue of command throughout the spring of 1942. The imperious MacArthur took umbrage that Nimitz would suggest an action in his sphere of influence. King moved swiftly to defuse this bone of contention, shifting the area boundary one degree to the west, giving Nimitz control over the lower Solomons, which included Tulagi and Guadalcanal.

King overruled Nimitz's choice of Adm. William Pye as his South Pacific commander, choosing the aloof Vice Adm. Robert L. Ghormley, who was then the American

naval observer in London. Pye had been interim Pacific
Fleet commander after Adm. Husband Kimmel was
sacked following the Pearl Harbor disaster and it was his
order that recalled the Wake Island relief mission on December 23. King, and other members of the Joint Chiefs of
Staff, couldn't forgive Pye's action to call off the rescue
effort, though many historians believe he made the right
decision.

Ghormley's primary asset was his diplomatic experience.
He was suave, gentle, patient and tactful, qualities he displayed during his two-year appointment to England. He,
like everyone else in the Navy Department, was almost
completely ignorant of the South Pacific and the intentions
of the Japanese in the area. His elevation to a wartime post
in the Pacific proved to be a disappointing one.

"I do not have the tools to give you to carry out that
task as it should be," King told Ghormley prior to the
latter's arrival in Auckland in mid-May. "In time, possibly
this fall, we hope to start an offensive from the South
Pacific."[7]

Ghormley had been handed the most critical job in the
fleet, one that would come to a boil much quicker than
anybody could imagine.

Meanwhile, the American Navy had just survived its first
big clash with the Japanese in what was to be called the
Battle of the Coral Sea on May 7–8. Tactically, the clash
was a stand-off but strategically, it was an American victory because it stopped a planned Japanese invasion of
Port Moresby. The Americans lost the carrier *Lexington*
in the battle and suffered heavy damage to the *Yorktown,*
which was quickly repaired to fight again four weeks later.

The Japanese lost a light carrier and suffered heavy
battle damage to another. More importantly, American

pilots shot down nearly half the carrier-based aircraft employed in the battle, taking with them their irreplaceable pilots.

A few weeks later, Nimitz, under constant prodding from King for some offensive action, proposed a quick strike on Tulagi, a small island off the coast of Florida Island and only twenty miles across the sea from Guadalcanal, by the 1st Marine Raider Battalion, which had recently arrived at Samoa. Tulagi, which was considered the best harbor in the Solomon Islands, had good deep-water ports and a seaplane base. The operation was quickly called off, however, because there weren't enough available forces to hold the island once taken. Planning continued for something more substantial but Tulagi was kept on the back burner.

King became energized again after the American victory at Midway in early June. He reasoned that the United States should seize the initiative with an attack in the Solomons by August 1. But the plan became mired in politics. General Marshall wanted General MacArthur to command the proposed offensive but King was adamant that the Navy should control the operation. King wired Nimitz in Hawaii in late June to prepare a battle plan on the assumption that only Navy and Marine units would be available.

MacArthur had no intention of letting the Navy take control. It was left to General Marshall to act as a mediator between the Navy and Army. Marshall offered a three-part operation designed to assuage MacArthur's objection over control. D-day would be August 1.

Task one would be the seizure of Tulagi and the Santa Cruz Islands under Navy control. The latter target was chosen because it had a good airfield site at Ndeni. Task two would be the capture of Lae, Salamaua and the northeast coast of New Guinea and task three would be the attack on Rabaul and adjacent positions in the New Britain–New Ireland area. MacArthur would be in control of the latter two operations.

On June 26, barely twelve days after the arrival of the 5th Marines of the 1st Marine Division in Wellington, New Zealand, Maj. Gen. Alexander A. Vandegrift and members of his staff were summoned to a meeting with Admiral Ghormley in Auckland. Vandegrift had no idea what was coming.

"Vandegrift, I have some very disconcerting news," Ghormley announced in a brusque manner immediately after the two had shaken hands.

"I'm sorry to hear that, admiral," Vandergrift answered.

"You will be more sorry when you read this," Ghormley said, handing him a top-secret dispatch from Washington.

"I pulled a chair up to his desk to concentrate on the document. It directed Ghormley to confer with MacArthur concerning an amphibious operation . . . and we were to land on August 1—less than five weeks away.

"I couldn't believe it."[8]

It was an "alert order" for an operation against Tulagi and "adjacent positions" and Ndeni in the nearby Santa Cruz Islands. Vandegrift would have operational control of the 5th Marines, the 1st Marines, which would arrive in New Zealand in two weeks, the 3rd Defense Battalion, currently in Hawaii, the understrength 1st Parachute Battalion and the 1st Raider Battalion, which had been training in Samoa for two months. To replace his 7th Marines, which were also garrisoned at Samoa, Vandegrift would be given one battalion of the 2nd Marines of the 2nd Marine Division, which had just left San Diego. The other two battalions of the 2nd Marines, however, would

be under the direct control of the amphibious commander, Rear Adm. Richmond Kelly Turner, who apparently had plans to use them in a separate operation.

Vandegrift was stunned. He was under the impression
that his division, much of it still en route to the South
Pacific, would not have to go into action until January 1,
1943. He was told that by the Marine Commandant, Maj.
Gen. Thomas Holcomb, who passed this information on
to him through Admiral King.

After Vandegrift had digested the message, Ghormley
asked him for his opinion.

"I knew only that my division was spread over hell's
half-acre, one-third in Samoa, one-third in New Zealand
and one-third still at sea," Vandegrift would write. "My
equipment, much of it new, had to be broken in; my supply had to be sorted and combat-packaged; shortages had
to be determined and filled."

After explaining all this to Ghormley, Vandegrift paused
to gather his composure and said: "I just don't see how we
can land anywhere by August first."

Ghormley nodded in agreement and said: "I don't see
how we can land at all, and I am going to take it up with
MacArthur. Meanwhile we'll have to go ahead as best
we can."[9]

Vandegrift saluted and left the conference to meet
with his staff.

"In addition to being totally unrealistic, the plan was
'Blue Water Navy' circa 1907 from start to finish with little or nothing in the way of specific reference to the role
of air power," Merrill B. Twining, an assistant operations
officer on Vandegrift's staff, later wrote. "Guadalcanal was
not even mentioned. There was a reference to adjacent
islands, obviously inclusive of the group of minor islets
close to Tulagi, such as Gavutu and Tanambogo. It most

certainly did not include the major island of Guadalcanal, some twenty miles to the south of Tulagi. Guadalcanal—ninety miles long and twenty-five miles wide—possessed the only extensive terrain in the area suitable for developing a major air base—an unsinkable aircraft carrier. Therefore, it was the strategic jewel in the Solomon Islands necklace. The Japanese, apparently aware of this, were believed to be constructing a fighter strip there."[10]

Assuming that these widely scattered units could be assembled in time, they still would be totally untrained in division-level tactics. Furthermore, most of the troops would have been at sea for several weeks and their physical conditioning would be less than optimum.

The 1st Marine Division was plainly not ready to go into combat especially without its best regiment. The 7th Marines, a force of some 3,200 men, was in Samoa, having been detached from the division since April. The unit had been stocked with the best personnel in the division and rushed to the South Pacific as a reaction force, only to sit around while the rest of the division was heading off to war.

The 5th Marines, which had been picked over to form the 1st Raider Battalion and to fill out the 7th Marines, arrived in Wellington, New Zealand with Vandegrift and his advance party on June 14. The 1st Marines, which had a strong leadership corps but was basically made up of new recruits, were scheduled to arrive in Wellington in early July. Replacing the 7th Marines would be the 2nd Marines of the 2nd Division, which Vandegrift had never seen before. Also under Vandegrift's command were three battalions of the division's artillery unit, the 11th Marines.

The division was far short of being in a satisfactory state of readiness for combat. The vast majority of the ranks were recent enlistees—Pearl Harbor Avengers. Many were in their teens but they were fit and willing. On the other hand, however, most of the NCOs and officers were crusty veterans, who gave the division its moniker as "The Old Breed."

The old salts and China hands, especially the seasoned gunnery sergeants—the "schoolmarms of the Marines"— had the tough job of turning civilians into killers and not much time to do it. What a colorful bunch they were, too.

"There were professional privates who had spent as much time in the brig as in the barracks," wrote historian Robert Leckie. "Gamblers, drinkers and connivers, brawlers in starched, creased khaki and natty 'pisscutter' caps, they fought sailors and soldiers of every nationality in every bar from Brooklyn to Bangkok; blasphemous and profane with a fine fluency that would astound a London cockney, they were nevertheless dedicated soldiers who knew their hard calling in every detail from stripping a machine gun blindfold to tying a tourniquet with their teeth. They were tough and they knew it, and they exulted in that knowledge."[11]

Vandegrift had no choice on when his division would be deployed. Time had run out. He absorbed the bitter news from Ghormley almost without comment, saluted and went about obeying his orders. Vandegrift's operations officer, Lt. Col. Gerald Thomas, asked why the 2nd Marines couldn't replace the 7th Marines at Samoa so that the 1st Division could go into battle with its best regiment. Ghormley had no answer, but said he would ask. Apparently Turner, who continued to act like a ground commander rather than an admiral, had plans to use the 7th in another operation at Ndeni in the Santa Cruz Islands, a plan that was quickly shelved. He would later propose forming his own Raider Battalion and also using the 7th Marines in a bizarre plan to establish scattered enclaves along the northern coast of Guadalcanal. He would be quickly disavowed of this latter plan when it was pointed out to him that there was no point in establishing other perimeters if the first could not be held.

Though secrecy was stressed, news of the impending operation spread quickly. A local newspaper in Wellington printed a story announcing the arrival of "a completely equipped expeditionary force of American Marines" and then conjectured that a force such as this is "not usually sent to bases where action is not expected." One of the headlines read: "Americans to Attack Tulagi."

As far as the Marines could see, the whole world knew where they were going to hit. It wasn't a very reassuring situation.

Overall tactical command of the operation, dubbed "Watchtower," was given to Rear Adm. Frank Jack Fletcher, who had won a Medal of Honor at Vera Cruz in 1916. He would be promoted to vice admiral on July 15. Fletcher had recently gained a reputation as an overly cautious officer, one who was predisposed to "play it safe." This hesitancy to close with and engage the enemy was undoubtedly caused by his losing the carrier *Lexington* at Coral Sea and the *Yorktown* at Midway.

Fletcher had also been in command of a third carrier, the *Saratoga,* during its failed attempt to rescue the Wake Island garrison back on December 23. Some in the Navy, particularly the aircraft pilots, believed he had failed to try hard enough at Wake, ordering his ships to refuel rather than make a quick run to the island. When ordered to call off that mission he quickly obeyed, reportedly throwing his cap to the deck in disgust.

"Marines blamed him for failing to relieve Wake Island,"

General Thomas told his biographer, Alan Millett. "Critics then and now thought that he would rather fuel than fight, a reference to his uncanny ability to avoid contact."[12]

Only fifty-seven, Fletcher was clearly showing signs of strain and battle fatigue.

Fletcher would have three carriers at his disposal for "Operation Watchtower"—*Enterprise, Saratoga* and *Wasp.*

The choice of Turner, who was brought in at the eleventh hour, to command the amphibious force was a good one. He was as audacious as Fletcher was cautious. Also fifty-seven, Turner had done much of the planning for "Watchtower." He was highly intelligent, and his wire-rimmed glasses and beetle brows gave him the look of a college professor. A man of "corrosive ambition," he was a tireless worker with little patience for those who couldn't keep up. He was often arrogant and sometimes difficult to get along with, and he had a furious Irish temper and a biting tongue, one that was as caustic as a shaving stick. Turner was known to some as the "Patton of the Navy" or "Terrible Turner." In many respects, he was just like King, a man who commanded little affection but much respect.

Second in command to Turner was Rear Adm. Victor Alexander Charles Crutchley of the Royal Navy. He would have tactical command of the destroyers and cruisers that had the job of protecting Turner's troop transports. Crutchley had not wanted the job believing that it was more appropriate for an American flag officer. Turner rejected any such suggestion.

Crutchley, fifty-one, was a tall man with a bushy red beard and mustache that hid a battle scar he received in World War I where he earned the Victoria Cross in a night action. Australian sailors called him "Old Goat's Whiskers."

Vandegrift, fifty-five, had assumed command of the 1st Marine Division in March. A quiet, unassuming man, he was a protégé of the legendary Gen. Smedley Butler, known as "Old Gimlet Eye" to his contemporaries. Butler was a man who had won two Medals of Honor, the first at Vera Cruz in 1914 and the second in Haiti the following year. Like his mentor, Vandegrift was a superb judge of men. Just under 5-foot-9, Vandegrift had been the quarterback of his high school football team in Charlottesville, Va. He had a sturdy build, a hard jaw and a large dimple in his chin.

His grandfather, Carson Vandegrift, fought as a soldier in the Monticello Guards in the Civil War and was wounded at Antietam and in Pickett's Charge at Gettysburg. He was also at Appomattox when General Lee surrendered. A deacon of the local Baptist church, the elder Vandegrift would pray to "the God of Abraham, Isaac, Jacob, Robert E. Lee and Stonewall Jackson." He dominated the family, instilling in his admiring grandson a firm resolve to make the military his career.[13]

Asked to explain later in his career why he admired Jackson so, Vandegrift replied: "Because he could do so much with so little." It was a quality that he would acquire over the next several months.

A perpetual optimist, Vandegrift had been given the nickname of "Sunny Jim" by his mentor, General Butler, for the lighthearted way he obeyed an order. Vandegrift, called "Archer" by his friends, was an extremely courteous man with large blue eyes, rosy cheeks, thinning sandy hair and a long belligerent nose. He was also afflicted with a night blindness that would in his declining years lead to the loss of his eyesight. He spoke in a soft voice with a Virginia drawl and almost always referred to the enemy as Japanese. Rarely did he use the term Japs and he never referred to the enemy as Nips.

"Vandegrift was a classic Virginia gentleman," Twining wrote about his boss. "I have heard him harden his voice but I never heard him raise it—not even at me."

Vandegrift had little stomach for personal battles, preferring to let his two key staff members, Thomas and Twining, do all the dirty work needed to run a division.

Although Thomas and Twining occasionally disagreed they quickly became allied in the battle for the heart and mind of Vandegrift. They had no challengers in the command post but worried that when Vandegrift was out of their sight he might be influenced by one of his regimental commanders that might get some Marines killed.

By the end of September, Thomas would dominate not only the division staff but the entire division, according to his biographer, Alan Millett. "He did not seek power for its own sake," wrote Millett, "but he rose to this position because he believed the division had come to Guadalcanal to give the United States its first offensive victory over Japan. His sure-handed, clear-headed management of the defense made him second only to General Vandegrift as the architect of victory. To play this role, he not only outthought the Japanese commanders he faced but outmaneuvered some Marines as well, including Vandegrift himself."[14]

Vandegrift would come to rely greatly on his staff, trusting that their judgment would more than offset any doubts he may have had about his own capabilities. He said as much in a letter he mailed to his wife, Mildred, shortly after leaving the country.

"When you remember me in your prayers, as I know you will," he wrote, "ask that I be given the judgment and ability to lead this splendid outfit so that it will accomplish its task with the least possible loss."[15]

2

Cactus

Turner and Nimitz met with King in San Francisco on July 3 to firm up the opening phase of the Pacific offensive, which at that time included only Tulagi and the Santa Cruz Islands. Much of that changed two days later when it was discovered that the Japanese were stepping up construction of an airfield on Guadalcanal. Detailed intelligence gathered from aerial reconnaissance and coastwatcher Martin Clemens revealed that a twelve-ship Japanese convoy had docked at Lunga Point and had unloaded four heavy-duty tractors, six road rollers, two generators, an ice plant, two tiny locomotives and a dozen hopper cars. Also coming ashore were two construction battalions and 400 fighting troops to guard them.

Allied planners temporarily deleted the Santa Cruz Islands from the operation and substituted Guadalcanal, giving it the code name "Cactus." Also added were the twin islands of Gavutu-Tanamboko near Tulagi. Tulagi had been given the code-name "Ringbolt."

Vandegrift's primary mission was to capture the airfield on Guadalcanal and hold it until relieved by Army troops. Little did he know that it would take his Marines four months to complete the job before being relieved by the Army.

MacArthur and Ghormley had been quick to express pessimistic views of the entire operation from the beginning. They sent a message to the Joint Chiefs that they were "of the opinion, arrived at independently, and confirmed after discussion, that the initiation of the operation at this time, without a reasonable assurance of adequate air coverage, would be attended with the gravest risk."[1]

Each wanted a delay to give them time to beef up their own forces but the Joint Chiefs voted on July 10 to proceed in order "to stop without delay the enemy's southward advance." The Chiefs also noted in their decision that a quick action would take advantage of the loss of some 400 aircraft suffered by the Japanese at Coral Sea and Midway. The Japanese, the Chiefs also reasoned, were not expecting any significant counterattack by the Americans until 1943.

Vandegrift's staff was under no illusions. They immediately began calling Operation Watchtower "Operation Shoestring" among themselves.

Vandegrift sent his intelligence officers to find out all they could about Guadalcanal, a large, jungle-covered island in the southern Solomons. Ghormley vetoed a proposal to land a small reconnaissance force on Guadalcanal by submarine as too dangerous.

The Marines gathered what intelligence they could from outdated and incomplete maps and a single photo flight over the island in an Army B-17. The flight showed there were no beach defenses on the north coast in the Lunga Point area where the Japanese had begun construction of an airfield. Although MacArthur's intelligence section had completed a detailed photo-map of Guadalcanal three weeks earlier, it never became available to the Marine planners. In a colossal screwup, the maps were mailed by the Army to an improper address in Auckland where they languished for over a month.

The Solomon Islands stretch for 600 miles southeast

from New Guinea in a long volcanic and coral chain. A sixteenth-century Spanish explorer had come upon the chain while in search of King Solomon's storied realm of Ophir and had named one of the largest of the islands Wadi-en-Canar after a village in Spain. In time that name became Guadalcanal. The British established a protectorate over the southern islands, which included Guadalcanal, in 1893 and set up their administrative headquarters on the nearby island of Tulagi.

Tulagi, with its great harbor, had been the capital of the British Solomons, featuring a street of shops, a hotel, a wireless station and a number of bungalows built for the administrators. It also had a cricket field and a small pitch-and-putt golf course. There were no cars on the island. People walked everywhere and took a launch to nearby islands.

Guadalcanal, on the other hand, was called "a bloody, stinking hole" by the Australians, which was exactly what it was.[2] From the air the island, a mere twenty miles across Sealark Channel from Tulagi, looked like a green jewel set in a blue-green sea. From ground level, however, the island was a teeming mass of untamed jungles that were wet, unfriendly and unhealthful, offering no natural resources but mud, coconuts and malarial mosquitoes.

The Solomons are one of the world's wettest areas. Rainfall in some places exceeds 200 inches per year. During a twenty-year period before the war, annual rainfall at Tulagi averaged 164 inches. Temperatures range from 73 to 93 degrees Fahrenheit and humidity is high. Northwest monsoons bring almost daily rain during the wet season from November to March. The term "dry" is relative, for southeast trade winds bring frequent rains during the dry season.

No complete topographical map of the island existed

nor would one be available during the entire campaign. Vandegrift's intelligence officers came to believe the enemy garrison in the area to be about 8,400. The actual count was 3,457. Of that total, some 2,571 were stationed on Guadalcanal, mostly Korean laborers working on the airfield.[3] There were about 1,000 infantry-trained naval troops on Tulagi and the nearby seaplane base on the conjoined islands of Gavutu-Tanambogo.

Vandegrift's plan was to split his division into two task forces. He would take the 1st and 5th Marines, the latter minus one battalion, and a battalion of the 11th Marines, some 11,000 men in all, and land just to the east of Lunga Point on the north coast of Guadalcanal. Their mission would be to capture and hold the airfield. The second group, under the command of the assistant division commander, Brig. Gen. William B. Rupertus, consisted of about 6,000 men and included a battalion from the 5th Marines (2/5), the 1st Raider Battalion (875 men), 1st Parachute Battalion (about 375 men), with the 2nd Marines in reserve. This force would seize Tulagi and the twin islands of Gavutu-Tanambogo.

The Guadalcanal landing would be supported by aircraft from the *Saratoga* and planes from the *Wasp* were assigned to Tulagi. Aircraft from the *Enterpise* would provide cover for the three carriers and engage in patrol missions.

Once Tulagi and the landing field on Guadalcanal had been taken, the Expeditionary Force would occupy Ndeni, some 350 miles to the east. Engineers were to be ready to work on airfields on Guadalcanal and Ndeni immediately. Airfield construction material and troops would be sent forward as soon as possible. To free the Amphibious Force for further offensive action, occupation troops were to be dispatched to relieve the Marines.

Operation Plan No. 1-42 did not specifically designate the forces to effect the relief and occupation but stated that orders would be issued at a later date.

To expedite combat loading operations of the troop transports in New Zealand, the Marines would take only what they needed to actually live and fight. All excess clothing, bedding rolls and company property was stored until they returned. Most heavy vehicles, the entire twelve-gun 155-mm heavy artillery battalion and much of the ammunition had to be left behind.

The reloading of the ships in Wellington, New Zealand took place during weeks of heavy rain and with a lack of cooperation from the local dock workers. The local unions, believing that the longer the job took, the longer the pay lasted, proceeded at a snail's pace. They stopped for morning and afternoon tea, and if it rained, they didn't work at all. Vandegrift fired them, replacing them with Marines, who did not drink tea and who worked in shifts around the clock. When the Marines could get to town, some amused themselves by scrawling obscene references to New Zealand dock workers on the walls of hotel lavatories. "All wharfees is bastards" was one of the most restrained of the recorded graffiti.

The dock area became a quagmire as "drenched men wrestled with rain soaked cartons of clothing, food, medicines, cigarettes and chocolate bars. The cheap card board containers containing Navy rations and Marine Corps supplies disintegrated; one officer remembers walking a hundred yards through a swamp of sodden cornflakes dotted with mushed Hershey bars, smashed cigar boxes, odd shoes and stained, soggy bundles of socks. Lack of time, restricted port facilities, terrible weather, improper packaging, and uncooperative labor combined to create what Vandegrift described, in language notable for moderation, as 'an unparalleled logistical problem.' Others in less elegant terminology described the dock area as 'a mucked-up swamp.' "[4]

It soon became apparent that the timetable for an August 1 landing could not be met. The second echelon of the division, the 1st Marines, were late reaching New Zealand—they arrived on July 11—and the ships had to be unloaded and then combat-loaded in the order of their need in an assault landing. On July 18, Vandegrift met with Ghormley in Auckland and asked for a delay. King agreed to move the landing up to August 4 and then, after further protest, he made a final compromise to August 7. The date could not be postponed further lest the Japanese complete their airstrip for use against the Allied forces. As it was, there was no time to combat-load several of the ships.

This hybrid, half-trained and thoroughly scattered division finally got underway on July 22 and headed to the island of Koro in the Fiji Islands about 1,550 miles southeast of Guadalcanal for a series of rehearsals. The convoy, the largest armada in U.S. history up to that time, would eventually consist of 82 vessels—three carriers (*Enterprise, Saratoga, Wasp*), one battleship (*North Carolina*), 14 cruisers, 31 destroyers, 19 transports, five minesweepers, five fueling ships and four converted destroyer transport ships (APDs).

The armada consisted of virtually every ship type in the U.S. Navy. Men rushed topside from each ship, staring in awe at the might and power of this huge naval force.

Not everybody went to look at the fleet, however, as a good-sized gale kept many buttoned up, as General Vandegrift noted in a letter to his wife, dated July 24.

"Lord, what a day. Woke up this morning with everything on the deck sailing across the room and the doors banging. It seems we ran into a storm during the night and this ship has been literally rolling her decks under. There are quite a few seasick. To tell the truth, I'm not feeling too well myself, but have made all the meals."

A council of war was held aboard Fletcher's flagship, the carrier *Saratoga*, on July 26. All the major players were there, except Vice Admiral Ghormley, who sent his deputy, Rear Adm. Dan Callaghan. Ghormley later said that he "was desirous of attending this conference, but found it impossible to give the time necessary for travel with possible attendant delays." At the time, Ghormley was busy moving his headquarters from Auckland to Noumea on the island of New Caledonia.

It was "a critical error of judgment,"[5] according to historian Frank.

Ghormley would remain "out of the picture" for the entire operation. He would be referred to by some of his contemporaries in the coming weeks as "the traffic cop of the Southwest Pacific" and "Nimitz's errand boy."[6]

The gathering got off to a comedic start for Rear Adm. John S. McCain, the man who commanded all of Ghormley's aircraft in the South Pacific. As McCain was climbing up a Jacob's ladder to board the *Saratoga*, a garbage chute swung open on the carrier and showered the admiral with milk.

"(McCain) managed to retain his hold but a startled officer of the deck soon faced one mad little admiral," Vandegrift wrote.[7]

It was an ominous beginning to what would become a highly contentious meeting.

"The conference took place in the wardroom, a big, pleasant cabin with drapes and leather sofas where the ship's officers ate their meals and relaxed when off watch (and where courts-martial were held)," wrote historian

John Foster. "The conferees sat at a long table covered with green felt, Fletcher at the head, Turner on his right, Vandegrift on his left.

"A Marine in fresh khaki, with a .45-caliber pistol on his hip, stood by the door, which was closed and dogged. The sliding panel to the officers' pantry was shut so the stewards couldn't hear."[8]

Vandegrift, who had never met Fletcher, later said he was shocked at the indifference shown by Fletcher to the task at hand, adding that he "seemed nervous and tired, probably the result of the recent battles of Coral Sea and Midway."

Fletcher seemed to regard the upcoming operation as an amphibious hit-and-run raid rather than the seizure of a permanent foothold in the Solomons and had made plans accordingly. He exhibited no enthusiasm whatsoever.

"(Fletcher) appeared to lack knowledge of or interest in the forthcoming operation," Vandegrift would later write. "He quickly let us know he did not think it would succeed."[9]

Turner spoke next, but before he could complete more than a few sentences, he was interrupted by Fletcher.

"How long will it take to land the troops and their gear?" Fletcher asked.

"About five days," Turner replied.

"I'm leaving in two days," Fletcher said matter-of-factly. "I can't risk an attack against my carriers any longer than that."[10]

There were only four American carriers left in the Pacific and three of them were here—only the *Hornet* was missing. Fletcher, who had already lost two carriers earlier in the year, was very sensitive about losing any more.

Fletcher turned to a stunned Vandegrift and told him

that many of the transport and cargo ships were on loan from MacArthur's command and must be returned in a couple of days. When the fleet left, they would have to go, too.

There was little time for discussion or argument. Fletcher passed out his operations plan and that was that. There weren't even enough copies to go around. Ghormley never did see one until a month later.

After a brief discussion, which consisted mostly of objections from Turner and Vandegrift, Fletcher compromised and agreed to keep his carrier forces around until the third day.

"My Dutch blood was beginning to boil, but I forced myself to remain calm while explaining to Fletcher that the days 'of landing a small force and leaving' were over," Vandegrift wrote. "This operation was supposed to take and hold Guadalcanal and Tulagi. To accomplish this I commanded a heavily reinforced division which I was to land on enemy-held territory, which meant a fight. I could hardly expect to land this massive force without air cover—even the five days mentioned by Turner involved a tremendous risk."[11]

"Although Turner heatedly backed me," Vandegrift wrote, "Fletcher curtly announced that he would stay until the third day. With that he dismissed the conference."[12]

Rear Adm. Daniel Callaghan, Ghormley's chief of staff and representative at the meeting, took a few notes but didn't say a word. Those in the room knew they would get no input from a man "whose principal qualification for the demanding post he occupied was that he had been President Roosevelt's naval aide."[13]

If Vandegrift was dismayed by what he heard from Fletcher, he was even more disappointed in the rehearsals conducted over the next several days. He likened it to a Chinese fire drill. Absolutely nothing went right.

"We had landing exercises today," Vandegrift wrote his wife on July 28. "It took too long to get the boats out and too long to get the troops in the boats."

One of the most serious handicaps was the necessity for maintaining radio silence, which made ground-to-air communication impossible and impeded the coordination of ground force attacks with close air support.

Firing exercises were limited to conserve ammunition. Reef conditions made landings too dangerous for the men and too hazardous to the fragile, wooden Higgins boats. Landings were canceled after only about one-third of the Marines actually landed. For most, landing operations consisted of getting in and out of the irreplaceable Higgins boats. Boat crews practiced assembling into formations and taking their positions for the ship-to-shore movement, then turning about and heading back to the mother ship.

The landing crafts were not in the best of condition. On one transport a dozen boats were out of service. Those that worked coughed, sputtered and snorted like buses. Some would not start at all, floundering in the sea like wounded whales. The newer boats with retractable bow ramps were not available. They had been reserved for the American landings in North Africa, which would take place in November. What were left were tired old training vessels dredged up from Kaneohe Bay in Hawaii, Quantico and Parris Island, veterans of hundreds of practice landing operations, many of them worn out and far from combat ready.

Ships of all sizes milled around in aimless pursuits, nearly running into each other or into the treacherous reef. Unit integrity was in absolute shambles. The first

casualty of the operation may have been a young lieutenant who was horsing around aboard ship with his
roommate.

"Two first lieutenants in the cabin next to mine were
seeing which could draw his pistol quicker. Frontier
stuff," wrote division historian Herb Merillat. "They not
only whipped their Colts from the holsters but clicked
the triggers. A .45-caliber bullet tore through a cabin-
mate's body. Tonight after chow the colonel gave officers
a lecture on playing with firearms. One officer is out of
commission, he said, and another probably will be, for a
different reason."[14]

Vandegrift, who firmly believed in the necessity for
complete rehearsals, called the training exercises "dubi-
ous" and labeled the rehearsal a "complete bust," but
later softened his opinion.

"In retrospect it probably was not that bad," he said.
"At the very least it got the boats off the transports, and
the men down the nets and away. It uncovered deficien-
cies such as defective boat engines in time to have them
repaired and gave both Turner and me a chance to take
important corrective measures in other spheres."[15]

"Sunny Jim" Vandegrift, ever the optimist, consoled
himself by remembering an old show business adage that
proclaimed that a "poor rehearsal traditionally meant a
good show."[16]

He could only pray that would be the case.

Most of the 1st Raider Battalion loaded aboard four old
converted destroyers—the USS *Little, Colhoun, Gregory*
and *McKean*—on July 24 at New Caledonia and set out for
the rehearsal area off the Fiji Islands. The high-speed
transports, called APDs, were former four-stack destroyers
of World War I vintage. The two forward boilers and stacks

had been removed to allow the ships to transport about 150 men. Of the original six APDs, only two, the USS *Manley* and USS *Stringham*, survived the war. (More about these tough little ships and their brave crews later.)

A fifth transport failed to show at New Caledonia, temporarily stranding Easy Company of the Raiders. Three days later, however, the unit embarked on the SS *Monowai*, a former New Zealand passenger liner that had been fitted with two 4-inch guns and several 20-mm anti-aircraft guns before being pressed into service as an armed cruiser.

Instead of a cramped troopship, Easy Company enjoyed most of the comforts of home while hurrying to catch up with the rest of the battalion.

"The officers aboard had their own staterooms and tea was served in the morning," Lt. John Sweeney of E Company remembered. "I thought it was a perfectly wonderful way to go off to war."[17]

The captain of the *Monowai* wanted to take the Raiders all the way to Tulagi but was denied permission. Instead, the Raider unit transferred to the USS *Heywood*, already jammed with troops from other units assigned to the Tulagi campaign.

The invasion would be well covered by the media. Richard Tregaskis, a tall, gangly reporter, who would write the famed novel *Guadalcanal Diary*, and Robert Miller of United Press were aboard the *Crescent City*, Ralph Morse of *Life* magazine was on the *Vincennes*, Joe James Custer of United Press was on the *Quincy* and Foster Hailey of the *New York Times* was aboard the *Minneapolis*. Aboard the *Wasp* were Clark Lee of the Associated Press and Jack Singer of International News Service. Tregaskis and Miller would land with Vandegrift's forces on Guadalcanal on the first day.

As the massive armada sailed into history, one anonymous Raider captured the scene perfectly with a verse to the song "Bless 'em All" that went:

> They sent for the Navy to come to Tulagi;
> The Navy responded with speed.
> In 10,000 sections, from 16 directions,
> Oh Lord, what a screwed-up stampede.

After dusk on July 31, the armada, concealed by low clouds and operating under radio silence, turned north in the Coral Sea and headed for the objective area and a date with destiny as the first U.S. amphibious invasion since the Spanish-American War.

3

Red Mike

As the convoy crept closer to its destination, Col. Merritt A. Edson nervously paced the deck of the USS *Little* while he wrestled with creeping doubts about the upcoming operation. Nothing this large had ever been tried before. The rehearsals went poorly and if things didn't improve on D-day, the operation could turn into a disaster.

Edson's Raiders were selected to storm Tulagi, which was believed to be the most heavily defended objective of the operation. Edson was given the toughest job because he had the best-trained and best-led battalion in the task force. Still, very few of his men had really seen combat before.

Many of the men were on deck busying themselves with last-minute preparations like cleaning and oiling weapons and sharpening bayonets. Some had brought along large bolo knives, others had homemade blackjacks—canvas sacks containing lead balls—for hand-to-hand fighting. Others were loading machine-gun belts, humming while they worked. "One, two, three, another Jap for me," they sang out as they snapped the individual bullets into the belt.

They looked—and sounded—ready. But, Edson wondered to himself if that was really the case.

Edson had met often with former coastwatcher Henry Josselyn, who would go ashore with the Raiders the next day. Josselyn had lived and worked on Tulagi before the war. He had provided the Raiders with valuable intelligence on the coral reefs and other terrain features as well as the strength and disposition of the Japanese garrison.

Edson and his Raiders knew more about Tulagi than Vandegrift and his invasion force knew about Guadalcanal. There had been no word from coastwatcher Martin Clemens on Guadalcanal for two weeks.

Edson strolled the deck of the USS *Little*, looking out into the blackness and trying to picture what lay ahead for his Raiders. It was an overcast night with only brief periods of moonlight peering through the thick clouds. Softly, Edson could hear his Marines singing in the holds below deck. The only sound above deck was the swish of rushing water as the ship cut its way ever forward.

Many of the men were sleeping on deck where the air was cleaner. It was hard to walk anywhere on the blacked-out ship without tripping over sleeping bodies who were curled up everywhere, including in the lifeboats.

Earlier that day, the men got the word where they were going. The zero hour was still to be announced. Orders were read and assignments given. One of the details concerned the burial of friendly forces. "Graves will be suitably marked. All bodies will bear identification tags," a young lieutenant told the men. That got everybody's attention. Then, to a chorus of laughter, the lieutenant added: "I recommend you take along a change of underwear."[1]

Edson reached to his collar and felt the eagle insignia of a full colonel, a promotion he received just after the rehearsals. His deputy, Sam Griffith, who would be promoted to lieutenant colonel in a couple of days, had pinned the silver eagle on his boss a few days before.

There would be a flurry of promotions during the first week of August as Marine Corps personnel had grown to over 100,000, nearly doubling since Pearl Harbor. Three of his company commanders—Lew Walt, Ken Bailey and Joe Chambers—all received early promotions to major on August 1 and more than a half dozen first lieutenants would become captains the day of the landing, August 7.

As his troops liked to say of Edson, he was "no oil painting." Barely 5-foot-7, he weighed only 140 pounds. In uniform he always appeared neat but he looked a tad misshapen—"kind of small and sort of shriveled up."[2] A little stoop-shouldered, he leaned to port when he walked, the result of an old and persistent back injury. He also suffered from poor night vision, a condition that helped disqualify him from flying a few years back.

"[Edson] was quietly impressive," John Sweeney said. "He may not have been a Hollywood figure but he had everything else."[3]

What did impress others, however, was his icy gaze, soft voice and quiet air of menace. He was "cool," according to intelligence officer Capt. Henry Adams, who had been an FBI agent prior to the war.

Sweeney remembered a postwar luncheon with his old commander where Edson told him the biggest regret of his career was not earning a Purple Heart.

"Lord knows he tried to get one many times, standing up in the front lines daring the enemy to shoot him," Sweeney said.[4]

"His normal voice, which could become a rasping bark in the heat of combat, was so soft and low that you leaned toward him to hear him," according to press officer Herb Merillat. "His lips often smiled when his eyes did not, as though he had a clever but not really funny joke on the Japanese, or they on him."[5]

Edson left a vivid impression with famed war correspondent Richard Tregaskis, whose classic book *Guadal-*

canal Diary is still in print, the first time they met on Tulagi five days after the landings.

"[Edson] was a wiry man with a lean, hard face partly covered by a sparse, spiky growth of grayish beard," Tregaskis wrote. "His light blue eyes were tired and red-rimmed in appearance, for he was weary now from long days of fighting, and his red eyebrows and eyelashes, being almost invisible, heightened the effect. But his eyes were cold as steel and it was interesting to notice that even when he was being pleasant, they never smiled. He talked rapidly, spitting his words out like bullets, his hard-lipped mouth snapping shut like a trap."[6]

Years later, Tregaskis wrote a magazine piece that summed up Edson nicely.

"He smiled rarely, and his pleasure—usually at a job well done—was signaled by a shy, lopsided grin which warmed the hearts of his troopers far beyond the measure of its candle power. The Raiders, the Marine elite troops, had an apt if unprintable Marine epithet for that grin—a publishable equivalent might be 'like a jackass eating briars.'

"He usually spoke in a hoarse whisper that had you leaning forward to hear him. But though he never raised his voice, his men trembled when he was displeased. He could wither a man with his China-blue, gimlet eyes . . . I thought of Edson's eyes as being as purposeful as a killer's and as unemotional as a shark's . . . But, although he did not look the part, he was the bravest, the most effective killing machine I met in fifteen years as a war correspondent."[7]

Some were put off by what they termed his diffidence, his driving ambition and perfectionism. He had his share of nicknames, including "Red Mike" for the color of his beard, which he grew during his adventures in Nicaragua in the late 1920s. He was also called "Eddie" by his peers and "Eddie the Mole" by his troops for the way he looked when his small head seemed dwarfed by his helmet and "Mad Merritt the Morguemaster" for his aggressiveness. Some of his troops also called him a "glory hound," though not to his face.

Whatever his peers or troops called him, he had gained a Corps-wide reputation as a man who got things done. The word had spread within the upper echelons of the Marine Corps that if you had a tough job that needed doing, give it to Edson because he wouldn't stop until the mission was accomplished.

Quiet and calm by nature, Edson was a good listener who was not given to loud outbursts or shows of emotion. To others, he was a mystery.

"I think he was in many ways a pretty cold man," his deputy, Sam Griffith, said. Edson never warmed to his second in command as he did with most competent officers who served close to him. Years later Griffith would tell a writer: "I never felt I knew Eddie."[8]

The two men often disagreed on the organization of the battalion and, to a lesser degree, tactical matters. It is a testament to their character and professionalism that neither man let their differences interfere with their official duties.

Edson was very concerned about the physical shape of the men after being cooped up in a crowded transport for two weeks. Many of the transports had to reduce the daily food ration to 1,500 calories. Without much fresh food most of the men subsisted on soup and bread. Some men lost up to twenty pounds, scarcely the best preparation for an amphibious landing. Diarrhea was a problem even before they hit the beaches.

Edson had no doubts Tulagi could be taken with his

force. The question was could they hold it. The Japanese would certainly try to retake the island. He also knew that time was of the essence. The landing force was in a race against the clock. Tensions were running high as planners in Washington and Canberra believed an invasion of Australia's western and northwestern territories was imminent. Ready or not, the Americans had to move quickly.

Still a couple of days from the objective, Edson was alone with his thoughts when his runner and loyal companion, Corp. Walter Burak, approached him standing by the ship's railing. Edson, staring off into the sea, was startled at Burak's sudden appearance.

"Don't worry, Colonel," Burak said, sensing Edson's edginess. "These kids will do all right. They're Marines."

Edson smiled, telling himself that if they were all like Burak, they would do very well, indeed.

Burak, who grew up near Pittsburgh in the small town of Greensburg, Pa., was more than just a runner to Edson. An All State football player in high school as a rugged 5-foot-9-inch, 190-pound running back, Burak was like a son to Edson. Every time you saw Edson you could be sure that Burak was nearby.

A deeply religious young man, Burak wasn't like a lot of Marines of his day. He didn't smoke, drink or visit tattoo parlors. And, he certainly never cursed. Once on Samoa when he was Corporal of the Guard, he instructed his men before going on duty to watch their language. "I don't expect much except while you're under my post I don't want any profanity to be used," he told his men.[9]

Normally, the men would snicker at something like this or even laugh out loud. Not with Burak. The men knew of his devotion and spirituality and held him in high regard. They respected him because of his faith.

He also took football very seriously, according to his good friend Fred Serral, who said Burak was generally a mild-mannered man until it came to football. He often played defense during scrimmages at Quantico and then later on Samoa. Some of the guys would just joke around but Burak would crash through the line and charge toward the quarterback.

When the play was over he would walk over to the guy he had knocked to the ground and help him up while apologizing for hitting him so hard, according to Serral. He would do the same thing on the next play. The guys who were watching couldn't help but notice his passion for the game and yet his genuine concern for his fellow man.[10] Edson noticed, too.

Burak's athleticism would prove to be a great asset during the bitter fighting to come on Tulagi and Guadalcanal.

Merritt Austin Edson was born on April 25, 1897 in Rutland, Vt., the third and last child of Erwin and Lelia Edson. Merritt's father, who had a strong but spare build, came from a long line of farmers. A year after Merritt's birth, the Edsons moved to Chester, in southern Vermont, not too far from the Connecticut River.

Growing up on a farm, Edson enjoyed the outdoor life. "He ran track, enjoyed skating, skiing, hockey and tennis but his favorite was always baseball. He hunted, trapped, fished and swam and took special delight in camping trips to nearby Lowell Lake."[11]

He was also a studious boy, graduating as the top male student in his high school class, earning a $100 scholarship to the University of Vermont. He enrolled in the fall of

1915 with the intention of studying agriculture. That fall he joined the local chapter of Alpha Tau Omega, a forerunner of the Reserve Officers' Training Corps (ROTC). The chapter was also a part of the Vermont Army National Guard.

In March of 1916, President Woodrow Wilson had sent a force led by Brig. Gen. John J. Pershing into Mexico to track down followers of Pancho Villa, a bandit whose men had killed seventeen Americans during a recent raid into New Mexico. Three months later, with tensions mounting between the two countries, Wilson called up the National Guard. The Vermont contingent was sent to Eagle Pass, Texas on the banks of the Rio Grande River where Edson, as a private, got an eyeful of what it was like to be a "real" soldier.

In a letter to his father, Edson recalled "one hang of a day" where he "got beautifully bawled out" for failing to notice the approach of his commanding officer. Between extra guard shifts and kitchen police duty, he was kept busy around the clock.

Even with all the hardships, Edson seemed to thrive on military life. Later, when he became an officer, the experience would give him an understanding of the perspective of those lowly privates at the bottom of the military ladder.

He was quite taken with the pageantry, particularly the regiment's evening parade, describing it as "one of the most beautiful sights I know of, a thousand men passing in review, good men most of them, who are ready to serve their country and their country's flag." While others looked forward to demobilization in September, Edson did not.[12]

On May 12, 1917, a month after America's entry into World War I, Edson submitted an application for an appointment as a second lieutenant in the Marine Corps. He never considered joining the Army. His reasons, according to his biographer, have never been explained but he may have been captivated by an aggressive advertising campaign by the Marines and its slogan of "First to Fight."

"That certainly would have appealed to him and may have prompted his unexpected decision."[13]

The Marine Corps was expanding rapidly at the time. Where there had been 341 Marine officers in June of 1916, there would be 874 a year later and an additional 300 by October of 1917. Edson signed his enlistment papers on June 26 and took a five-day test in early July. Then he waited to hear how he did.

By mid-August, and still without word, Edson thought the war was surely passing him by. Edson had passed his entrance test but the overworked Marine Corps administrators had forgotten to notify him. Eventually, after it was noticed that he had not reported for duty, new orders were cut and delivered to him on September 17. He left for Parris Island, S.C. the next day.

Because he had missed his officer candidate class, Edson was very nearly assigned to the standard twelve-week boot camp for enlisted men (he was still technically a private in the reserve). While waiting a decision on the matter, a displeased Edson was put to work on a detail cleaning the mess halls. The situation was finally cleared up and he took the oath of office as a second lieutenant on October 10, leaving the next day for Officers Training School at Quantico, Va.

The original clerical error continued to dog Edson at Quantico where he arrived too late to participate in the training class currently nearing completion. When the next class graduated in mid-February, forty of the 124 candidates were assigned to France as replacements.

Much to his disappointment, Edson was not one of them. He despaired of missing the war altogether while his classmates were fighting and dying and winning medals.

Edson didn't sulk, however. He used his time stateside to improve his shooting and leadership skills.

"You asked me if I was a very stern officer," Edson wrote his mother. "I am afraid not, not nearly as stern and commanding as I should be to succeed A#1 in this work. Why, I have been here a week and I haven't even bawled a fellow out once, yet."[14]

He had been on the receiving end of tirades from superiors as a private in the Vermont Guard. He would never forget that experience.

Finally, Edson got his orders to France. He sailed with the 5th Brigade from Philadelphia on October 1, arriving in Brest, France on October 13 where they were promptly assigned to stevedore and guard duty. The Germans had already put out peace feelers. The war would end in four weeks before Edson could see any action.

Edson would remain in Europe for another thirteen months, unsure of his future and if the Marine Corps would be a part of it.

"About my staying in the service," he wrote his mother. "I doubt it very much, for there is nothing in it."[15]

Still, he applied to remain in the Marine Corps and took the required four-day written test that covered eleven different subjects, from tactics to naval gunnery. He did so, he said, to avoid the "disgrace" of being "bounced out."[16] Meanwhile, he had been reduced in rank from captain to first lieutenant as the Corps had begun reducing its size. He arrived home just before Christmas of 1919 not knowing if the career he once loved so much was about to come to an end.

Three months later, Edson learned he had scored very

well on the retention exam he had taken in France and received an outstanding fitness report. In August of 1920, he married his long-time sweetheart, Ethel Robbins, in Burlington, Vt. With new responsibilities he no longer had the freedom to resign his commission and strike out in another field of work.

Edson felt he needed to make a name for himself if he was going to compete with the World War I heroes for advancement. He applied to flight school in Pensacola, Fla., looking forward to the adventure and danger of flying. Edson was one of seventeen pilots accepted by the Marine Corps in 1922, bringing to fifty-two the total of flyers in the service. Four of the eight officers in his training class would die in aviation accidents during training.

Edson would spent the next three years in an uneventful assignment in Guam before returning to Quantico in late 1925. The following year he was finished with flying when a physical examination revealed that he had defective depth perception. In late 1927, he sailed to Central America where he was to have the most formative experience of his career in the jungles of Nicaragua the following year.

Another important event occurred in 1928. His long-awaited promotion to captain came through on February 11. Except for a three-month period during the war as a captain, Edson had been a first lieutenant for almost a decade.

In March, Edson led a three-week patrol up the Coco River in eastern Nicaragua in search of rebels under the command of one Augusto Cesar Sandino. Sandino and his Sandinistas, as the rebels were called, had rejected the political leadership of their country and American intervention, breaking off on their own a year before. They took to the jungle, pillaging villages and gathering recruits along the way.

Edson's first patrol had penetrated 260 miles into the interior but had not found any rebels. The experience was but a taste of two more patrols, each of a longer duration, that tested his endurance, aggressiveness, tactical skill and leadership. Each time he came out of the jungle he sported a full reddish beard, giving him a nickname— Red Mike—he carried with him for the rest of his life.

Edson's third and longest patrol, from late July of 1928 to March of 1929, was designed to catch up with and destroy Sandino and his rebels once and for all. Despite nagging illnesses, Edson kept the pressure on, finally driving Sandino into Honduras. His reputation was made. He became a symbol of aggressiveness and persistence, all the while perfecting the concept of constant roving patrols.

One of the important lessons he learned, one that stuck with him throughout his career, was the danger of night movements in a jungle environment. "In my opinion," he wrote, "the supposed advantages of night marches in bush warfare can not begin to equal their disadvantages."

It was a lesson he put to good use more than a decade later in thwarting the Japanese on Tulagi and Guadalcanal.

He did admit to one failure in Nicaragua, however. "I would like to (have been) lucky enough to bag old Sandino himself—that would be something to write home about," he said.[17]

Ethel wrote her husband that the newspapers were full of his name. "Everyone knows who you are now. You're famous," she wrote. "I bask in the glow shed from your aura."[18]

On June 15, 1929, Edson received the Navy Cross, his country's second highest award, for his skill and leadership in Nicaragua.

Edson spent the first half of the 1930s as a tactics instructor at the Basic School for new lieutenants and developing a reputation as a deadly marksman. Promoted to major in March of 1936, Edson became captain of the national championship Marine Corps Rifle and Pistol Team that year. In late May of the following year he, his wife and two small sons shipped out to Shanghai where he became the operations officer for the 4th Marines, witnessing firsthand Japanese aggression in China.

A day after the Edsons arrived, July 7, Japanese troops on maneuvers clashed with Chinese troops at the Marco Polo Bridge near Peking. Using that incident as a pretext, the Japanese Army in Manchuria launched a full-scale invasion of north China. Peking fell within a month and the Japanese moved to reinforce its garrison in Shanghai. Ethel and the boys left the city on August 20 for the temporary shelter of Manila.

In 1937 the 4th Marines was at a peacetime strength of just fifty-nine officers and slightly more than a thousand men, about a third of its authorized strength. Elements of the 6th Marines arrived in September to bolster the American enclave but they could do little more than watch the Japanese and Chinese fight it out on their own. By November 9, the Japanese had driven the Chinese from Shanghai.

On December 12, Japanese planes bombed and sank a U.S. gunboat on the Yangtze, infuriating the Marines. The Japanese expressed their regrets but it was clear they were testing American will, a tactic they would use again and again in the coming years.

Edson left China in the spring of 1939 after building a solid reputation as a man who got things done. His commanding officer, Col. Charles F.B. Price, praised him for his "devotion to duty, initiative, energy, intelligence, tact and professional ability" and added that he considered him "the most valuable officer on my staff."[19]

With war heating up in Europe, President Roosevelt authorized an expansion of the Marine Corps from 19,000 to 25,000, opening the way for faster promotions. Edson was nominated for promotion to lieutenant colonel in the fall of 1939 and finally pinned on the silver oak leaves in April of 1940, four years after he had made major.

A little over a year later, an invigorated Edson was hand-picked by Gen. Smith for command of the 1st Battalion, 5th Marines, then training at Quantico, Va. The 5th Marines had won glory at the battle of Belleau Wood in World War I. Recent commanders of the 5th included Alexander Vandegrift, now the assistant commandant, and Harold Utley, Edson's mentor in Nicaragua. The 1st battalion was earmarked by Smith for special amphibious training, operating aboard special high-speed transports called APDs and utilizing inflatable boats for beach landings.

Change was afoot throughout the Marine Corps in mid-1941. Earlier in the year, the 1st Marine Brigade had become the 1st Marine Division, encompassing the veteran 5th Marines and the brand-new 7th and 1st Marines. It was largely a paper division at first, existing well below its authorized strength of 15,000 men. A similar reorganization was underway on the West Coast with the 2nd Marine Brigade.

Joint exercises that summer with the Army's 1st Division did not go very well. Edson found out quickly that his battalion was in poor physical condition and that the APDs and Higgins boats were ill-equipped to conduct efficient amphibious landings. The men were crammed aboard the APDs, which offered stark living conditions. There were no bunks or showers for the men and ventilation was very poor. At the prompting of a congressional investigation, most of these conditions were improved over the next few months as the Raiders grew very fond of these heavy-duty ships.

Following the exercises, Edson wrote a twenty-seven-page report on his views on the organization and functions of his new battalion, coming to the conclusion that using a standard infantry battalion as a permanent mobile landing group was unsound. His critique recommended streamlining the unit to fit the space provided by the six APDs (about 150 men per ship) and equipping them for mobility rather than burdening them with heavy weapons.

Slowly, Edson watched his battalion grow in ability and confidence. By November, they had finally reached the levels of physical conditioning and performance he had demanded of them. Just in time, too, for the events of December 7 would change all of their lives forever.

4

A Wake-Up Call

Edson's battalion might have been reasonably well trained by the outbreak of the war but few other military units could say the same. The sudden and destructive attack by Japanese aircraft at Pearl Harbor on December 7, 1941 clearly demonstrated how unprepared America was for war. It was a stroke of luck, however, that all three carriers in the Pacific had been at sea or they too would surely have been destroyed.

It was also good fortune that Japan didn't follow up with a ground assault of Hawaii and an invasion of the West Coast. Many military leaders believed they had the manpower and equipment to do both.

"The country had allowed its reserve to sink so low that if the Japanese had continued from Pearl Harbor with an amphibious force and landed on the West Coast they would have found that we did not have enough ammunition to fight a day's battle. This is how close the country was to disaster in 1941," Marine General Holland "Howlin' Mad" Smith wrote after the war.[1]

John Sweeney, a young second lieutenant in the 1st Battalion, 5th Marines, remembers plenty of apprehension on the East Coast of the country as well. He and a couple of his buddies in the battalion were driving to Washington, D.C. to visit a couple of "watering holes" and have dinner when they heard about the attack on Pearl Harbor on the car radio.

"We were listening to the Redskins game," Sweeney said. "The sportscaster suddenly shifted his attention from play calling to reporting that large numbers of spectators were leaving their seats for the exits. Then came incredulous and somewhat excited bits of information that the Naval base at Pearl Harbor had been bombed by the Japanese.

"We pulled off the side of the road and decided we should go back to Quantico," Sweeney said. "When we got there we didn't know what to do. Somebody found a copy of the war plan. The gist of the plan was to 'double the guard.' "[2]

There was an air raid alert that night in the Washington, D.C. area although there were no enemy aircraft carriers anywhere near the East Coast. Edson spoke to his battalion staff and told them to assure the men that the radio messages they had heard were true. He urged all of them to stay calm and wait for orders.

"It got everybody's attention," Sweeney said of the attack. "There was a new focus, without any doubt. There was very little talk about the Pacific at the time. It was not a great concern. We thought we'd be going to war against the Germans, not the Japanese. The pace of training really picked up. There was a war."[3]

Sweeney was like a lot of the young officers in the Marine Corps at that time. Having graduated from Xavier University in 1940, he worked as a sales trainee for Procter & Gamble for a few months. Knowing he was ripe for the draft, he signed up for a Marine Corps officers program for college graduates in the spring of 1941. One of his instructors was Major Merrill Twining, who would later command the 1st Marine Division, retiring in 1959 with the rank of a four-star general.

"Going through Officer Candidate School was a real education in itself," Sweeney said. "There were 300 or so guys in my class from all over the country. It was a real melting pot. The NCOs called us 'goldfish eaters.' That fad was what college kids were into during those days. The training was great, though. [The cadre] made it a level playing field for everyone."[4]

Sweeney reported in to Edson in September and was assigned to a machine-gun platoon in Dog Company under Capt. Henry Cain.

The attack on Pearl Harbor galvanized America like she had never been before. The outrage was universal and recruiting offices were overwhelmed with enlistments. They called themselves "Pearl Harbor Avengers."

There were so many volunteers that the recruiters had to delay acceptance of some of them. There weren't enough training facilities, equipment or qualified instructors to handle the deluge of new recruits.

America was in a state of shock those first few weeks after the Pearl Harbor disaster. Even those who witnessed the carnage at Pearl could not believe that Japan was powerful enough to inflict such damage and escape virtually unchallenged.

"We were so proud, so vain, and so ignorant of Japanese capability," said Gene LaRocque, who was aboard the USS *Maryland* at Pearl Harbor. "It never entered our consciousness that they'd have the temerity to attack us. We knew the Japanese didn't see well, especially at night—we knew this as a matter of fact. We knew they couldn't build good weapons, they made junky equipment, they just imitated us. All we had to do was get out there and sink 'em. It turns out they could see better than we could and their torpedoes, unlike ours, worked. We'd thought they were little brown men and we were the great big white men. They were of a lesser species. The Germans were well known as tremendous fighters and builders, whereas the Japanese would be pushovers."[5]

Authorized Marine Corps strength doubled from September of 1939 to June of 1941 to about 54,000 and it was a little over 66,000 by December 7. By war's end, nearly half a million men wore the Marine uniform. Priding themselves on having high recruiting standards, the Marines accepted only 38,000 first-time enlistees in the three years prior to the war from an application pool of 205,000.

During the first month after Pearl Harbor 18,000 men were accepted into the Marine Corps. More than half the initial volunteers were rejected for medical reasons, however. The long and harsh Depression had taken its toll on the health of America's youth. Many of the volunteers were suffering from anemia or malnutrition as a result of poor eating habits and the lack of vitamin-enhanced diets. Medical and dental needs had also been neglected because they simply could not afford to pay for such services.

As the war wore on, however, the armed services, including the Marines, became a lot less picky on who they accepted for military duty. Draftees were not accepted as Marines until mid-1943, and were then listed as "Selective Service Volunteers."

There was a tremendous cry in America for revenge against the Japanese and an accountability from the U.S. forces for allowing this sneak attack. Something had to be done quickly to restore the public's faith in its military and to assuage the severe morale problems in the armed services. Roosevelt quickly came to the conclusion that the blame for the disaster must fall on Adm. Husband

Kimmel and Army Lt. Gen. Walter Short, the two senior officers in charge in Hawaii, though there was plenty of evidence that others may have been more directly responsible for the debacle.

Roosevelt sent Secretary of the Navy Frank Knox to Hawaii on December 11. Three days later, he returned to Washington, arriving at the White House at 2200. He told the president that "the damage was so horrendous" that he had not detailed everything in his twenty-nine-page report for fear of some leak. He said that "if the American people knew what had happened at Pearl, they would panic and the war would be over before we ever got into it."[6]

Roosevelt moved swiftly, relieving both Kimmel and Short and naming a board of inquiry to thoroughly investigate what had happened at Pearl Harbor. On December 17, Roosevelt resurrected the post of commander in chief, U.S. Navy, which he had abolished a year earlier, and gave the job to Adm. Ernest King. Adm. Chester Nimitz was a quick choice to succeed Kimmel as commander of the Pacific fleet, such as it was.

Among those who thought Roosevelt's actions were too rash was Kimmel's chief of intelligence Edwin T. Layton. Layton, who retired as a rear admiral, wrote after the war that Kimmel's firing only "served to draw attention away from any responsibility that Washington might bear for the Pearl Harbor disaster. It smacked of firing the office boys to conceal skullduggery in the boardroom."[7]

Layton, who like the rest of Kimmel's staff was kept on by Nimitz, was very bitter about Roosevelt's hasty decision to relieve his boss.

"Although (Kimmel's) dismissal was not unexpected, we all regarded it as premature. We wondered what would happen to the Wake operation. It may be an established American tradition that losing baseball teams have their manager fired, but not during the first game of the World Series.[8]

"A December victory at Wake . . . would have been a stunning blow to Japan. It would have opened the way to a transpacific relief of Corregidor and the Philippines. And it would have rallied the Navy and provided a tremendous boost to the morale of the American people who were facing a bleak Christmas."[9]

Wake Island, 2,000 miles west of Hawaii, had a garrison of 450 Marines, assorted Navy and Army personnel and 1,200 civilian construction workers. A dozen F4F Wildcat fighter planes had been delivered to the island on December 4. Eight of them were destroyed on the ground during the December 7 attack. Four days later, a Japanese landing party was repulsed. In radio contact with Hawaii, the Wake defenders were asked if there was anything they needed. "Send us more Japs," came the reply, prompting a stunned America to stand up and cheer.

Meanwhile, a relief operation for the defenders was being planned. A few hours after the U.S. carriers had left for Wake on December 16, Kimmel was notified he was to turn over his command to his deputy, Vice Adm. William S. Pye, the next day.

Pye, who had expressed little enthusiasm for the Wake relief plan, eventually called off the mission when intelligence revealed the presence of three enemy carriers near the island. The recall was issued on December 22 when Adm. Frank J. Fletcher, aboard the USS *Saratoga*, was only 425 miles from the island. The Japanese landed the next day.

When the message to abort the mission reached Fletcher, he reportedly threw his cap to the deck in disgust. Even more upset were the *Saratoga* pilots, who took the abandonment of their fellow Marines personally. Several threatened to climb into their fighters and fly to Wake. Others broke down and wept.[10]

Many naval officers felt that the political moves to change fleet commanders to quickly provide a scapegoat for the Pearl Harbor disaster resulted in the loss of the Wake Island garrison. Pye's decision to write off Wake cost him the trust and respect of many of his subordinates.

Roosevelt reportedly told an aide that he considered the recall "a worse blow than Pearl Harbor." Roosevelt castigated his Navy for bungling the Wake mission and sarcastically demanded that the Pacific Fleet find some way in the near future to hurt the Japanese.

When Pye turned his command over to Nimitz on December 31, he quietly stepped to the sidelines of history. He ended his Navy career without ever receiving another major combat command. The Navy never forgot or forgave him for the loss of Wake Island.

In hindsight, however, most military historians generally agree that Pye made the right decision. Had the *Saratoga* been lost as Pye feared might happen—a very distinct possibility considering the available intelligence— the great victory at Midway the following June might never have happened.

Admiral Nimitz knew before accepting his assignment that President Roosevelt had agreed with British Prime Minister Winston Churchill that the first priority for military action would be in Europe, not the Pacific. Nimitz would have to hold on to what he had until the American war machine was able to produce the bullets, bombs, ships and airplanes to go on the offensive in the Pacific. Accordingly, Nimitz's first orders from Admiral King were to cover and hold the Hawaii-Midway line and secure the sealanes between the West Coast and Australia.

The brutal attack at Pearl Harbor had enraged the American people and unified them in their quest for revenge. They would have to be patient, however, and that proved difficult as the war news from the Pacific kept getting worse and worse.

There was no darker period in American history than the winter and spring of 1942. The Japanese landed on northern Luzon in the Philippines on December 10 and made their first attempt to take Wake Island the next day. Guam fell on December 22, followed by Wake on December 23 and Hong Kong on December 25. Additionally, the Japanese had sunk the British battleship *Prince of Wales* and the battle cruiser *Repulse* off Malaya on December 10. They had been the only two allied capital ships in the whole western Pacific. Singapore fell on February 15. Gen. Douglas MacArthur arrived in Australia on March 17 after having been evacuated from the Philippines six days earlier. The two biggest blows were the surrender of Bataan on April 9 and Corregidor on May 6. More than 75,000 men, a third of them Americans, were taken prisoner in the Philippines. It was the greatest capitulation in U.S. military history.

Among the defenders on the island fortress of Corregidor, which was called "the rock" by the Americans, were elements of the 4th Marines, the "China regiment" in which so many of the older Marines had served during the 1920s and 1930s.

The surrenders at Bataan and Corregidor were particularly humiliating. Outnumbered and decimated by hunger, disease and battle wounds, without supplies and any hope of relief, the "army" of the Philippines was humbled by the well-disciplined and battle-hardened Japanese. The prisoners, who were forced to march nearly a hundred miles in six days to squalid prisoner-of-war camps, endured blistering heat, exhaustion, starvation, unspeakable cruelty and murder. Thousands died along the way, either from disease or from a Japanese bayonet.

By the late spring of 1942, Japan had conquered the Philippines, Singapore, Hong Kong, the Dutch East Indies, Malaya, Borneo, the Bismarck Islands, Siam, Sumatra, the Gilberts, the Celebes, Timor, Wake, Guam, most of the Solomon Islands and half of New Guinea. Japanese bombers had pulverized the key Australian port of Darwin, and citizens of Brisbane, Melbourne and Sydney feared an imminent invasion. The Japanese empire had expanded some five thousand miles from Tokyo in nearly every direction, covering one-seventh of the globe, some 12.5 million square miles of new territory in only five months of war.

In Washington, gloom contended with chaos. Generals and admirals were stunned by the power, speed and skill of the Japanese advance and reached a grim conclusion: With full mobilization of manpower and resources, and at a frightful cost in casualties, it would require at least ten years to reconquer the Pacific. That was just the initial assessment.

Still, there was no shortage of optimism or patriotism in those early, dark days of the Pacific war. Parents of those serving in the military proudly displayed in a front window a pennant with a blue star for each son or daughter in uniform. A gold star meant that their loved one wouldn't be coming back. By war's end, there were very few homes that didn't have either a blue or gold star hanging in a front window. Many houses had more than one.

5

Birth of the Raiders

During the 1920s, the Marine Corps often had to defend itself and its mission of amphibious assaults from those who believed there was no need for such a specialized force. Old-timers, in both the Army and Navy, held to the doctrine that hostile and defended shores could not be seized from the sea. One only had to look at the disastrous campaign at Gallipoli in World War I to realize the impossibility of sea-borne assaults by infantry forces.

Many generals and some admirals derided Marines as "beach jumpers" and nothing more than "the Navy's police force." The Marines persisted in their beliefs, however, and continued amphibious training in the Caribbean. At the time, the basic strength of the Marines consisted of two brigades, the First Brigade on the East Coast, which were referred to as the "Raggedy-Ass Marines," and a Second Brigade near Los Angeles, also known as "the Hollywood Marines."

Two of the most important boosters of this kind of warfare were President Roosevelt and British Prime Minister Winston Churchill. Churchill regaled the president with stories of the dash and bravery of his British commandos, which had been formed in the summer of 1940. Roosevelt was so impressed he sent several U.S. officers, including future Raider Sam Griffith, to Great Britain to observe their training.

The first so-called "rubber boat battalion" was the 1st Battalion, 5th Marines, which was redesignated the "1st Separate Battalion" on January 6, 1942. A similar unit, called the "2nd Separate Battalion" (which would become the 2nd Raider Battalion), began forming later that month in San Diego as part of the 2nd Marine Division.

The concept of "separate elite" units within the Marine Corps didn't go over very well with the senior officers, who, almost to a man, objected in very strong terms.

Marine Commandant Maj. Gen. Thomas Holcomb believed that the term "Marine" was alone sufficient to indicate that a man was ready for duty at any time, and the injection of a special name such as "commando" would be undesirable and superfluous.

"Neither General Holcomb nor I favored forming elite units from units already elite," General Vandegrift wrote in his memoirs. "But Secretary of the Navy Colonel Frank Knox and President Roosevelt, both of whom fancied the British commandos, directed us to come up with a similar organization."[1]

Things may have come to a head on January 13, 1942 when Marine Capt. James Roosevelt, with the full backing of his father and the obvious encouragement of maverick Maj. Evans F. Carlson, wrote the commandant to recommend the creation of "a unit for purposes similar to the British Commandos and the Chinese Guerrillas."[2]

Normally, reserve Marine Corps captains do not correspond with two-star generals. But, because of who Jimmy Roosevelt was, Holcomb knew he'd better take a long and hard look at it. There was also another idea floating around Washington that really rankled the Marine Corps. A plan was afoot to give reserve Army Col. Bill Donovan, a longtime friend of the president, a Marine rank of brigadier general so that he could take charge of the "commando" project.

Donovan had won a Medal of Honor in World War I as commander of the 165th New York Regiment (the old "Fighting 69th" of Civil War fame). Following the war he and Franklin Roosevelt became classmates at Columbia Law School and, despite being a lifelong Republican, Donovan and FDR became fast friends. Donovan failed in a bid for Governor of New York in 1932 and slipped quietly back into his successful New York City law practice, specializing in international cases. When World War II came along, FDR, trying to give his administration a bipartisan look, called Donovan to Washington in 1940 to become Coordinator of Intelligence. Donovan reported directly to the White House.

It has never been completely determined who suggested the appointment of Donovan to head up the Marine commando project. His name was probably floated at a meeting at the White House on December 22, 1941, attended by FDR, Churchill and Navy Secretary Frank Knox. Other opinions on the matter were probably sought from Admiral King, General Marshall and FBI Director Herbert Hoover. The latter three undoubtedly saw Donovan as a threat to their own power and would have been happy to see him leave his present position as "coordinator of intelligence." Hoover had been openly bitter that he didn't have the president's ear exclusively on matters of intelligence and counterintelligence.

What was purely a military situation quickly became a delicate political problem. When Holcomb got wind of the Donovan affair in a letter from Admiral King on January 8, he swallowed hard and then sought the advice of his top two Marine officers, Maj. Gen. Holland M. Smith, the commanding general of Amphibious Force, Atlantic Fleet, and Maj. Gen. Charles F.B. Price, commanding general, Department of the Pacific. He asked each to comment on the commando concept and the appointment of Donovan as its leader. Not surprisingly, both were cold on the former and adamant against the latter.

Smith, a tough, egocentric and cantankerous sort, told Holcomb it wouldn't look very good if the Marine Corps had to go outside its ranks to secure leaders. Going further, he said that the "appointment of Colonel Donovan to brigadier general could be compared to that of Lord Mountbatten in Great Britain—both are 'royal' and have easy access to the highest authority without reference to their own immediate superiors. The appointment would be considered by many senior officers of the Corps as political, unfair, and a publicity stunt . . . The commandant would lose control of that number of Marines assigned as commandos. We have enough 'by-products' now. No strictures are cast upon Colonel Donovan. He has a reputation for fearlessness but he has never been a Marine and his appointment would be accepted with resentment throughout the Corps. It would be stressed that the Marines had to go outside their own service for leaders. It is the unanimous opinion of the staff of this headquarters that commando raids by the British have been of little strategical value. We have not reached the stage where our men are so highly trained and restless for action that they must be employed in commando raids."[3]

In truth, most, if not all, of the British commando raids were abject failures. Conceived by a Lt. Col. Dudley Clark, a staff officer at the War Office in Whitehall, at the urging of Churchill, the commandos were trained for cross-Channel forays on the continent of Europe.

"Enterprises must be prepared with specially trained troops of the hunter class who can develop a reign of terror down the enemy coast," Churchill told his military chiefs.[4]

Formed in June of 1940 just after the debacle of Dunkirk, the first "butcher-and-bolt" raid took place three weeks later after the briefest of training. Four air-sea rescue boats crossed the English Channel with 115 hastily chosen volunteers. They blackened their faces with makeup supplied by a London theatrical costumer, which they found very amusing. The plan was to land at four points along the French coast south of Boulogne to test German defenses and take prisoners.

One boat found nothing and promptly returned. Another found a German seaplane anchorage straddling its intended landing site and none made it ashore. The third group surprised two German sentries and killed both but left without searching the bodies or finding out what they were guarding. The fourth boat, with Colonel Clark aboard as an observer, nearly blundered into Boulogne harbor. A German patrol drove them off with Clark sustaining a wound to his ear.

Returning to England, one of the four boats was refused entry to Folkestone harbor until the identity of its occupants could be established. While the men drifted off the harbor boom, they drank the rum that such boats carried for reviving downed airmen who were plucked from the chilly waters of the channel. As a result, many of them were distinctly unsteady on their feet when they were at last allowed ashore. As a final indignity, they were arrested by the military police on suspicion of being deserters.[5]

A second raid, consisting of thirty-two officers and 107 enlisted men, took place three weeks later, on July 14, 1940. The target was the Le Bourg airfield at Guernsey, one of the Channel Islands. Only forty men made it to shore, and after finding nothing, most had to swim out to their launch in heavy seas.

Both raids were comic failures, but Churchill was far from being discouraged. He decided that individual recruiting, longer training and special equipment would be necessary before any more commando raids would be attempted. Several camps were established for this specialized training in the Scottish highlands in the fall of 1940.[6]

The commandos did achieve a level of success in subsequent forays, particularly on the northern Norwegian island of Vagsoy on March 4, 1941 and on a German radar station on an isolated channel headland near Bruneval, France, on February 27, 1942, but their contributions to the war effort were minimal.

Nonetheless, U.S. officers like Army Brig. Gen. Lucian Truscott, Army Col. Bill Donovan and Marine captains Sam Griffith and Wallace Greene were sent by Roosevelt to observe the commando training and returned to America with glowing reports of its effectiveness. It was their recommendations that helped launch the formation of the American Army's Ranger program and the Marine Corps's Raider battalions.

General Smith opposed the commando concept on philosophical grounds, noting that all Marines could be trained in raiding techniques by their own officers if it were deemed important. He felt that all Marines were considered as commandos, expressing a view that would become increasingly common among senior Marine officers, namely, that there was no task that the "elite" commando units could perform any more effectively than regular line units.

General Price warned of another problem, noting that the rapid expansion of the Marine Corps would result in an extreme shortage of qualified officers and senior NCOs with the requisite command experience. He concurred with the commando concept but only if the personnel were recruited directly rather than by drawing on already thin Marine Corps ranks.

"If, on the other hand, our very limited resources in trained officers must be further disbursed," Price wrote, "and if the best of the adventurous spirits and 'go-getters' among our men must be diverted from the Fleet Marine Force in meeting the requirements of this additional activity, then the undersigned would recommend seriously against assuming this additional commitment."[7]

Some of Price's contemporaries thought this opinion was formed to curry favor with his commander-in-chief.

Price also wrote a personal letter to Holcomb that delved more deeply into his true feelings about the Raider project.

"There is another thing in this connection which I could not put in my other letter and that is the grave danger that this sort of thing will develop into a tail which will wag the dog eventually," he wrote. "I know in what quarter the idea of foisting this scheme upon the Marines originated, and I opine that if it is developed along the lines of a hobby in the hands of personnel other than regular Marine officers it would very easily get far out of hand and out of control as well.

"It appears pretty clear to me that you are in a position of having to comply and that nothing can be done about it so please accept my sympathy."[8]

Clearly on the horns of a dilemma, Holcomb admitted as much in a letter he wrote to a friend in mid-January of 1942.

"The Donovan affair is still uppermost in my mind. I am terrified that I may be forced to take this man," Holcomb wrote to an old friend and former Marine, Samuel Meek, who was then an executive with Time-Life. "I feel that it will be the worst slap in the face that the Marine Corps was ever given because it involves bringing into the Marine Corps as a leader in our own specialty, that is, amphibious operations . . . It will be bitterly resented by our personnel, both commissioned and enlisted, and I am afraid that it may serve to materially reduce my usefulness in this office, if any, because I am expected, and properly so, to protect the Marine Corps from intrusions of this kind."[9]

On February 10, Holcomb sent a long personal letter to Maj. Gen. Clayton Vogel, who was forming the 2nd Marine Division in San Diego, offering to send him Edson to head up the 2nd Raider Battalion. Holcomb never made clear his reasons for the offer. Perhaps he felt Carlson would become a political liability or perhaps he was just trying to be even-handed. In any event, Vogel declined the offer.

An uneasy agreement seems to have been reached among all the parties concerned. Donovan, who would later head the Office of Strategic Services, the forerunner of today's Central Intelligence Agency, remained in the Army while Holcomb accepted the controversial Maj. Evans F. Carlson, who some thought to be a Communist sympathizer, as commander of the west coast Raider battalion.

Carlson, who had gained fame marching with Chinese Communist guerrillas behind Japanese lines in the late 1930s, had become a confidant of the president and his son while stationed at Warm Springs, Ga. in the mid-1930s. Carlson had corresponded directly with the president on his long march in China at FDR's request, drawing the ire of Marine Corps brass, who resented his breach of the chain of command. Claiming he was being muzzled by his superiors, Carlson resigned his commission in 1939. After

two years of writing and lecturing, he returned to active
duty in the spring of 1941.

Nine months later, Carlson took command of the 2nd
Raider Battalion with Capt. James Roosevelt as his executive officer. Both were reserve officers.

President Roosevelt never wavered in his determination to have a Marine commando force and, in the end,
he prevailed.

"Many historians have looked to the Donovan-Carlson-
Roosevelt nexus as the source of the Marine Raider concept," wrote Jon Hoffman. "While these men did have an
impact, they served more to accelerate a process already
underway. [Gen.] Smith and [Col.] Edson had created a
battalion fully capable of raid duty long before the propos-
als of Roosevelt and Donovan stirred the pot in late 1941
and early 1942."[10]

The question wasn't if there would be special commando
outfits but what they would be called. Nobody liked the
name "separate" battalion, according to John Sweeney.

"Who wanted to rally around an outfit called the 1st
Separate Battalion?" Sweeney asked. "Calling us commandos wasn't much better. That's what the British called
their outfits. Let them have it, we felt."[11]

Edson suggested the use of "1st Destroyer Battalion."
General Smith came up with "1st Shock Battalion." General Price didn't mind the "commando" appellation but
also liked the term "raiding." General Holcomb short-
ened it to the "1st Raider Battalion" and signed an order
to that effect on February 12, 1942, effective on February
16. A similar order created the 2nd Raider Battalion
three days later, on February 19. While the 1st Battalion
was a restructured infantry battalion (1st Battalion, 5th
Marines), the second would be built from scratch.

The basic mission of the two new Raider units was threefold: to be the spearhead of amphibious landings by larger forces on beaches generally thought to be inaccessible; to conduct raiding expeditions requiring great elements of surprise and high speed; and to conduct guerrilla-type operations for protracted periods behind enemy lines.

Within a week of the name change, Edson was ordered to ship one of his reinforced rifle companies to help stock the 2nd Raider Battalion, then forming at Camp Elliott near San Diego. This move greatly affected his unit's combat effectiveness and would lead to a bitter feud with Carlson over the shoddy treatment of one of Edson's hand-trained units.

Carlson, who was under the impression he was to have a free hand to form his battalion, bristled when Marine Headquarters shipped him a ready-made company (seven officers and 190 enlisted men). To him, it was a clear case of "interference" from above. He summarily broke up the outfit and insisted that each individual reapply for his battalion, subject to the same "Gung Ho" selection process that all his other volunteers underwent.

Carlson had already raised a lot of eyebrows within the Marine Corps with his unorthodox training methods, which included the absence of saluting and no special privileges for the officer corps. His adoption of the motto "Gung Ho," a Chinese phrase meaning "work together" or "work in harmony," rankled many feathers among the brass, who thought the term was giving the Chinese Communists undesired publicity.

Though Edson certainly didn't like the idea of losing a company of men he had assiduously trained over the past six months, he quickly complied with the order. "To Edson's credit," historian Jon Hoffman wrote, "he did not comb the battalion for the weakest links, but simply selected Capt. Wilbur Meyerhoff's Company A."[12]

Nobody wanted to be shipped to the West Coast, according to Sweeney, who was a platoon leader in the weapons company.

"We were normally assigned to A Company during exercises but when A Company was picked to go, they took another weapons platoon with them. I felt as if I had dodged a bullet," Sweeney said.[13]

Many of the others, however, were excited about the move because they expected the West Coast unit to see combat first.

Much to their disappointment, Carlson dissolved the company when it arrived in San Diego and made each member requalify to meet his own unorthodox standards.

"This was a hell of a mess and most of us tried to qualify," Lt. John Apergis, a platoon leader in Able Company, wrote to Edson. "We were proud and just could not stand rejection by the West Coast mob."[14]

Apergis described the treatment he and the rest of A Company received from Carlson as disrespectful. According to Apergis, Carlson greeted the company at a formation by asking who among them wanted to volunteer for a commando outfit. Only half stepped forward. Those who remained were subjected to not only physical testing but psychological testing as well.

Some of the latter testing was "conducted in a darkened room; occasionally a knife flew by and thudded into the wall, or firecrackers went off under the interviewee's chair. Few seemed to meet the intriguing standards Carlson had set."[15]

Carlson's treatment of Edson's company ignited a firestorm within the Marine Corps, according to the latter's biographer, Jon Hoffman. General Price, who was keenly aware of President Roosevelt's friendship with Carlson, bluntly wrote Edson privately that the company he had sent to the West Coast had made "a very bad impression" on Carlson, so bad that he had accepted only a quarter of them for his command.

"I am trying to stop an official complaint on the case, not because I feel that one is not warranted but because I hate to see you get hurt over the matter . . . this commando business is a hobby with high authorities in our nation and Capt. James R. is the Exec of the Battalion," Price said. He ended by saying: "Either there is an entirely different impression in the East as to what these men are to do and the type of men required effectively to do it or someone has made a serious bust."[16]

Edson was furious with Carlson and pulled no punches in answering Price's letter.

"Whatever Carlson's so-called standards may be," Edson wrote, "his refusal to accept three out of four of these men only confirmed my opinion that the Marine Corps had lost nothing by his resignation a few years ago and has gained nothing by his return to active duty as a reserve major.

"The statement in your letter to the effect that the men rejected by Carlson were distributed to units in the 2nd Division 'where no one wanted them' is not so much a reflection upon the quality of men sent as upon this prejudicial attitude and ignorance of the officers under your command. It is true that Jimmie Roosevelt has connections with high officials in this country. It is also true that he is a reserve captain with very limited military experience as an officer in the Marine Corps. I have already stated my opinion of Major Carlson.

"I have given you many years of loyal, faithful, and, I believe, efficient service . . . If, as implied in your letter, you feel that an official complaint is warranted based on Carlson's reports to you, I shall not ask you to withhold it on my account. I have no apologies to make nor anything to conceal in the transfer of this draft to the West Coast."[17]

Edson would harbor a grudge against Carlson that would last even after the latter's death. It is worth noting that the troops Edson sent Carlson were more mature and better trained than those already in the battalion and would go on to play key roles in the unit's success. Two, Sgt. Robert V. Allard and Sgt. Dallas H. Cook, would win Navy Crosses but lose their lives on the Makin Raid in mid-August of 1942.

To fill the vacancies left by the detachment of one of his companies, Edson was authorized by the commandant to handpick replacements now pouring out of the Recruit Depot at Parris Island, S.C. It didn't make him a popular man.

"Merritt Edson, armed with appropriate orders, arrived to comb our units for officers and men deemed suitable for his 1st Raider Battalion—a new organization," Gen. Vandegrift wrote in his memoirs many years later. "Edson's levy against our division coming at such a critical time, annoyed the devil out of me, but there wasn't one earthly thing I could do about it."[18]

The 1st Division was also being picked over by the 7th Marines, who had been alerted to duty in Samoa as a deterrence to Japanese expansion. That order came on March 21, two days before Vandegrift assumed command of the 1st Marine Division and received his second star.

Edson was relentless in recruiting men for his battalion, which produced a solid group of company commanders to compliment the charismatic Ken Bailey of C

Company. Bailey was renowned throughout the Marine Corps as the very model of a commanding officer.

"[Bailey] was the Hollywood version of a Marine officer: tall, six-foot-three or so, handsome, with . . . broad shoulders and lean of hip. His men loved him, and every junior officer in the outfit wanted to be just like Captain Bailey," according to John Sweeney.[19]

Capt. Ira "Jake" Irwin, who would command the battalion for a brief period later in his career, stepped in to take command of D Company when Capt. Henry Cain died of a heart attack during a forced march in March. Taking D Company into battle, however, would be Capt. Justice M. "Jumping Joe" Chambers. Chambers, who was related on his mother's side to Valentine Hatfield, the patriarch of the Hatfield clan in the notorious Hatfield-McCoy feud, was plucked from the division staff where he was serving as adjutant.

By mid-March, most of A Company had been reconstituted with Capt. Lew Walt as its commanding officer. Edson found Walt, who would eventually hold the post of assistant commandant, at Quantico where he was company commander of the Officer Candidate Class. Even then, the charismatic Walt was thought of by the Marine brass as "a comer."

Bailey, who was killed on Guadalcanal, Chambers and Walt would go on to account for two Medals of Honor, two Navy Crosses, three Silver Stars and seven Purple Hearts in distinguished military careers. Each would be promoted to major just prior to the landing on Tulagi.

Edson didn't get everybody he was after, however. General Smith flatly turned down his request for Capt. Victor "Brute" Krulak, who was then the general's aide.

The last piece of the command puzzle was finding a dynamic executive officer. Edson finally settled on Maj.

Sam Griffith, who had just returned to the States after serving a five-month assignment in England and Scotland observing commando training, much of which would find its way into the curriculum of the 1st Raiders. Edson and Griffith made for a strange combination. The former was small in stature and quiet by nature while the latter was strong, durable and very intelligent.

"Where Edson is able and courageous, he looks small and sort of shriveled up," Raider Lee Minier wrote his parents. "Griffith is big, rugged, a real fighter."

Griffith graduated from the U.S. Naval Academy in 1929 and later studied tactics under Edson at the Basic School. A skilled and prolific writer, he had a gift for languages. While serving in Nicaragua he became sufficiently fluent in Spanish to read Cervantes' *Don Quixote* in the original. And, when he was sent to Beijing, China in 1935, he learned Chinese and studied Chinese military theorists such as the classical Sun Tzu and the contemporary Mao Zedong. Upon retirement as a brigadier general in 1956, he undertook graduate studies at Oxford, where he earned the degree of doctor of philosophy in Chinese military history. He was, as one of his colleague's commented, "a special breed of cat."[20]

"He could communicate at all levels from buck private to general," said Raider "Tiger" Erskine. "He was physically fit for the field and he knew his craft. He was a professional in every sense of the word."[21]

Soon after joining the 1st Raider Battalion, Griffith was sent to San Diego to observe the training of the 2nd Raider Battalion. Griffith, who had met Evans Carlson in China several years before, was highly impressed with the "Gung Ho" spirit of the unit. He also liked Carlson's organization of the rifle squad into three fire teams for greater firepower and better control in battle. His endorsement of

Carlson's methods created an awkward situation with Edson, who loathed everything about his West Coast counterpart.

To the credit of each man, Edson and Griffith managed to put aside their conflicting views of Carlson and got on with preparing the 1st Raider Battalion for military action, which came sooner than either one had anticipated.

6

Off to Lava-Lava Land

Training moved into high gear in February. Edson divided his program into four areas: physical fitness, marksmanship, individual skills and small-unit tactics. There was a heavy emphasis on hiking, speed of execution and the ability to perform silently and in the dark.

Edson was blessed with a solid cadre of noncommissioned officers, all under the direction of the "first soldier," Sgt. Maj. Edwin C. "Parson" Clark. Clark's knowledge of the Marine Corps was encyclopedic and his "sea stories" were as endless as they were entertaining.

The lower ranks were an eclectic bunch, representing every walk of life in the country. All were double volunteers. Many were recent high school dropouts "whose youthful appearance suggested enlistment without parental consent."

The training quickly separated those who could "cut it" and those who couldn't. Some of the old-timers, who had grown fat and lazy during garrison duty between the wars, dropped out and were replaced by younger, more energetic men.

Recruits poured into the Marines during the first few months of 1942. Those from states west of the Mississippi River went to San Diego for boot training while those born east of the river were sent to camps at New River and Parris Island. All the recruits hit the ground running.

Other than a heavy emphasis on physical fitness, much

of the training centered on surprise and mobility. Raiders could not expect to have on call heavy fire support from artillery, tanks, aircraft or naval gunfire when operating deep within enemy territory. They would have to take what they needed to live and fight with them. Weapons would have to be light, durable and powerful.

There were many eighteen-hour days and seven-day weeks, completing a syllabus that covered everything from weapons training to physical conditioning, from armed and unarmed hand-to-hand combat to scouting and patrolling. The men fired hundreds of rounds from all the weapons and hiked hundreds of miles with full packs and equipment. Ample opportunity to quit was given to all the men. Few did.

Edson also spent a lot of time after hours giving special education to his runner, Corporal Burak. The two had grown close, developing a father-son relationship. Burak proved to be a willing student in all things military, a tireless worker who had a great thirst for knowledge. Many nights the two sat together at battalion headquarters after the day's work was done, Edson tutoring his willing student in the art of compass and map reading.[1]

Edson was very much a hands-on commander with all the men.

"His men are simply tools which he uses to do a job," one of his Raiders said. "But he takes good care of his tools just like you take care of your rifle."

Gunny Sgt. Robert Jernigan said Edson rarely showed emotion, preferring a quiet, calm approach to leading.

"He'd come to someone who'd maybe forgot to fill a canteen or whose pack was on crooked," Jernigan said. "He'd put his hand on the lad's shoulder and tell him, 'Better get that fixed, son. Might be awful important to have it right out there.' That man could sure handle men."

One Raider aptly described his last six weeks in Quantico as a "preparatory course in physical endurance and deliberate mayhem."[2]

On March 21, 1942, barely a month after their designation as a Raider Battalion, Edson's reconstructed unit was detached from Amphibious Force, Atlantic Fleet and received alert orders to proceed by rail to San Diego for further movement overseas. Limited troop space required Edson to leave behind at Quantico a rear echelon of some 234 men under the command of Major Griffith. At the time, Griffith believed he was being left behind as the heir-apparent to form the nucleus of a 3rd Raider Battalion, an opportunity that he felt he was more than ready for. A kind of rivalry had developed between Edson and the more cerebral Griffith over the months and would continue to build throughout their association.

Under utmost secrecy, Edson's party of twenty-nine officers and 638 men departed Quantico by train on April 1 and arrived in San Diego five days later.

As the train headed south some of the men thought they were headed to Florida for some more rubber boat training, perhaps on some nice warm Caribbean island.

"Things look interesting down here," Private Minier wrote his parents on March 27. "We have drawn full equipment and have our bayonets sharpened and heavy marching order packs ready. We are ready to move anytime but it may be quite a while. When we do leave it will just be to go to Florida or somewhere for more training probably."[3]

Minier's next letter home was dated April 13 and said: "I have arrived safely at my destination beyond the seas."

"None of the men knew where we were going," Sweeney recalled. "But when the train made a right turn and soon rattled over the Mississippi, they had a good indication we were heading west, but they still weren't sure of our destination."[4]

The train would pull over to a siding a couple of times during the day so the men could get off for some calisthenics and stretch their legs. An extra baggage car served as the galley and it was never closed.

Edson used the time in San Diego to add a couple of valuable lieutenants to his staff, Henry Adams Jr., a crack pistol instructor, and John Erskine, a Japanese language specialist. Erskine, who would earn the appellation of "Tiger" during his stay with the Raiders, was a funny-looking specimen of a Marine. Rejected by Marine recruiters in early 1941 because he was "too short, too skinny and too myopic," his language skills made him a valuable commodity when war with Japan broke out.

Erskine was the son of missionary parents, spending the first sixteen years of his life growing up in Japan where he became proficient in reading and speaking Japanese. He knew almost nothing of the Marine Corps and its history and traditions, however. He had never spent a day in training. He didn't know how to render a proper salute, he had no idea how to erect a shelter half and he couldn't find the safety on a .45 pistol or field strip an '03. But, he was fluent in Japanese, had a great heart and a terrific sense of humor, all assets in short supply in a combat unit.[5]

After six days of temporary duty in San Diego, which included lots of calisthenics and cleaning of equipment, the stripped-down battalion embarked aboard the USS *Zeilin* and sailed for "permanent duty beyond the seas." The word "permanent" had an ominous ring to many of the men, who quickly made up jokes about it. The humor served to mask their fear.

The destination—Samoa—was kept a secret until they were well on the way.

Surprisingly, the Raiders endured the sixteen-day trek across the Pacific with a minimum of seasickness. All that training aboard rubber boats and in the holds of the rough-riding APDs must have conditioned them to endure ocean-size swells. Most of them settled in and had a pleasurable trip except for one time when a huge wave doused everyone on deck and scared the wits out of them.

"We didn't have movies, of course," Sweeney remembered. "We played a lot of charades. Some read books and wrote letters. We had meetings every day and we heard about the Doolittle raid on the radio."[6]

On April 22 the ship held the traditional ceremony for crossing the equator. The first-timers, or "pollywogs," were subjected to the ritual dunkings that turned them into "trusty shellbacks."

Edson watched the ceremonies with bemused interest. His mind was on the 234 men left behind in Quantico. Edson sensed there was a move afoot to use his rear-echelon forces under Major Griffith as the nucleus of a third Raider Battalion. Griffith even traveled to southern California in late April to observe the 2nd Raider Battalion as a guest of Carlson. There is no record that Edson, whose feelings toward Carlson were well known, had given Griffith permission to make the visit.

Before he left San Diego, Edson had written a polite but forceful request to the Commandant to expedite the deployment of the balance of his battalion to Samoa. Holcomb's reply gave Edson cause to be concerned. "The disposition of the Rear Echelon . . . is under consideration," it said. "You will be advised if it is found practicable to transfer this unit to your command."[7]

Edson was determined to get them back—and get them back quickly.

• • •

The *Zeilin* pulled into Pago Pago Harbor on the island of Tutuila during a driving rainstorm on April 28. On the next day, a bright morning sun revealed to the men the paradise before them. The harbor was like a postcard with crystal-clear green water surrounding the towering tree-covered mountains.

Edson was not in a sunny mood, however. After setting up camp on the southwest coast near Leone Bay, he composed an urgent message to the Commandant once again asking for the early deployment of his rear-echelon forces at the first opportunity. It was important to him that the entire unit train together. Edson was also unsure of his exact mission. Was he to train his men for hit-and-run amphibious actions or gear them toward behind-the-lines guerrilla combat?

Edson didn't wait for an answer before shaking off the effects of a long ocean voyage. He and his operations officer, Maj. Robert Brown, quickly laid out a plan of heavy training to get the unit combat ready as soon as possible. For some reason, Edson assumed his unit would be called to action almost immediately.

Samoa's rugged hills and pounding surf provided excellent training venues. The sparse population also presented opportunities for live-fire exercises. As the Raiders shook off the effects of a long sea voyage, the training grew longer and more difficult.

"We are off on an overnight hike to Leopards Point which compels us to cross the mountains," Pfc. Henry "Popeye" Poppell wrote in mid May. "The hike is very tiresome. We have a schedule of from five in the morning to ten or twelve at night along such lines as: rubber boating, judo, bayonet fighting, stalking, demolition, first aid, mountain climbing, communication work."[8]

Much of the equipment being used was leftover from

World War I. There was a serious problem with communications. Short-range walkie-talkies proved unreliable in a jungle environment. The long-range radios, called TBXs, were bulky, erratic and prone to break down in the humidity. They had a range of less than twenty miles on land and a little more over water. The TBX weighed 120 pounds and broke into three parts for transportation, requiring a three-man team to lug it into place, assemble it and then operate it. When the unit moved, it had to be disassembled and carried to the next location, where it was reassembled.

The most reliable means of communications proved to be hand and voice signals and the liberal use of runners.

The weaponry wasn't much better. The bolt-action Springfield '03 rifle, "Old Betsy" of World War I fame, was a long-range weapon, better suited for open areas than jungle fighting. The Browning air-cooled .30-caliber machine gun was a superb, lightweight weapon (thirty-one pounds), capable of firing between 400 and 550 rounds per minute. It needed an experienced and steady hand to deliver consistent fire on a target without burning out the barrel, however.

The new M-50 Reising .45 caliber submachine gun, four pounds lighter than the Thompson machine gun, was adopted by the Marine Corps as a personal weapon for company grade officers (captains and lieutenants) and noncommissioned officers. Featuring a twenty-round magazine, it was hailed as an improved version of the Thompson. The Reising, however, never lived up to expectations and was roundly cursed for its unreliability. Intended to be a quick, inexpensive replacement for the "Tommy Gun," it would prove to be too fragile for a jungle environment. If not kept spotlessly clean, it had a tendency to jam or malfunction in battle. Sam Griffith called it "an absolute dud." Other Marines derisively called it the "Rusting Gun."

The weapon of choice was the reliable Browning Automatic Rifle (BAR), which proved its worth time and again on Tulagi and Guadalcanal. It had its drawbacks, however. It was a bit heavy (seventeen pounds) and it had a strong recoil.

Frank Guidone, then a corporal, was like a lot of enlisted men at the time who had fond memories of their stay on Samoa.

"I loved Samoa," Guidone said in a 2002 interview. "We hiked the jungles and over the hills. We were lean and we were eager. We had the finest junior officers in the Corps. Our NCOs were seasoned. Several of them fought in Haiti and Nicaragua. I was a rifleman in A Company and Lew Walt was our company commander."[9]

Guidone thought the world of Walt, who went on to glory at Cape Gloucester, Peleliu, Korea and Vietnam before retiring in 1971 as a four-star general and assistant commandant of the Marine Corps.

Walt was tenacious and determined to complete a mission or project, according to Guidone, who remembered one time when he challenged his NCOs on a steep march up a mountain called "The Rainmaker" on Samoa.

"Walt took off at a gallop and we followed. It was straight up," Guidone said. "Most of us were about to give up but we were determined to keep going as long as Walt was still on his feet." Suddenly, Walt, gasping for breath, stopped and sat down. "This was the first time I ever saw Captain Walt halted in his tracks and it was just in time for us. But then shortly he was on his feet again and away he went to the top."[10]

The quality that set Walt apart, according to Guidone, was his compassion for the enlisted man and his sense of teamwork.

"No matter what we were doing he always made me feel as though I was the expert. He relied on his subordinates to a great extent," Guidone said.

"We trained in the surf with our rubber boats, traversed the jungles in the darkness with our compasses and did hand-to-hand fighting with bayonets and knives. We did all this on two meals a day. We got a jelly sandwich for lunch. Samoa is where we cut our teeth and turned into an elite jungle fighting unit.

"It was in Samoa where we added the toggle ropes that would enable us to climb some steep slopes," Guidone said. "We each carried a length of rope in each of our packs. These ropes could be hooked together making a solid line of rope that we all could grab and climb or drop. On Tulagi my squad utilized this technique to lower ourselves down a sheer cliff while under fire."[11]

Although most of the training was offensive, the battalion was also assigned a defensive mission. Should the Japanese attack Samoa, the Raiders would become the island's mobile reserve.

Most of the time, the Raiders trained in the rugged mountains, thick jungles and sandy beaches of this tropical paradise. A heavy emphasis was placed on physical conditioning, marksmanship, night operations and small unit tactics.

The realistic training claimed two lives and nearly a third. One Raider was accidentally killed by a gunshot wound to his stomach and another died after falling from a 150-foot cliff. Edson took time to write the families of the two men, explaining that their sons had given their lives for their country as fully and honorably as if they had died in battle.

Gunny Tony Yelanich, who served with Edson in Nicaragua, broke his back on a fall and would be sidelined for a full year until it healed.

Samoa was Lt. John Erskine's boot camp. The diminutive Erskine, who went from civilian life directly into the Marines as a Japanese language expert, tried to keep up with the rigorous training but soon fell ill to fatigue. A few days later, Edson spotted an obviously recovered Erskine in the mess tent wolfing down a huge plate of food.

"My God, you're eating like a tiger," Edson said to his little intelligence officer.

"Sir," Erskine is said to have replied, "we're going into combat soon, and I want to at least rate a flesh wound."[12]

Erskine would be called "Tiger" by his comrades for the rest of his life.

Barely 5-foot-4 and scrawny as a scarecrow, Erskine was like a battalion mascot. Though small in stature, he was a beloved figure among the fighting men of the battalion and one who was every inch a Raider. Though he went on to a distinguished career in the Central Intelligence Agency after the war, he remained ever proud of his time with the Raiders, attending all the reunions. When he died in 1996, he was eulogized by John Sweeney, who praised him for his devotion to and affection for the Raiders.

The men also had time for recreation on Samoa. Boxing matches had long been a tradition in the Marines. Called "smokers," the matches developed toughness and stamina, as well as pride among the men.

There were other more leisurely pursuits, as well. Gathering around the radio looking for news, reading, writing letters and playing cards were favorites. One of the most popular card games was acey-deucey. There were also moonlight swims.

Going to church on Samoa was an interesting experience as the Marines listened to the native congregation sing their religious hymns to the tune of "I've Been

Working on the Railroad" and "You Are My Sunshine."

Samoa might have been the only place where Marines looked forward to work details unloading ships. That's where they "appropriated" most of the lumber and building supplies needed to construct their galleys—and much of the food and beer to stock them.

Though off-limits, it was impossible not to notice that many of the Samoan women strolled the island in their native dress, which is to say topless. Many a Raider cast his inquisitive eyes on the native shower stall, hoping to catch more than a glimpse only to be disappointed as the women, according to Guidone, "made skillful use of their lava-lavas, showering very well without exposing very much of their bodies."[13]

Guidone, who grew up in eastern Ohio, was typical of a lot of young Marines at the time. After graduating from high school in 1939, he grew bored helping his father tend bar in Wellsville. He wanted to see some of the world. A year later and against his father's wishes, he let a friend talk him into joining the Navy. When the Navy said there would be a two-week waiting period, he went down the hall to the Marine Corps recruiter and left the next day for Parris Island.

Guidone was home on leave when Pearl Harbor was bombed on Sunday, December 7. He didn't even know where Pearl Harbor was. Now, almost five months later, he was in Samoa. He had no idea where Samoa was, either.

Tom Pollard, "T.D." to his friends, joined the Marine Corps in 1940 as a seventeen-year-old high school dropout. "I hated school and was anxious to do something exciting. I joined to see the world," said Pollard, who was assigned to the 60mm mortar platoon. "When we got to Samoa I thought it was the most beautiful place I'd ever been before but, in truth, there wasn't much to do there. You'd like to have a little recreation."

Pollard spent many of his nights playing poker with other Marines or with the natives.

"One time we were playing poker in a hut with this chief—we called all the natives chief—and he kept winning most of the hands," Pollard said. "Finally somebody asked him where he learned to play poker.

"Bob Hope," he said in his fractured English. He had learned from celebrities who stopped in Samoa on cruise ships in the 1930s.[14]

Pollard's squad had the detail of policing the area around the latrine on Samoa, an important but thankless job.

"It was a six-seater with lids and everything. We made a tarp to put over it to make it more private. It was real fancy," Pollard said.

"When we policed the area we'd throw everything in the hole, add a little gas and then try to set it on fire by lighting some paper. Sometimes it would catch and sometimes it didn't. One of the men, Sgt. Joe Connolly, said he had a friend who could get him some aviation gas. So, the next time we poured a little aviation gas in the hole and it wouldn't light. Then we poured a lot of gas in. The whole thing blew up and the tarp caught on fire. Believe me, everybody had some shit on them."[15]

Edson's mood soared in mid-May when he learned that the Commandant had changed his mind about using his rear echelon as the nucleus for a 3rd Raider Battalion. They would, instead, rejoin their unit on the first available troop ship to Samoa.

In the meantime, Edson was still on the lookout for good men. He and his operations officer, Maj. Robert Brown, who was "double-hatting" as executive officer until Griffith arrived, made it a habit to look over personnel on ships passing through Samoa and trying to convince some of them to become Raiders. They found some, too.

On June 6 came the glorious news of the American victory at Midway and the loss of four Japanese carriers. Edson was exultant, for he knew that this would certainly speed up the deployment of his unit.

The only damper on Edson's enthusiasm was the news that his battalion wouldn't be the first Raider unit to see action in the war. Two companies of Carlson's 2d Raider Battalion had been on Midway during the attack and some of the men had fired off a few rounds at Japanese aircraft.

The battle of Midway was the first decisive defeat by the Japanese Navy in 350 years. Furthermore, it put an end to the long period of Japanese offensive action and restored the balance of naval power in the Pacific. The threat to Hawaii and the west coast was automatically removed and except for operations in the Aleutians area, where the Japanese had landed on the islands of Kiska and Attu, enemy operations were confined to the South Pacific. Edson knew instinctively that the war had changed direction and that all eyes were now on the islands north of Australia and New Zealand.

On July 3, Edson had his full battalion back but there was no time for a reunion. The entire battalion, which had been alerted for combat in the Solomons, embarked two days later for the French colonial island of New Caledonia, arriving on July 7.

On the journey to New Caledonia, Edson tinkered with the makeup of his battalion and made some last-minute reassignments. Impressed with Chambers' performance on Samoa, Edson made him company commander of D Company, moving the more laid-back Capt. Ira Irwin to Battalion Quartermaster and gave E Company to Capt. George Herring.

A Demolitions Platoon was established within E Company under Lieutenant Sweeney. Assigned to the new unit was Gunny Sgt. Angus Goss, who had been through a special demolitions course back at Quantico. Goss would use his talents to earn a Navy Cross on Tulagi the following month.

In addition, Edson arranged the meritorious promotions of veteran sergeants James "Red" Sullivan and Astle "Spike" Ryder to second lieutenant and assigned them to C Company

Edson continued to drive his men hard, particularly D Company, which had just arrived from the States as part of the rear echelon. He was pleasantly surprised to find them in good shape considering their long sea trip and absence from the rest of the battalion. He gave due credit to Griffith for their state of readiness.

Lt. Col. Merrill B. Twining, assistant Operations Officer of the 1st Marine Division, flew to New Caledonia from New Zealand on July 20 to brief Edson on the upcoming operation. Part of the briefing concerned the whereabouts of Guadalcanal coastwatcher Martin Clemens, who had not been heard from for the past few weeks. If he had been eliminated by the Japanese, it would make the mission much more difficult.

Edson offered to send a night patrol to try and locate him. Twining got General Vandegrift to approve the plan and Edson gave the assignment to Lt. Ed Wheeler of D Company. Three days later, however, the plan was scrapped by area commander Vice Admiral Ghormley, who said it was too dangerous.

Edson and Twining were both very disappointed. Twining would later castigate the Navy for its timidity, something he and others would have occasion to do often in the coming campaign.

"Dangerous? I thought everybody realized that this whole war business was dangerous . . . This particular patrol would have been a piece of cake for Edson's men," Twining wrote in his memoirs.[16]

Edson had a good feeling about his men as they got ready to go to war. He felt comfortable that he had done all he could to prepare them. He assembled the entire battalion after a grueling all-night exercise and told them exactly how he felt about them.

"I'm ready to stack you men up alongside any other outfit in the world," he said with obvious pride. "The next time we pull this operation it'll be for keeps."[17]

The next day, July 24, four rifle companies of the Raiders boarded the familiar APDs—*Little, Calhoun, Gregory* and *McKean*—and slowly headed to a rehearsal area off the island of Koro in the Fiji Islands. A couple of days later, the remainder of the Raiders (Easy Company) left for the training area aboard the New Zealand luxury liner *Monowai*.

Sailing with the Raiders were two valuable passengers, former coastwatchers Dick Horton and Henry Josslyn.

"Both men had served on Tulagi and Guadalcanal. Both were invaluable to us with their advice and hand-drawn maps," Sweeney said.

7

Into the Fray

As darkness fell on August 6, General Vandegrift peered into the gathering gloom from the deck of the *McCawley* and tried to put a positive face on the upcoming invasion. He was pleased that the massive convoy had arrived without detection. The element of surprise was crucial because he expected a hard battle. The men had done all they could to get ready. He was confident they would succeed.

Just after midnight on Friday, August 7, the task force approached Savo Island and split off into two attack groups, each dropping off picket destroyers to guard the entrances to the channel. Task Force Yoke, an eight-ship formation that included the 1st Raider Battalion, headed straight for Tulagi while General Vandegrift's Task Force X-Ray, comprised of fifteen transports, turned right toward Red Beach on Guadalcanal. The day dawned clear and hot as the objectives came into view.

A Japanese communications gaffe had contributed to the surprise arrival of the Marines this morning. A postwar study of enemy radio traffic revealed that the Japanese were under the impression that a U.S. task force had left Pearl Harbor. Enemy outposts in the central Pacific—the Marshalls, the Gilberts and the Carolines—were alerted immediately but other areas received the warning on an "information only" basis. Tulagi received the information at 0430 hours on D-day, five minutes after the task force had been sighted entering Sealark Channel.

One hundred miles to the south, meanwhile, Admiral Fletcher's three aircraft carriers turned slowly into the wind and, just before dawn, began to launch their warbirds.

Like most of the Raiders, Pfc. Henry "Popeye" Poppell didn't get any sleep this night.

"I am thinking of home. Those I left behind," Poppell wrote in a diary. "Would I return to them? Before I could realize the time, chow was given. We are eating in the dark as we glide past the islands. The dawn is breaking. We are ready. We can now see the flash of bombs as they scream to meet their objective and a few cans on the outer rim are opening up with salvo after salvo of shells, and we can see them as they land on the beach and in the jungles."[1]

Raiders on deck strained their eyes to catch a glimpse of their objective but the small island of Tulagi was completely overshadowed by the much larger Florida Island behind it to the north. At 0630 all Marines were ordered below just before the ships began their bombardment.

The cruiser *San Juan* lobbed 280 five-inch shells on the southeast corner of Tulagi, nearly a mile from the landing beach. At the same time, thirty-six fighters and forty-four dive bombers from the three U.S. carriers swept over the area. On Tulagi, seven moored Kawanishi flying boats were sunk and nine Zero float planes were wrecked. Several more planes were destroyed at Gavutu-Tanambogo as the planes strafed dockside warehouses, fuel storage tanks and other assorted buildings.

Officers on deck carried on a running description of the events taking place to those below by the on-board speaker system. During the bombardment, a Raider in the intelligence section was accidentally killed when the trigger on his rifle became caught on a bedspring. Some viewed this as a bad omen.

The first troops ashore belonged to B Company, 1st Battalion, 2nd Marines, who landed on Florida Island to secure the promontory sheltering Tulagi and to ensure that the Japanese could not enfilade the force making the major landing. They landed without opposition at about 0740 and never did meet any Japanese. The rest of 1/2 had a similar mission, landing on Florida Island east of Gavutu-Tanambogo at noon to support the 1st Parachute Battalion. They, too, encountered no Japanese.

H-hour for the landing on Tulagi had been set for 0800, one hour prior to the landings on Guadalcanal, but Rupertus radioed Vandegrift that he was ready to go at 0740.

"I know I'm jumping the gun, General," said Rupertus, "but we're all ready to go and I'd feel better about it."

"Take off," Vandegrift said.[2]

Up from below came the Raiders, armed to the teeth and ready to go to war. The noise was deafening and smoke drifted over much of Tulagi. Sailors came up to them as they crossed the deck, slapping them on the back to wish them luck.

"Chocolate cake tonight,"[3] one of the cooks said to a squad from Able Company. Many thought this would be a quick raid and everyone would be back on board in a matter of hours. Earlier, they had gotten an entirely different message when their lieutenant had told them that by this time tomorrow some of them would be dead.

Whichever way it turned out to be, the Raiders went ashore with full stomachs. Some were fed hunks of tinned corned beef for breakfast. Others had steak and eggs. Some of the men had seconds.

"If we had only known of the lean days ahead," one of the Raiders said, "I'm sure many of us would have stuffed steaks in our pockets."

"Stand by to land the landing force," came the order.

Mixing with the gunfire were the sounds of beating hearts and the rattle of winches as the first landing craft was maneuvered into position. Some of the men stepped aboard the Higgins boats as they were lowered to deck level while others went over the side on cargo nets when their boats were lowered some forty feet to the water. The movement of the ships swung the cargo nets back and forth, slamming the men into the steel hulls. Still, the debarkation was a moment of almost welcomed relief.

Many of the men had painted their faces to make themselves look combat ready.

"What a comical detail the camouflaging of our faces turned out to be," Sgt. Hugh Davis of Baker Company later wrote. "Some of the weird designs would have put to shame many an Indian war tribe. I have often wondered what the battalion supply sergeant thought when he received the shipment of vaudeville makeup. Whether this stuff served any useful purpose other than giving us a few laughs may be doubtful but it was well worth its weight in gold for some of the comical scenes created while waiting for the show to get on the road."[4]

Many of the men carried extra bandoleers of ammunition and had hand grenades strung all over them. Others carried extra ammunition boxes. Their packs contained canned C-rations of concentrated coffee and biscuits, meat and beans, vegetable stew and D-ration chocolate bars—enough for two or three days until field kitchens could be set up. Helmets, which had been covered by strips of burlap to cut down on the glare, were worn with the chinstraps unfastened in case a man hit the water instead of the Higgins boat. Even after all their training climbing down the landing nets, Raiders still stepped on the hands of those preceding them and felt their own hands squashed by the men above. Most were too tense to yell out. Once in the boats, the men fixed bayonets and hunkered down below the gunwales. Each boat team consisted of thirty-six men.

"We must have looked mean enough to scare the pants off a brass monkey," one Raider told a reporter afterward. Another wondered if his grin looked as sickly as the guy next to him. Yes, he was told. It did.

PFC Poppell's boat filled quickly and headed away from the USS *Little* to meet up with other landing craft.

The Raiders had been told not to pack much food. "Don't worry about the food," Edson told one company commander. "There's plenty there. Japs eat, too. All you have to do is get it."[5]

Admiral Turner had sent a message to all ships a couple of days before that was pinned on all the bulletin boards.

"On August seventh this force will recapture Tulagi and Guadalcanal Islands which are now in the hands of the enemy," it said. "In this first forward step toward clearing the Japanese out of conquered territory we have strong support from the Pacific Fleet and from the air surface and submarine forces in the South Pacific and Australia. It is significant of victory that we see here shoulder to shoulder the U.S. Navy, Marines and Army and the Australian and New Zealand Air Naval and Army services. I have confidence that all elements of this armada will in skill and courage show themselves fit comrades of those brave men who have already dealt the enemy mighty blows for our great cause. God bless you all."

Edson also had given the Raiders a little pep talk the night before. He repeated a radio propaganda intercept he had heard from the Japanese that asked, "Where are the United States Marines hiding? The Marines are supposed to be the finest soldiers in the world, but no one has seen them yet."

The men looked at each other with questioning looks and then after a few seconds, one Raider in the back yelled out: "We'll be up your ass in the morning." The remark caused some nervous laughter and then it grew into a roar. A thin, bloodless smile crept over Edson's face.

The naval guns were still firing when the Raiders commenced loading the Higgins boats, one by one. The noise was constant. The five-inch guns, belching yellow clouds of smoke, sounded like machine guns, pumping out round after round.

Above them, the men could see the carrier planes swarming over Tulagi. The dull "thump" of bombs from the dive bombers echoed off the surrounding islands.

As each Higgins boat was loaded, it swung away from its mother ship and headed for the rendezvous point to circle until all were ready for a coordinated run to the beach.

The scheme of maneuver called for Baker and Dog companies to land abreast across Blue Beach, to be quickly followed by Able and Charlie companies, with Easy Company bringing up the rear. The Raiders would then cross the island in a column of companies, wheel to the right to form a battalion front and advance abreast.

Easy Company, minus its four machine-gun platoons, which were attached to the line companies, provided beach security in the landing area of Blue Beach. At 0916, just after the last Raider unit had hit the beach, the first elements of the 2nd Battalion, 5th Marines landed on Blue

Beach, releasing E Company of the Raiders from the task of securing the beachhead. Once ashore, 2/5 proceeded across the island, formed a line abreast and turned left to sweep northwest.

Tulagi is an island about two miles long and half a mile wide lying just a scant 125 yards south of Florida Island. A ridge rising over 300 feet above the sea marks the northwest-southeast axis of the island. About two-thirds of the way down from the northwest tip of Tulagi the ridge is broken by a ravine and then rises again in a triangle of hills, the southeastern-most of which was designated Hill 281 after its elevation in feet.

"Everyone down," came the order as Sergeant Davis' Higgins boat plowed dead ahead for the landing beach.

"All is quiet," Davis said. "Soon the old Lewis guns in the bow of the Higgins boat began to rattle. Someone screams. Could this be our first casualty? No, just a hot extracted round from one of the Lewis guns [dropping] down the collar of one of the men."[6]

Every one of the landing crafts either scraped or got hung up on the coral reef, some thirty to 100 yards from Blue Beach. The jolt of hitting the reef threw the men against the bulkhead, causing a few bumps and bruises. A few were tossed overboard. As they had been taught, the men rolled over the side and into water up to their armpits as the Higgins boats swayed back and forth on the reef. Once unloaded, the lighter Higgins boats had no trouble maneuvering off the reef and heading back to the APDs to take in another wave.

"Over the side," came the order in Sergeant Davis' boat. "Fortunately, we all could swim and made the beach in good order," Davis said. "Gunner [Cecil] Clark is standing at the edge of the undergrowth now giving us the word to keep moving. We moved. Through the graveyard, shell holes and felled trees."[7]

"This is war, boys—nothing like starting it in a graveyard!" bellowed Clark."[8]

Other than a few scrapes and abrasions from the coral, no one had been injured on the landing. But, most of them were soaking wet.

By 0815, the rifle companies were ashore and the lead elements from Baker and Dog companies were making their way up and over the central ridge. Some sporadic small-arms fire could be heard in the distance but it didn't affect the landing operation.

Practically the last man ashore was Colonel Edson, through no fault of his own. His Higgins boat stalled and floundered helplessly after leaving the APD. He tried to flag down another boat that was returning from the beach empty but apparently he couldn't be heard. Another empty boat approached Edson's boat warily. Ordered to come alongside and take his men ashore, the coxswain replied that his orders were to return to his ship. Edson exploded in a rare display of uncontrolled temper. After much shouting and threats of court-martial, the coxswain brought his boat alongside and delivered the Raiders to Blue Beach—but not before getting hung up on the coral reef. By the time Edson got to shore, mad as the proverbial wet hen, his battalion had crossed the island and was proceeding to the southeast not yet under fire.

Commandeering John Sweeney's demolition's platoon, which had been guarding the beachhead, Edson hightailed it inland to find his battalion.

Earlier, the Japanese radio station on Tulagi, which had spotted the American armada at first light, began sending messages to Rabaul. The first one, at 0625, simply said:

"Large force of ships, unknown number or types, entering the sound. What can they be?" A half hour later, another more urgent message was sent from Tulagi saying: "Enemy task force of twenty ships attacking Tulagi. Undergoing severe bombing. Landing preparations under way. Help needed."

The station got off another message at 0805, saying that the "landing of enemy troops has commenced," and promising to "burn our documents" and "fight bravely to the last man." There were no radio messages sent from Guadalcanal.

The first thing the Raiders saw when they landed at Blue Beach was an old Church of England (Episcopal) cemetery. Lieutenant Colonel Griffith led Baker and Dog companies ashore and quickly formed a defensive cordon around the landing beach, waiting for Able and Charlie companies to arrive before pushing inland. As hoped, Blue Beach was not defended. The Raiders had come in through the back door. The only casualties were from the slime-covered coral reef, which bloodied some hands and knees and ripped some clothing.

Everyone was soaking wet. Because the Higgins boats did not have bow ramps, the men had to roll over the side to disembark. Some found themselves in waist-deep water, some neck-deep and some in over their heads. Others fell into holes in the reef. Those carrying extra loads of weapons and equipment struggled mightily as all landed safely. Only one rifle was lost coming in.

The first man up the hill and across the ridge was Pfc. Cliff Fitzpatrick, a scout with the 1st Platoon of Baker Company. Hot on his heels was his squad leader, Corp. Ben Howland. Lt. Eugene "Tex" Key, the platoon leader, wasn't far behind. They led a push 1,000 yards straight across the island, with the rest of the battalion following. When Baker Company's lead squad reached the crest of the ridge, they looked down on the harbor on the other side and saw five Japanese float planes sinking at their seaplane ramp. A four-engine patrol bomber lay nearby and other Japanese planes could be discerned beneath the water. Meanwhile, not a shot had been fired at the Raiders.

Lieutenant Key reported to the troops behind him that all was clear and then formed his platoon in a skirmish line along the harbor. Maj. Lloyd Nickerson, the company commander, arrived on the scene and gave the order to proceed down the reverse slope to the inner harbor and sweep through the village of Sesapi and a section called Chinatown.

Shortly after forming up and starting their advance, B Company spotted a Japanese flag flying over a building on a small island in Tulagi Harbor. Gunnery Sergeant Clint Haines approached Major Nickerson and asked permission to set up his 60mm mortars and fire at the flag. The request was denied. Nickerson thought there would be better targets for his mortars.

Another group from Baker Company entered a store in Chinatown and saw evidence of a panic departure by its occupants. Blankets were strewn on the floor, furniture was overturned and some weapons were left behind in their flight. Fearing booby traps, the Raiders were ordered not to touch anything and continue the advance along the inner harbor.

The rest of the battalion, once they had moved inland, wheeled right and started down the island four companies abreast. Meanwhile, the 2nd Battalion of the 5th Marines came ashore on Blue Beach, crossed the island behind the Raiders and wheeled left. After completing its mission without opposition, the 5th Marines later reversed course and headed southeast where they would be in position to provide support for the Raiders.

The original plan called for all four companies to be lined up abreast (B, D, A and C companies from top to bottom) and start its sweep down the island within an hour after landing. But, because of the rugged terrain and heavy bush, it was closer to three hours—even without any significant enemy resistance. By 1100, the men were sweating profusely and already showing considerable fatigue. Many canteens were already empty.

"What the hell is this, another training exercise?" quipped one Raider during the early going. Three hours after landing, the Marines still hadn't met any opposition.

All that would soon change.

At about 1100, Edson called a conference of his company commanders at his temporary command post in an abandoned Japanese trench on the nose of the ridge and told them there would be a coordinated air and naval bombardment on the terrain ahead of his battalion prior to a sweep to the southeast.

Edson, still spitting mad after his experience getting ashore, took time to chew out one of his company commanders, Maj. Justice Chambers, for an action he deemed disrespectful. Chambers had left the conference briefly to rush to the site of some firing on his Dog Company. Moments later, a grinning Chambers returned to the conference in high spirits because his men had wiped out a Japanese patrol. Edson fixed him with a cold stare and, in a voice loud enough for everyone to hear, said, "Major, don't you ever leave my presence again without my permission."[9]

It was an act of rash behavior by a commanding officer that would happen again later that day to Lieutenant Key and Maj. Ken Bailey, who all-too-willingly rushed to the sounds of gunfire without regard for their personal safety, much as Edson, himself, would do quite often in his career. While Edson was extremely lucky to escape injury, Key, the son of a Dallas preacher, and Bailey would each lose his life before the end of the campaign.

Baker Company drew first blood of the operation along the left flank bordering the harbor. As the advance guard approached Carpenter's Wharf they ran into about two dozen natives, mostly women and children, who appeared confused and scared. They were escorted to the rear and the patrol continued.

Moving beyond the cover of a stone jetty, Pvt. Thomas F. Nickel was hit by a sniper. Lieutenant Key, probably too far forward, saw Nickel fall. Key instinctively jumped over a stone wall and rushed to his aid only to be cut down by more sniper fire. Then, with others providing covering fire, Dr. Sam Miles, a twenty-eight-year-old Princeton and Johns Hopkins Medical School graduate, grabbed his black bag and crawled out to see if he could help Nickel and Key. He, too, was struck by a sniper's bullet before he could open his bag in a deadly display of marksmanship. All three died on the spot—the first battle casualties of the Tulagi-Guadalcanal campaign.

"Lt. Key first ordered me to move out and then said, 'No, stay here and cover me,'" recalled Pfc. John A. Van Ness. "He took one step and was shot in the chest. He fell and, as he rolled over, mouthed the words, 'stay back,' then died. I was sure then and now that Lt. Key took that bullet for me because the entire squad knew the sniper was behind that barrel."[10]

Pvt. John Gilligan was also killed in this initial skirmish but Pvt. Thomas Church was luckier. An enemy bullet had pierced the front of his helmet and glanced upward, ripping through the top of his helmet without touching his head. He didn't know how close he came to getting killed until someone later asked him about the hole in his helmet.

With Key's 1st platoon pinned down behind the sea wall, Major Nickerson ordered Lt. Rex Crockett to move his 2nd Platoon past the 1st down the beach. After advancing a short distance, the platoon reached a point where the sea cut in almost to the main ridge, leaving a very narrow passage that allowed only one man at a time to cross. The Japanese allowed about two-thirds of Crockett's platoon to pass this bottleneck before opening fire on the rear squad, killing one man and wounding two others.

Pfc. Vince Cassidy came to the rescue, displaying a pitching arm he never knew he had.

"I remember passing a group of grave markers at the base of the cliff inscribed in Japanese [but] no sign of living Japs," Cassidy said. "[We] approached a place where the space between the sea and the cliff narrowed, cautiously moving through expecting the enemy to be just beyond.

"Still no sign, then suddenly shots, shouts, screams and the horrible realization that those behind us were under fire . . . the frantic look on Lt. Crockett's face . . . other shouts from which we knew that [Pvt. John J.] Gilligan was badly hit . . . can't remember how many of us were cut off, at least all of our squad, I think . . . the desperate feeling that something had to be done . . . scaling the cliff, an awareness of sniper fire from a high point and the grateful realization that he wasn't a very good shot."[11]

Cassidy recalled pulling himself over the crest of the cliff and, while hanging on to a shrub to keep his balance, throwing his two grenades, then going back down to get some more and doing it again until the sniper fire stopped.

"I don't believe any of us in the squad had ever thrown

them before," said Cassidy, whose heroics helped defuse what could have been a very dangerous situation.

Meanwhile, the Marines had received word at about 1115 from Australian coastwatcher Paul Mason on southern Bougainville of an impending Japanese air attack. "I say, old boy, we've got something stirring over here. Looks like you've got twenty-seven meatballs coming to tea," was Mason's way of saying that twenty-seven twin-engine Japanese bombers, called "Bettys" by the Marines, were on their way from Rabaul. The news forced the American transports to halt unloading and prepare to hoist anchor for evasive action.

The Japanese had reacted quickly by diverting a planned air strike at New Guinea to the Guadalcanal area. In their haste, however, the flotilla commander sent the planes off with 550-pound bombs instead of rearming them with torpedoes, a huge stroke of good luck for the American transports hovering off the beaches.

Some of the Allied ships picked up the message direct from Mason. However, most got it by a complicated but highly effective relay through Port Moresby, then relayed to Townville, Australia, which had the strongest transmitter in the region. The news was next flashed to Canberra, then to Pearl Harbor and, finally, to the fleet off Guadalcanal. One way or another, every ship in the invasion fleet got the word within twenty-five minutes.

The bombers, along with seventeen Zero fighters, arrived over the area at 1300 and were met by waiting Wildcats from the three U.S. carriers for the first dogfight of the Guadalcanal campaign. Only one American ship (the destroyer *Mugford*) was hit during the air attack but the unloading of much-needed supplies was delayed for several critical hours.

Thanks to the timely warning from Mason, the carrier planes were able to launch their Grumman Wildcat fighters and get into position to intercept the enemy planes when they arrived. They needed every advantage they could get because the Zero was much more maneuverable than the Wildcat.

At about 1320, the Wildcats dove into the covering flight of Zeros as the surface ships opened up on the bombers. Bombers began dropping out of the sky, trailing smoke as they crashed into the sea. The rest came on but their bombing was wild. The Allies claimed they shot down sixteen Japanese planes that first day, thanks to the early warning from Mason. The Americans lost eleven fighters and one dive bomber.

The network of coastwatchers on neighboring islands would play a vital role in the survival of the American force on Guadalcanal in the coming weeks. The 1,200-mile round-trip from Rabaul pushed the fuel capacity of Japanese aircraft to their limit, leaving them little room for maneuver and precious little time over the target. They had to fly a straight line, northwest to southeast and back again, both times right over the coastwatchers on Bougainville. Any deviation and they might run out of gas and be forced to ditch in the sea.

The Raiders resumed their march down Tulagi after the enemy air raid and, in no time Dog Company forces had occupied the Residency building in the lower center of the island, which would later become Edson's command post.

The Residency wasn't taken without cost, however. While conducting a fire mission near the Residency on a target to the right, Major Chambers was seriously wounded, apparently by one of his own 60mm mortar rounds that either exploded prematurely or struck an overhanging tree limb. The blast, which injured several other Raiders, broke Chamber's right wrist and injured his left wrist and right leg.

Chambers, temporarily dazed by the blast, came to when he was being treated by a corpsman. Noticing that his watch was blown to bits in the explosion, one of his men gave him a British-made lady's wristwatch he had liberated from a dead Japanese officer. It drew a weak smile from Chambers, who regained his feet and tried to carry on.

"We kept arguing with the Major about the angle of the mortar tube," Pvt. Finley Foden said in describing what happened. "He kept raising the angle. We were under a tree and the round hit a branch."[12]

The energetic Chambers, who had been chewed out earlier in the day by Edson, was again probably too far forward but that appeared to be the order of the day for all the Raider officers. Two and a half years later, the man his troops called "Jumping Joe" and "Joe Potts" would be awarded the Medal of Honor for his aggressive leadership on Iwo Jima.

Major Bailey, who would also receive the Medal of Honor for his heroism in a future engagement, was also seriously injured in a foolish way. Leading Charlie Company on the right flank along the southern part of the island, he ran into heavy sniper fire from a cave-like bunker in the south face of Hill 208 overlooking the cricket field.

According to Platoon Sgt. Robert Jernigan, Bailey dashed forward, jumped atop the bunker and tried to kick open the firing ports so his men could stuff grenades in the holes.

"Six enemy troops rushed out of the bunker with bayonets fixed intent on liquidating Ken," Jernigan later reported. "[Bailey] sprayed them with his Reising Gun, killing all six of them within twenty feet of where he was standing. [Bailey] received a Jap bullet in the thigh which had been fired through one of the remaining firing ports and had to be evacuated."[13]

Like Chambers, Bailey wouldn't leave right away. Temporarily patched up and limping badly, he and Jernigan went off to reconnoiter the front line. A sniper's bullet from the top of a coconut tree, one probably aimed at Bailey, struck Jernigan in the chest and exited out the center of his back near the spine.

Moments later, Bailey again charged a bunker, this time with weapons platoon leader Lt. "Spike" Ryder. Both men were knocked flat by an explosion. Both officers, along with Jernigan, were immediately evacuated to the battalion aid station and Edson sent Major Griffith forward to temporarily take over Charlie Company from Bailey.

Meanwhile, Lt. Clay Boyd had pushed his 2nd Platoon of Charlie Company through enemy-held territory to the southeastern point of the island where they were to link up with a platoon from Dog Company. When the latter didn't show and with darkness settling in, Boyd would find himself on his own and cut off from the rest of the Raiders.

In the center of the line, Maj. Lew Walt led Able Company forward across the small pitch-and-putt golf course. He, too, was probably much too far forward for his own good. He missed getting killed by a matter of inches.

"As we were approaching one of the trees," Walt later wrote, "one of the scouts hollered at me, 'Look out, there is a Jap,' and he pointed toward the old road bed about 40 yards to my right. As I turned my head, I just by chance saw the flash of light on a Jap bayonet and a Jap, with gold buckteeth and black-rimmed glasses, was lying flat on his belly among the bushes and was sighting down his rifle barrel at me. I dropped as fast as I could and his first shot hit the tree about four inches above my head. He reloaded rapidly and for some reason I was unable to move. I saw him aiming in on me again when he was hit by a burst from Red Hills' BAR and [Cliff] McGlocklin's Reising. The Jap's second round hit the tree above my head just two inches below the first round. Two years later, I returned and looked at that tree. The two bullet holes were still discernible and I thanked God again that 'Red' and 'Mac' saved me from being the first casualty of A Company."[14]

Later, Walt would rush out into a hail of bullets and carry a mortally wounded Marine to safety, earning the everlasting respect of his men. Also exposing himself to fire time and again was Colonel Edson, who seemed to have a protective shield around him. Edson, and the rest of his officers, often led from the front rather than rely on the faulty communications systems then in place. Orders were often delivered by runners or in person rather than by the unreliable walkie-talkie radios.

Able Company ran into stiff opposition later in the afternoon when it approached a ridge at the far end of the golf course just before the cricket field. The enemy had barricaded themselves in houses and bunkers at the foot of the ridge, preventing any further advance of Walt's company. By nightfall, Able Company had fallen back around the Residency with orders to hold it against expected counterattacks during the night.

Charlie Company, located on the extreme right flank, also pulled back a bit to set up night defensive positions. Capt. Robert Thomas, who had now assumed command from Griffith, who had temporarily taken over when Bailey was shot, suddenly realized he was missing Lieutenant Boyd's 2nd Platoon, which left a gap between his unit and Able Company in the night deployment. It would nearly result in disaster.

The Raiders found out that first day that Japanese soldiers were not the stereotypical scrawny, buck-toothed, four-eyed draftees they saw in movies or in the funny papers and magazines. They were tough and they were good shots. In fact, they were deadly marksmen. Many of the Raiders who were killed on Tulagi were shot through the temple.

The Raiders were also good shots. Edson, the former captain of the Marine rifle team, had seen to that. One of the Raider sharpshooters who attained legendary status on Tulagi was Pfc. John Holladay of B Company. Holladay, a thirty-year-old native of Florence, S.C., called his Springfield rifle "Ole Lucifer." Earlier that first day, legend has it, Holladay took aim at a Japanese sniper in a distant palm tree and squeezed the trigger. When nothing happened, 1st Sgt. Brice Maddox supposedly told Holladay he'd better shoot the sniper again. Holladay shook his head slowly from side to side and said: "Top, ole Lucifer don't lie; he'll fall in a minute."[15] Maddox smiled and shook his head. Sure enough, a few seconds later, the Japanese sniper slid out of the tree and crashed to the ground—dead on arrival.

The first day of combat had more than its share of highs and lows as well as tears and laughter. One of the lighter moments of the day came when baby-faced Pvt. William Dodamead Jr. stood up during a lull and shouted to anyone who would listen that "this is a helluva way to spend my seventeenth birthday."[16]

Another occurred when Sgt. Tom Pollard of A Company found himself in the same foxhole with Sgt. "Peep Sight" Mills, an old campaigner from the 1930s, during an enemy mortar barrage.

" 'Peep Sight' used to tell us all these war stories about fighting in Nicaragua," Pollard said, "so when the shells started coming close I turned to him and said, 'Hey "Peep," was it like this in Nicaragua?'"

"Damn you Pollard," he said, "we didn't have any mortars like this in Nicaragua."

At 1625, Edson phoned General Rupertus, who was still aboard ship off Tulagi, and told him the enemy force had broken contact and withdrawn to strongholds around Hill 281 at the southeastern tip of the island. He would need another day to complete the sweep. He ordered his companies to pull back a bit and dig in for an expected counterattack during the night.

Red Mike tried to give Rupertus a feel for what had been going on all day so that he could brief General Vandegrift.

"Snipers were everywhere, in the trees, in caves, behind rocks," Edson said. "Many times the snipers would let us go by and then open up on us from the rear. Some of their holes were natural caves. Others were blasted out of rock. The only way to get them was by dynamite and hand grenades."

Edson also gave Rupertus some casualty figures. They were nearly 20 percent, including two company commanders (Bailey and Chambers).

Edson was concerned about the loss of Bailey and Chambers so early in the campaign and the effect it would have on his battalion's first night of combat. He passed the word for everyone to remain awake and alert for an all-out effort by the Japanese to retake the island.

He was determined to hold the ground they had won.

• • •

Over at Gavutu-Tanambogo, 3,000 yards east of Tulagi, the fighting had been vicious from the outset. The 1st Parachute Battalion, only 377 men, was actually outnumbered by the Japanese, who had been well concealed in caves and bunkers awaiting the landing. The Japanese garrison consisted of some 536 men, 342 members of an air group operating a seaplane base on Gavutu, 144 from a construction unit and fifty from a special naval landing force.

Each of the tiny islands (Gavutu was barely 500 by 300 yards, Tanambogo even smaller), which were joined by a 500-yard causeway, was dominated by a well-fortified hill and coral reefs that only allowed landings from the east. The net effect of the terrain and coral configuration was to channel attackers into a narrow funnel dominated by high ground on two sides. A shortage of landing craft dictated that the landings begin around noon after all troops were ashore on Tulagi. This gave the enemy added time to prepare for the invasion.

After a brief air and sea bombardment, the defenders let the first wave of Parachutists land on Gavutu before riddling the second and third waves. Among the first Marines killed during the landings were two staff officers, and those seriously wounded included the battalion commander, Maj. Robert H. Williams, who was evacuated on the same Higgins boat he arrived in. With initiative and a ton of courage, the "Chutes," as they were called, moved out at 1400 to take Hill 148 on Gavutu, which eliminated one area of withering fire. However, shortly after taking the hill, they were accidentally attacked by American aircraft, which resulted in several deaths and injuries.

Late in the afternoon, with Gavutu still unsecured and Tanambogo yet to be attacked, the Chutes requested reinforcements. Told there were only a few snipers on Tanambogo, General Rupertus decided to send Company B of the 1st Battalion, 2nd Marines (1/2), the same unit that had provided flank security for the Tulagi landings earlier that morning. Unfortunately, naval gunfire had ignited a huge gasoline fire that illuminated the five boats bringing in the fresh troops at about 1845. One of the shells landed amid the boats, wounding a coxswain and sending it off course. Two other boats, unaware of the wounded coxswain, followed the boat away from the landing area. As a result, only two of the five boats reached shore where heavy fire caused them to reembark shortly after landing.

Rupertus would have to request the other two battalions of the 2nd Marines, which were being held in reserve, before the campaign was over. The 2nd Battalion would head for Tulagi and the 3rd would be needed to secure Gavutu-Tanambogo.

Gavutu was declared secure by noon of the next day but Tanambogo needed more softening before it could be safely assaulted by Lt. Col. Robert Hunt's 3rd Battalion, 2nd Marines. Two sorties of Dauntless dive bombers swept over the little island but once again some of their bombs fell short, resulting in the deaths of several Marines.

A livid Hunt got on his radio and asked that he be spared further air "support." Instead, he requested naval gunfire. The destroyer *Buchanan* maneuvered through the treacherous reefs into point-blank range and blasted Tanambogo so that reinforcements could be landed. It wasn't until the third day that the islands were finally declared secure.

Meanwhile, the landings on Red Beach on Guadalcanal, five miles east of Lunga Point and the airfield, had gone off without a hitch. The only injury reported was when a Marine cut himself trying to open a coconut.

One of the early arrivals ashore was writer Richard Tregaskis, who captured the mood of the debarkation with crystal clarity.

"I walked among the troops gathered on the forward deck, and found them silent and nervous—a contrast to the gaiety and song which had filled the few preceding days," he wrote. "There did not seem to be much to say, although a few lads came up with the inevitable, 'Well, this is it.'

"The first of our Marines clambered over the rail and swung down the rope nets into the boats. The boats pulled away and more came up, and the seeping waterfall of Marines continued to slide over the side."[17]

The Marines could see two columns of smoke and fire rising to the west where a fuel dump must have been hit by naval gunfire. Once the bombardment ended, a haze of black smoke hung over the landing area almost obscuring the beachhead. Moments later, a covering screen of fighter planes streaked over the island, strafing targets of opportunity. The loaded Higgins boats headed for the smoke and ground ashore on the white sandy beach as Marines quickly raced to the tree line. Each of the little boats, sporting a small American flag at the stern, backed up and headed back to the transports for more passengers.

"In our boat there was no talking, despite the excitement of the moment," Tregaskis wrote. "The motor was making too much noise, at any rate. We sat and looked at each other and occasionally peeped over the side to glimpse other boats plunging shoreward in showers of spray around us, or to cock an eye at the strangely silent beach."[18]

Once on land, too many Marines milled around waiting for orders, creating a backup on the beach. The first order was to get off the beach and into the coconut palms. It didn't take long to work up a sweat. The Marines, showing the effect of being cooped up aboard ship for over two weeks, had underestimated how tough it would be to maneuver in the thick jungle. They were slow to advance on the objective, drawing the wrath of Vandegrift. In fairness to the ground commanders, had they been able to study aerial photographs before the landing, they might have been able to pick out easy, natural routes instead of a straight compass course through the thick jungle.

Many Marines, unlike the Raiders over on Tulagi, were burdened with excessively heavy packs and extra ammunition. Some men began to lighten their loads by discarding spare articles of clothing until the sergeants got it under control. Many were drained by the heat and stupefying humidity. Short of water (because of shortages, the men were issued only one canteen instead of two) and salt tablets, they bogged down quickly. Twilight found the Marines one mile from their starting point, dispersed and exhausted.

"We had allowed more time than we needed," Lieutenant Colonel Twining said of the sea voyage to Guadalcanal. "This miscalculation required the Marines to spend an unnecessarily long wait in the boats wallowing in a choppy sea, so there was a good deal of seasickness before we got ashore."[19]

There was something sinister and forbidding about Guadalcanal that gave the men "the creeps" when it was first spotted from the transports. Some of the men expected King Kong to come out of the jungle and meet them on the beach. Once ashore, they found the terrain covered with huge trees with knobby roots, thick tangles of vines with sharp thorns and vegetation so dense as to be almost impenetrable.

Probably the most colorful description of Guadalcanal came from an unnamed Marine pilot who told one of his comrades during the dark days to come that "if the world needed an enema this would be the right place to put in the hose."

When Vandegrift came ashore he discovered what his assault troops had already found out for themselves. Guadalcanal might be beautiful from afar, but the island stunk. It stunk with a particularly offensive odor of rotting vegetation that had accumulated over untold centuries in the past. No man who got it in his nostrils would ever forget the awful smell of Guadalcanal.

"The rain forest was truly something to see and feel," wrote historian John Foster. "Tall, thick trees rose straight up to a height of ten stories or more, like columns in an enormous lost cathedral, to a roof of muscular green leaves that blocked out Mount Austen and even the afternoon sun. In the deep oppressive gloom, the only sounds were the angry cries of white cockatoos, mynah birds, and other wild fowl screaming at the interlopers—and the drip-drip-drip from leaf to leaf of the last South Pacific rain."[20]

By dusk, the invaders held a beachhead a mile wide and a half-mile deep. Vandegrift, who arrived on shore at about 1600, was clearly disappointed with the day's effort and decided to call a halt. He ordered his men to dig in for the night. For passwords they used words like "Honolulu," "lollipop" and "lollygag," believing that the Japanese would have difficulty pronouncing the letter "l."

"I never understood that," historian William Manchester would later write. "I think their problem was the letter 'r.' They called us Malines."[21] (Actually, the Japanese had trouble with both l and r and the word Marine came out sounding more like "Madeen.")

Occasional shots rang out all night as nervous Marines fired on shadows and strange noises.

"Once, near midnight, I heard a submachine gun cracking very near the grove," Tregaskis wrote of the first night ashore. "Then a rifle barked. Then another. And soon, five or six guns were firing simultaneously, and the bright tracer bullets were zipping in several directions over the grove where we lay. Some of the slugs whined through the trees close by. Then the firing fell off and died, and we went back to sleep again."[22]

The passwords often proved difficult for the Marines, as Robert Leckie described during his first night ashore. The password was "Lilliputian" and Leckie challenged one of his pals who had gone off to relieve himself.

"Halt!" Leckie cried out.

"Fer Gawd's sake, Lecky, don't shoot. It's me, Briggs."

"Gimme the password."

"Lily-poo . . . luly . . ."

"C'mon, c'mon! The password, or I'll let you have it."

"Luly-pah . . . lily-poosh . . ." Silence, and then, in outrage:

"Aw, shit—shoot!"[23]

After a nervous night, the Marines regrouped the next morning and swept over their objectives. By late afternoon, advance patrols from the 1st Battalion, 1st Marines occupied the airstrip. Rifles at the ready for expected resistance, they instead found the area deserted. Huge stores of ammunition, weapons, food and machinery were abandoned by an enemy who had fled into the jungle without firing a shot. Also left behind were many personal diaries, which proved to be a great source of intelligence.

"We burst in upon a breakfast table left in a rush. It looked as if the Japanese had left by the back door as we came in the front," Tregaskis wrote. "Serving dishes, set in the middle of the table were filled with meat stew, rice and cooked prunes. Bowls and saucers around the edge were half full of food. Chopsticks had been left propped on the edges of dishes, or dropped in haste on the floor mat."[24]

Tregaskis looked around and saw a small group of prisoners, who turned out to be laborers, being marched to the rear. "There were three of them," he said, "walking in single file, and the Marines, looking huge by comparison, shooed them along like pigeons."

The enemy had fled in a panic when the high explosive shells of the naval bombardment had ripped through their camp. Most of their tents were either flattened or shredded by the fire. "In one little grove we found two shell-blasted bodies, now well attended by flies," wrote Tregaskis. "One body sat at the foot of a tree, eyes staring straight ahead. The left leg had been nipped off at the knee, and the lower part of the leg, with the shoe still on the foot, lay a few feet to one side."

William Whyte, an intelligence officer with the 1st Marines, was surprised at some of the luxurious conditions the Japanese had erected.

"Our enemy were sybarites!" he later wrote. "The officers, we discovered, lived in a tent city at Kukum with concrete floors, and they had brought with them a perfectly astounding collection of pornography. They had electric lights, steel-covered air-raid shelters, and elaborate concrete privies."[25]

White was also amazed at the amount of alcoholic beverages left by the Japanese, much of which was confiscated by his commanding officer, Lt. Col. William "Wild Bill" McKelvy, whom he described as "an original, a character, and an eccentric. He was also bibulous."

Before any of the Marines could lay claim to the copious amounts of beer and sake, according to Whyte, "McKelvy stepped forward and impounded all of it. The booze, he said, was off-limits to everyone, officers and men alike. Except, no surprise, himself. For the rest of the time we were on Guadalcanal, McKelvy nipped. He was never actually falling-down drunk. He was always just a little squiffed."[26]

"We named everything we captured for the Japanese premier, General Hideki Tojo. The trucks, then, were the Tojo Truck Works. We even picked up an ice-making machine. It became the Tojo Ice Company."

Nearby, the gravel-and-coral runway, 2,600 feet long and 150 feet wide, was nearly nine-tenths finished. All that remained was a 200-foot section in the center of the strip. Japanese fighter planes had been scheduled to make their first landings in a matter of days. Using captured trucks and earth-rollers, the Marines would have the field operational for American aircraft in less than two weeks. Under constant sniper fire, the work crews were forced to dig foxholes every few yards so they would have a place to take cover. On August 12, they named the airstrip Henderson Field in honor of Maj. Lofton Henderson, a Marine squadron leader killed in the Battle of Midway.

The strip lay in the middle of a cleared field, mostly surrounded by the coconut palms of the Lever Brothers' plantation. It ran approximately northeast to southwest, with the latter end just short of the Lunga River. The prevailing tradewinds of the area came from the southwest.

Radio Tokyo immediately derided the Marine landings as "summer insects which have dropped into the fire" and vowed to push them back into the sea.

The Americans had other plans, of course. On August 8, just after the airfield had been captured, one young recruit ran up to a small blackboard nailed to a coconut tree near the center of the Japanese camp, took out a piece of chalk and wrote: "Tokyo your [sic] full of shit, Pvt. M. Shapiro."[27]

8

Banzai

As darkness fell on Tulagi the first night, the Raiders could hear groups of Japanese chattering away all along their front. It sounded very much like a football crowd chanting "push 'em back, push 'em back, way back." More than a few fueled their fervor with copious amounts of rice wine.

Though they were not front-line infantry troops, the infantry-trained Special Naval Landing Force (called "rikusentai" in Japanese) on the island fought savagely, adhering to their Bushido Code that preferred death to surrender. They slapped bamboo sticks together, yelling such things as "Hey, Babe Ruth" and "We drink American-boy blood." The howled threats were supposed to make the Americans "scatter like leaves." That tactic had worked well in China and other areas of southeast Asia.

The strongest attack came at 2230 as Japanese forces broke through the line between A and C companies, temporarily cutting off the latter. It was the first of many banzai attacks to come during the Pacific war.

"[The Japanese] came to within fifty to seventy-five yards of my command post," Edson later wrote. "They were using hand grenades, rifles and machine guns. We suffered quite a few casualties as our men fought hard to hold them back. One machine-gun company lost fifty percent of its noncommissioned officers."

The Japanese did occupy a building near the Residency but were repelled in their attack on the latter, according to Captain Sweeney.

Edson, of course, was not content to sit around his battalion command post that first night and get his news secondhand. Though his night vision was poor, he insisted on visiting his front-line commanders. Sweeney, who was in charge of the overall security of Edson's CP, was enlisted to escort his boss on this risky venture.

"We all had code names. I was John Wolf and Edson was Red Mike," Sweeney said in a 2001 interview. "It was pitch-dark. Edson held on to my cartridge belt and every four or five steps we were challenged by a Raider voice. I would answer, 'John Wolf with Red Mike.' At one stop I heard a Raider mutter, 'Goddamn, what's he doing here?' "

"Colonel, this is scary for me and dangerous for you," Sweeney finally said a half hour into the mission. Edson saw Sweeney's logic and agreed. The two men returned to the CP, with Sweeney calling out "John Wolf with Red Mike" all the way.[1]

The next morning, Edson and Sweeney learned that Able Company's Lt. Arthur Gewehr was fired on and hit in the shoulder by one of his own men as he was checking his front line.

Other interesting nom de guerres, which would be used throughout the campaign, included "Ken Dill" for Bailey, "Silent Lew" for Walt and "Joe Potts" for Chambers.

On the advice of language officer Tiger Erskine, the Raiders had chosen passwords that used the letter "L," believing that the Japanese would have a difficult time pronouncing them. Often, however, the jumpy Raiders would shoot before the password could be answered. That's how Lieutenant Gewehr was wounded.

Shepherding Edson around the front lines in the middle of the night wasn't the only special assignment Sweeney had on Tulagi. On the second day, Sweeney was handed the job of burial officer, an assignment he remembers very well to this day. Because of the tropical climate, the dead had to be put underground quickly. Sweeney used six or eight of his men from his demolition's platoon. Most of them did so under protest.

"I had a tough time getting them to do the job," said Sweeney, who would replace the fallen Lieutenant Key as 1st Platoon leader of Baker Company the next day. "They kept telling me they were Marines, not grave diggers. We didn't have any shovels so we had to use entrenching tools. We wrapped the bodies in shelter halves. All the graves were clearly marked. We knew they were just temporary."[2]

Disposing of enemy bodies, which had littered the battlefield in greater numbers, was a simpler problem. Many of the bodies were buried in bomb craters and others were stacked in houses and then the building was set afire. The smell was horrible either way.

That first night on Tulagi was a frightening experience for all the Raiders. Sgt. Frank Guidone's squad in Able Company, which had moved into a gap in the line next to Charlie Company, was typical of most.

"It was already too dark to dig in properly and most of us threw our packs on the ground and took up a prone position behind them," Guidone remembered. "The skyline to our front was lit from a fire somewhere along the ridge. I am not sure what the source was but it silhouetted the top of the ridge to our advantage."[3]

Off in the distance, the Raiders could hear the din of battle coming from the fierce fighting on Gavutu-Tanambogo.

The first attack came at 2230 and although it was noisy and bold, it was stopped cold. It lasted just a couple of minutes before the Japanese withdrew.

"We noticed forms creeping over the ridge line to our front," Guidone said. "And suddenly, to our right, a heavy machine gun opened fire and the tracer rounds seemed to float over our heads. The gun was nearer to C Company's front and some men started to make a move to the rear but were soon herded back into position. We heard Japanese voices to our direct front which sounded like commands and we commenced firing to our front despite being unable to distinguish targets and our fire undoubtedly was well over the heads of the approaching Japanese. When the forms were in range directly in front of us, [Pete Sparacino] and I lobbed our grenades—we only had two apiece—and it became quiet to our front but the Japs were there. I made a trip back to the CP for a box of grenades, our choice of weapons in situations like this. We heard groans and wailing coming from our front and we lobbed more grenades in the direction of the wailing of wounded Japanese."[4]

The attack at 2300 was more successful, making a deep penetration at the juncture of Able and Charlie companies and resulting in the capture of two machine guns and a walkie-talkie from the latter. A Japanese soldier, speaking perfect English over the captured radio and pretending to be Major Walt, tried to talk Edson into pulling his company out of its position. Edson recognized the fraud right away and hung up. That's when he and Sweeney decided to go forward and assess the situation themselves.

Pfc. Henry "Popeye" Poppell was in the last foxhole on Able Company's right flank, about fifty yards from the nearest Charlie Company position to his right. That was the gap the Japanese exploited to capture the two Charlie Company machine guns. Firing broke out to Poppell's right rear and he began to realize a breakthrough had occurred. As he withdrew he could see that Sgt. Clifford "Red" Hills had organized a skirmish line and was moving forward. Hills then led a charge that recovered the machine guns and stopped the penetration, an act of bravery that earned him a Navy Cross.

Another Navy Cross winner this night was little Edward Ahrens of Able Company. Only five-feet-seven and 130 pounds, PFC Ahrens was a whiz with a BAR. At about 0300, Ahrens spotted a group of men, led by what appeared to be an officer, approaching his foxhole. He couldn't tell they were Japanese until they were almost on top of him. Although shot twice and bayoneted several times, Ahrens managed to kill the Japanese lieutenant, a sergeant and several others with his BAR before he fell seriously wounded back into his foxhole. He was found the next morning by Major Walt, who was inspecting his lines.

"As I came upon his position that morning he was slumped down in one corner of the foxhole covered with blood from head to foot," Walt said. "In the foxhole with him were two dead Japs, one a lieutenant and the other a sergeant. There were eleven more dead Japs on the ground in front of his position."

Walt called out for a corpsman as he carried Ahrens to the rear.

"As the corpsman was administering morphine, Ahrens held the Jap sword up to me and said, 'Major, here's a souvenir for you. Those yellow bastards tried to come over me last night. I guess they didn't know that I was a Marine.'"[5]

Edson had no reservation about recommending Ahrens for the Medal of Honor and did so, only to see it downgraded to a Navy Cross.

Baker Company, positioned in front of the Residency, also experienced several attacks that night. Pfc. Vincent Cassidy, who had demonstrated his grenade-throwing technique earlier in the day, and his buddy Pvt. Michael F. Nee took up positions along a path leading to the Residency when they heard movement to their front.

"I heard Mike Nee yell something about moving out and turned toward him only to hear him scream as a burst of automatic fire, from what seemed to be right in front of us, . . . cut him down," Cassidy said. "I fired madly . . . Suddenly everything was quiet. Cautiously I looked around. Everyone I could see, most of these being to my right, was dead."[6]

Sergeant Guidone's exhausted squad in Able Company stayed awake all night, lobbing grenades until they ran out just before dawn.

"At daybreak we heard a rooster crow," Guidone said. "Man, that was a good sign. We knew that daylight was coming. It was gray and getting lighter. As I looked out toward the ridgetop I couldn't believe what I was seeing. There was about twenty-five to thirty Japs piled up. They were slaughtered. We threw about two cases of grenades that night—easily.

"One Jap was still alive. He got up and started running and got picked off; he didn't get very far. Later that morning, I went back to the CP [command post] area. I knew this was for real when I noted seven or eight bodies under ponchos—they were in a row. Gifford, Jerry DiSalvia, and Sergeant Luke were among the dead, along with four or five others. This first loss of our brothers was difficult to digest, but it was just the beginning."[7]

Guidone was nominated for a Navy Cross but wound up with a Letter of Commendation, instead.

• • •

The next morning, with the help of two companies from the 5th Marines, the Raiders pushed over the rest of the island, wiping out machine-gun positions in several caves. By late afternoon, Edson declared that his Raiders had complete physical control of the island. The Japanese, without food or water, fought to the last man, however, and it took a couple more days before the island was truly secure.

"[The Japanese] had evidently made a dash for their dugouts when the naval bombardment came, without stopping for provisions," Edson told writer Richard Tregaskis a few days later. "In one case there were three Japs cornered. They had one pistol. They fired the pistol until they had three shots left. Then one Jap shot the two others and killed himself."

Most of the fortified caves on Hill 281 on the southeastern end of the island had to be cleaned out one at a time. There were no flame-throwers or bangalore torpedoes. Grenades were the weapons of choice and caution was advised as Gunny Sgt. Angus R. Goss found out early on the morning of the second day. Goss, the ranking NCO of the Demolition's Platoon, had fashioned a short-fused "stick" charge that he lobbed into a cave only to see it tossed back at him. The explosion slammed Goss into a nearby shack, blew his trousers off and wounded him painfully. In a cold rage, Goss grabbed his Reising gun, staggered back to the cave opening and hosed down the astonished occupants, killing them all. Edson had recommended him for the Medal of Honor but it would be downgraded by the Navy Department to a Navy Cross. He also was honored by the British with that country's Conspicuous Gallantry Medal.[8]

Although Tulagi was declared secure, it didn't seem that way to Dog Company Platoon Sgt. Gene Martin. His platoon had settled down for the night on August 8 on both sides of a wide, flat path that bordered the cricket field. The path actually cut the island in two and ran through a deep, narrow cut that contained a well-fortified cave. Earlier in the day, the platoon had set off a big charge of TNT in the cave, which supposedly sealed it shut.

Martin's men took up positions in the ditches that ran alongside the path.

"By the time we were in place, it was dark," wrote Martin. "No one had slept for at least 48 hours and this was about the first time that we were not busy with some kind of active detail."

The men quickly fell fast asleep. Martin made a couple of "buddy checks" to make sure his men remained awake before sleep overtook him, too, around midnight.

"I dozed. Two minutes, five minutes? I don't know. It wasn't long," he said. "I knew before I opened my eyes that a Jap was near, damned near; for I could smell the unmistakable sweet odor of rice powder—strong.

"I opened my eyes and was jolted, but good. Standing so close to me that I could have reached out and touched him, was Jap number one. He was flanked closely on either side by number two and three, and about four paces away stood number four."

Across the path, Martin could barely make out the helmet of one of his men. The four Japanese had their backs to Martin and were peering into a ditch. One was an officer and carried a sword and another was carrying a machine gun. They whispered something to each other. Martin, who had fallen asleep while gripping his Reising gun, knew the safety catch was on.

"I knew that when [the safety catch] was moved it would sound like someone had snapped on a light switch," Martin said. "I very slowly elevated the muzzle of the Reising and at the same time eased my left hand over to the safety. It clicked off. I guess no one heard it but me.

"They're Japs, give 'em hell," Martin yelled as he pulled the trigger. "The first round—a tracer, damn it—was for the leader. The second stopped the guy on his left. The others spread like the wind, ending up, it turned out later, in the ditch with other Raiders."

Martin's outburst woke everyone up and led to a hail of gunfire. One of the fleeing Japanese stepped on Capt. Ed Wheeler, the platoon commander, in his haste to flee the scene and was quickly killed. The other was also quickly dispatched. The firing soon subsided but no one went back to sleep. It began to rain and then the men could hear the booming sounds and see the flashes of a terrific sea battle going on to the west.

In the morning, Martin discovered that the four Japanese had exited the cave in the cut and walked 100 yards or so down the path looking to set up a machine gun. They had walked through the entire length of D Company without being challenged. Everyone assumed they were Marines.[9]

Martin also appropriated the antique samurai sword that was dropped by the officer and brought it home with him when the war ended.

Others weren't as lucky. Pfc. George Johnson of Baker Company never got to enjoy his souvenir.

"[Johnson] picked up a Japanese hara kari knife, a very beautiful thing, and made the remark that he was going to keep it until he died," according to Sgt. Hugh Davis. "He walked about twenty yards and died with a bullet between the eyes. As far as I know, that knife stayed on his body unless someone in a burial detail removed it."

The Raiders had learned many valuable lessons that would later serve them well on Guadalcanal. One of them was to stay awake at night. Another was that "dead" Japanese can be dangerous. Enemy soldiers were experts at playing dead so they could rise up and take an unsuspecting Marine by exploding a grenade or firing a pistol. Taking no chances, the Raiders were instructed to shoot first and ask questions later.

Only three Japanese prisoners were taken alive on Tulagi. Perhaps as many as forty others may have escaped to Florida Island by swimming across a narrow channel. About 350 perished on Tulagi, many of them committing suicide rather than surrendering.

The Raiders lost a total of 39 men killed and 42 wounded on Tulagi, about nine percent of their force. Most of the casualties occurred on the first day. The 2nd Battalion, 5th Marines had eight killed and 16 wounded. On Gavutu-Tanambogo, the "Chutes" had suffered 30 killed and 45 wounded of the original roster of 377 men (20 percent).

Counting seven sailors lost on supporting naval vessels, a total of 122 Americans died to secure Tulagi and Gavutu-Tanambogo. The Japanese total came to about 863,347 on Tulagi and 516 on Gavutu-Tanambogo. It would take almost a week to find and bury all the bodies that were hidden under rubble or in caves. There would be thirty Navy Crosses awarded for extraordinary heroism during the two battles. Nine would be earned by the men of the 1st Raider Battalion.

Just after midnight of the first day, a highly agitated General Rupertus had phoned Vandegrift on Guadalcanal with the first reports of casualties. Rupertus told him that the Raiders had suffered 22 percent casualties on Tulagi and that the word from Gavutu-Tanambogo was that the 1st Parachute Battalion had suffered a staggering loss of 50 to 60 percent.

Though these percentages proved to be much too high, Vandegrift was aghast.

While Vandegrift and his main body of Marines continued to consolidate their gains on Guadalcanal on the second day, they could hear some of the battle noises from Tulagi and Gavutu-Tanambogo echoing twenty miles away across Sealark Channel. Another noontime Japanese air raid on August 8 scattered the American transports and delayed the critical unloading of supplies. This time, the Japanese bombers, or "Bettys" as they were called, came armed with torpedoes.

Flying at twenty to forty feet above the water, some twenty-three Bettys bore in on the transports through a hail of deadly antiaircraft fire. One by one, they exploded and splashed into the sea, some so close to the transports that crewmen had to duck to avoid getting hit. "Sailors on one transport swept the legs, arms and torsos of Japanese airmen over the side that day."[10]

Prior to the air raid, coastwatcher Jack Read on Bougainville had reported forty bombers en route. Shortly after noon, Read saw one Betty flying northward.

The Japanese did succeed in crippling one transport, the *George F. Elliot*, which was struck by a crippled bomber in the war's first kamikaze maneuver. The *Elliot* stubbornly refused to sink, burning throughout the night as a fiery beacon off the island of Tulagi where it was beached.

When the Marines completed the seizure of the abandoned airstrip on Guadalcanal late in the afternoon of the second day, they came into possession of three antiaircraft batteries, ammunition dumps, radio stations, a refrigerating plant, an air compressor plant, vehicles and stacks of supplies. Cups and bowls of warm rice, meat stew and prunes sat at deserted tables as if the diners were to return momentarily. Nearby was a row of brand-new wooden barracks.

"The failure of the Japanese to put up any formal organized resistance around the airstrip is as baffling now as it was to the Marines then," wrote historian Richard B. Frank in his definitive account of the battle in 1990.[11]

The biggest problem occurred on the beaches where unloading of equipment and rations quickly became chaotic. The morale of those doing the unloading was not helped by a driving rain and a lack of shelter. Cardboard containers of foodstuff, softened by the rain, broke open, spilling cereal, sugar and canned goods all over the beach.

In the absence of bow ramps, crews had to struggle in the water to lift boxes and crates over the gunwales, an exhausting and daunting task. As darkness fell on the first night, 150 landing craft, loaded with needed supplies, were either on the beach or standing off, waiting for hours for a chance to unload.

By late afternoon, 100 boats had landed with supplies and they were still not unloaded. Fifty more boats, bobbing gently in the swells, stood off at the surf line searching vainly for an open stretch of beach to land on. Tempers ran short and it threatened to develop into a major intraservice battle. The Navy believed their job was to land the supplies and it was the responsibility of the Marines to handle the unloading and moving the goods inland. The Marines disagreed, claiming they were fighting men, not stevedores. By nightfall, the situation was entirely out of hand, so much so that Admiral Turner ordered the unloading to cease until it could be better organized.

To expedite unloading the next day, Vandegrift doubled the length of the beach, extending it some 500 yards westward. Still, the situation improved only slightly.

Except for the delay in landing supplies and the logistical logjam on the beaches, Vandegrift was feeling pretty good about the performance of his green troops as night fell on the second day.

"The fighting is now over and we have the place we set out to take," Vandegrift wrote his wife on August 8. "The outfit did beautifully in a very trying situation. I am feeling well and very fit after a night in the jungle, and the worry of what was going to happen to the men. The show opened before dawn and we got in without their knowing it. At first it was exciting but then came the anxious hours of waiting to hear how things turned out on all sides. It went as planned. I deeply regret the men lost and the wounded, but we had to expect that and it was less than expected."

This sense of confidence was to be short-lived.

9

Bugout

Shortly after 1800 on the second day, Turner's communications room aboard the *McCawley*, respectfully referred to as the "Wacky Mac," intercepted a dispatch from Admiral Fletcher to Admiral Ghormley that changed everything.

"Fighter-plane strength reduced from 99 to 78. In view of large number of enemy torpedo planes and bombers in this area, I recommend the immediate withdrawal of my carriers. Request tankers be sent forward immediately as fuel running low," the message stated.[1]

Fletcher, who had promised earlier to stay in the area three days, did not bother to consult with Turner or Vandegrift and had, in fact, already begun his withdrawal before he got approval from Ghormley.

Turner was irate. Not a single Japanese plane or submarine had discovered Fletcher's carriers as far as Turner was concerned. And, he couldn't have been low on fuel. Most of the ships had topped off after leaving the rehearsal area. A subsequent examination of the ship's engineering logs proved Turner correct. The three carriers had enough fuel for ten to twelve days.

Turner surmised that Fletcher was scared off by the torpedo-armed Japanese bombers that attacked the Guadalcanal area on the second day. Fletcher knew well the damage torpedoes could do to ships of war. Hadn't he lost both the *Lexington* and *Yorktown* to torpedoes? Fletcher didn't need any more evidence to make a decision. He turned south, not only removing his three carriers from the scene but also taking his screening force of the battleship *North Carolina,* six heavy cruisers and sixteen destroyers out of action.

"Desertion" was a word the outspoken Turner used to describe Fletcher's withdrawal. There were those in the Marine Corps who openly speculated that Fletcher "wanted to add a fourth color to the American flag."[2]

Turner knew that if the carriers and the air cover they provided left, he would have to leave, too. He was determined, however, to stay the night and continue off-loading for much of the next day.

He called Admiral Crutchley and General Vandegrift at 2030 for an emergency meeting aboard the *McCawley,* which was anchored off Lunga Point. Crutchley, commander of the screening force of cruisers and destroyers, didn't arrive until 2230 because he had trouble finding the *McCawley* in the dark. And Vandegrift, who was accompanied by his operations officer, Colonel Thomas, didn't show until 2315 for similar reasons.

Turner came right to the point. He said he had been notified that Admiral Fletcher would be removing his three carriers from the area that night because of heavy aircraft losses and that he, Turner, tentatively planned to withdraw his transports at daylight. Turner called the meeting to learn whether enough supplies had been landed for the Marines and whether Crutchley thought he could keep his naval covering force in the area for another couple of days without air support.

Turner explained that without air cover his transports had to leave, but he said he would defer a decision on his actual departure time until Vandegrift could determine just how many additional stores General Rupertus needed on Tulagi.

Vandegrift pleaded with Turner to reconsider. The transports had more than half his division's equipment still aboard, including almost all of the barbed wire and most of the heavy equipment. Turner was sympathetic. He knew that without the warships, the Marines would be at the mercy of Japanese bombardment from the sea and the air.

"This was the Koro conference relived except that Fletcher was running away twelve hours earlier than he had already threatened during our unpleasant meeting," Vandegrift wrote in his memoirs. "We all knew his fuel could not have been running low since he refueled in the Fijis . . . [it] was a fait accompli, and we knew it.[3]

"Maybe we won't need four days to unload," Vandegrift told Turner. "Give me two days. Even one. Why, my engineers tell me we can patch up the runways on the airfield in a day, and we can have land-based aircraft on the field, if that's what's worrying you."

As an equally sympathetic Crutchley looked on, Turner just shook his head no.

"We're in fair shape on Guadalcanal," Vandegrift said. "But I don't know about Bill Rupertus on Tulagi. He's been fighting ever since the landing, and I doubt if he's got much supply ashore. I must certainly check with him first."[4]

The Marine commander tried to remain calm but he was boiling mad on the inside. He had no one to turn to.

"The navy brass was on edge," wrote Robert Edward Lee in his book *Victory at Guadalcanal*. "In the council of war aboard the *McCawley*, the marine commander's protest carried little weight. And the one man to whom an appeal might logically have been made was a thousand miles away, out of touch, out of mind: Adm. Robert Lee

Ghormley, the theater commander, the court of last resort. Ghormley had made his final delegation of command in absentia, at the Fiji conference, before Operation Watchtower was launched."[5]

Vandegrift turned to Thomas on the way out and said, almost incredulously: "They're leaving us bare-assed. Plain ol' bare-assed."[6]

The two men left just before midnight and boarded the destroyer-minesweeper *Southard* for a trip across Sealark Channel to Tulagi for a conference with General Rupertus. Leaving the *McCawley*, an already wounded Vandegrift wrenched his knee on a rung of the Jacob's ladder and the leg swelled quickly.

On the way out of the meeting, Admiral Crutchley saw the hurt in Vandegrift's face and moved to console him. "Vandegrift," he said, "I don't know if I can blame Turner for what he's doing."[7]

Turner, too, was sympathetic. He was also spitting mad at Fletcher.

Vandegrift was as mad as he had ever been in his long military career.

Shortly after the *Southard* got underway for Tulagi, a huge naval battle broke out to port near Savo Island. Neither Vandegrift nor his staff would understand the gravity of that battle until the middle of the next day. By the time they reached Tulagi the sea action was over.

Vandegrift met with Rupertus and his staff aboard the transport *Neville*, which was anchored off Tulagi. The USS *Neville* had been hastily converted to a hospital ship. Vandegrift went below to visit with the men and was struck for the first time by the consequences of war. Many of the wounded he saw and talked to died that night, unable to be evacuated out of harm's way because of the fierce naval battle that had gone on.

"The pathetic sight of rows of helpless men, some of them only boys, brought home the crushing responsibility of command," Vandegrift wrote. "Some of these Marines were in a bad way but the spirit they displayed deeply moved me and made me terribly proud."[8]

"It's been one helluva day, general," Vandegrift said to Rupertus when they met in the wardroom over hot coffee. Vandegrift had a sense that it would get a whole lot worse before it got better.

"I just left a conference with Admiral Turner and what I have to tell you isn't good. I don't mean our job. We've done just about everything we've been sent to do. But this," he said, brandishing his soggy notes on the withdrawal of Turner and Fletcher's forces, "this is pretty grim stuff. As far as I know, the carrier force has already sailed."[9]

He was right. Fletcher had begun withdrawing his carriers even before he got official permission from the theater commander, Admiral Ghormley. Turner had already radioed Fletcher to tell him that Vandegrift was "as mad as hell." Fletcher responded by telling Turner that Vandegrift would "just have to stay mad."

Rupertus asked about air cover.

"What air support? We won't have a Piper Cub between us in a few hours," Vandegrift raged in front of Rupertus.[10]

Returning to Guadalcanal before first light, Vandegrift looked over the rail where he could see a half dozen ships afire and hear the explosions of ammunition cooking off. He couldn't tell whose ships they were, American or Japanese. For all he knew, the enemy might have landed a force on Guadalcanal and overrun his tenuous toehold on the island.

Landing safely at the port of Kukum within the Marine enclave, Vandegrift called an emergency meeting of his top officers where he gave one of the best pep talks of his career.

"Singly or in pairs they straggled to my CP," Vandegrift wrote in his memoirs, "a sorry-looking lot with bloodshot eyes and embryonic beards and filthy dungarees . . . They were tired. Some smoked, others sipped black coffee . . . Most of them watched the beach and the parade of small boats landing survivors whose semi-naked bodies black from burns and oil of the sunken ships claimed the ministrations of our doctors and corpsmen. Even as they watched, the cruiser *Chicago*, her bow shot away, limped past transports busily hoisting landing craft to their decks."[11]

Vandegrift told his staff what he knew, which was very incomplete. He said that the carriers, which had provided air cover for the landings, had left the area and that the transports, only half unloaded, would be leaving later that day. He did not know when they would be back. They were now vulnerable to every conceivable attack—by land, sea and air.

Vandegrift let those bombshells sink in before he stood up and looked his staff in the eye. Clenching his jaw and looking as determined as he could, he told his officers to tell the men that Guadalcanal would not be another Wake Island or Bataan.

"Since 1775 Marines had found themselves in tough spots," Vandegrift told them. "They had survived and we would survive—but only if every officer and man on Guadalcanal gives his all to the cause."[12]

Vandegrift turned and kicked over an empty coffee tin. "What's wrong with the defensive, it's part of our job, too, huh? Just tell [the men] to forget about the Navy. We're Marines!"

Later that day, Vandegrift walked up to Bill Twining,

who was gazing out to sea off Red Beach, and softly asked: "Bill, what has happened to your navy?"

Twining paused for a moment and said: "I don't believe the first team is on the field yet, General."[13]

The Marines would be assuming a new role. Trained as assault troops, they were now being forced to hold and wait for the enemy to come and hit them. They didn't much like the situation, but there was nothing they could do about it. Dig in, they were told.

Colonel Thomas took over and outlined the courses of action over the next few days. The men would organize the defense of the island, get the supplies off the beach and moved inland, patrol, and perhaps most importantly, finish the airfield.

The Marine perimeter at Lunga Point was about five miles wide and some three miles deep. The beach defenses stretched some 9,600 yards from a lagoon-like body of water called Alligator Creek in the east to a high ridge overlooking the Matanikau River in the west. A thousand yards before the western end of the perimeter was the small coastal village of Kukum, which would serve as the main port facility.

Lovely coconut groves dotted the shoreline and provided for easy defense. "It was a machine gunner's dream," one Marine said. The enemy must have realized this as well because they never did try to assault the perimeter's beachfront.

Constructing fortifications was back-breaking work. Most of the shovels and axes were still on the transports and would never be unloaded. Only eighteen reels of barbed wire had made it to shore. Vandegrift sent the men out to strip wire from cattle fences, which later caused some scary situations. Japanese bombardments often stampeded the frightened animals, which sent them crashing into tents and foxholes in a blind fury. Many of the cows were shot by jumpy sentries as they thrashed about in the jungle.

All of the heavy equipment used by the Japanese to construct the airfield was left in place. This included six road rollers, four generators, six trucks, about fifty handcarts for hauling dirt, about seventy-five hand shovels, a quantity of explosives and two gasoline-powered locomotives that pulled hopper cars for earth moving.

The men were already starting to look ragged. Redeyed from lack of sleep, their unshaven faces were covered with mosquito bites. Their dungarees were caked with sweat and mud. Most of their conversation consisted of curses.

Everyone knew the Japanese would mount a counterattack to try and retake the airstrip and it could come at any time. Vandegrift knew he would need reinforcements from the troops on Tulagi but with the enemy in control of Sealark Channel it would be suicidal to try and bring them over until he had air cover. And that wouldn't happen until the airstrip was operational.

The damage inflicted on allied warships during the Savo disaster delayed the departure of Admiral Turner's transports, which remained in Sealark Channel until the late afternoon of August 9. At 1500, ten of the transports, one cruiser, four destroyers and the minesweepers departed the area. The rest, including Turner's flagship, the *McCawley*, followed at 1830. The transports were still half full. The retirement of Turner's forces left Ironbottom Sound devoid of allied shipping—at least on the surface.

The transports took away more than just equipment. Some 1,400 troops from the 2nd Marines, many of whom had been commandeered as stevedores, left as well.

On Sunday morning, the radio watch in Fletcher's

ships, far off to the southeast, could hear the beachhead at Guadalcanal calling, "Any friendly planes in the area, come in. Any friendly planes in the area, come in." There was no answer. Foster Hailey of the *New York Times,* who was with Fletcher's force on the *Minneapolis,* said the sailors were ashamed to look at each other.[14]

By sundown of that Sunday, Vandegrift's men had a new name for their outfit. The 1st Marine Division became the "1st Marooned Division."

The naval battle off Savo Island had been a disaster for the Allies, one that was hidden from the public for several months lest it give comfort and aid to the enemy. In a violent action early on the morning of August 9, one that lasted just over half an hour, Japanese ships sank three American cruisers (*Quincy, Vincennes* and *Astoria*), badly damaged another (*Chicago*) and sank an Australian cruiser (*Canberra*)—with no ship losses to themselves.

Shortly after midnight, Vice Admiral Gunichi Mikawa, one of the Japanese Navy's boldest tacticians, silently led his force of five heavy cruisers, two light cruisers and a destroyer into the deep-water channel hard by the volcanic cone of Savo Island, eight miles northwest of Guadalcanal and eighteen miles due west of Tulagi. He was counting on surprise and he achieved it despite being spotted earlier by two Royal Australian Air Force planes.

"Only one [of the pilots] bothered to make his report [and] that report was filed after the pilot flew another four hours, returned to base in New Guinea and had tea," one historian wrote."[15]

Many of the crews of the Allied ships were tired after their long journey and, obviously, not as alert as they should have been.

"It was a hot, overcast and oppressive night," wrote Morison, "heavy with destiny and doom, as a novelist would say, inviting weary sailors to slackness and to sleep."[16]

Several Japanese float planes flew lazily over Skylark Channel around midnight looking over Turner's fleet. The beached transport *Elliot,* still burning near Tulagi, helped illuminate the area for the Japanese planes. The American ships could see and hear the planes but assumed they were friendly. Nobody had passed the word to them that Admiral Fletcher and his carrier planes had left the area long ago.

Mikawa's ships had no radar, but his lookouts, equipped with excellent binoculars, were experts in night fighting. The Japanese Navy had a long history of training their men for night actions, selecting men with the best eyesight to act as lookouts. They were, in effect, their "human radar."

Also, their "Long Lance" torpedoes far exceeded those used by Allied ships. Each torpedo was capable of propelling its thousand pounds of high explosives more than ten miles at a speed of fifty knots. Illuminated by flares and caught in searchlight beams, the Allied crews were stunned by the torpedoes and naval gunfire.

Ensign Harris Hammersmith, aboard the *Quincy,* later told a reporter that his ship was taken by complete surprise.

"[There was] fire all around, shells hitting our superstructure. There were dead, so many of them. The captain. The exec. The chief engineer. The navigator. They all got it," Hammersmith related. "There was firelight shining on the flag. Those of us who saw the colors in the light never forgot what we saw. There was a shell hole in the blue field. And a hole in the red and white stripes. But the flag was there, still."

First light of August 9 revealed over 1,000 oil-covered sailors, many burned, others seriously wounded, clinging desperately to empty shell cases, life rafts, orange crates or to any flotsam or jetsam that would hold their heads above the water. Trails of blood attracted sharks; during the long night men had occasionally disappeared with appalling suddenness. Rescue operations inaugurated at dawn proceeded during the morning. In five hours more than 700 wounded were saved. A dozen sharks were killed by sailors who shot them with rifles from the rescue craft and decks of destroyers.[17]

"Those of us on shore watched the whole thing—we had front-row seats for a thrilling sea battle," Lieutenant Whyte of the 1st Marines wrote. "It was a spectacular sight—ships exploding in the rockets' red glare. We had no idea who was winning, at first, but we began to get an inkling when the operators of our radio transmitters reported they couldn't get through to our principal ships. The reason they weren't getting through, of course, was that our big ships were eight fathoms deep.

"Now was the key moment—the time to destroy the American landing on Guadalcanal, for the cargo ships were still lying off the island and they were helpless. Instead, Mikawa turned away, in a typical example of the failure of the Japanese to seize the initiative. The death stroke to those of us on Guadalcanal was averted."[18]

News of the one-sided naval battle sent shock waves throughout Australia and New Zealand, which viewed the disaster as a renewed threat of a Japanese invasion.

Radio Tokyo proclaimed that the Japanese Navy had sunk twenty-four warships and eleven transports "filled to capacity with Marines" and that Australia had "absolutely become an orphan of the southwest Pacific." The propagandists were absolutely giddy, warning the Americans that there was still "plenty of room at the bottom of the Pacific for more American Fleet, ha, ha!"[19]

The Marines who heard these broadcasts laughed and hooted out loud. But they knew some of it was true.

The disaster—which it clearly was—could have been much worse. Unaware that the U.S. carriers had already withdrawn, Mikawa decided to retire rather than hunt down the vital transports, which had been the main target of his mission. Had the Japanese destroyed the twenty-three Allied transports, which had been huddled at their anchorage off Lunga Point, the battle for Guadalcanal might have been decided then and there. Instead, the enemy turned northward and left the scene, happy with their obvious victory.

"There can be little doubt that destruction of the transports by Mikawa, or by Yamada's airmen on the morning of August 9, would have ended the campaign shortly in ignominious defeat for the Allies," wrote Richard Frank.[20]

Morison called the battle "probably the worst defeat ever inflicted on the United States Navy in a fair fight." Admiral King called it "the blackest day of the war. The whole future then seemed unpredictable."[21]

The Navy would later hold an investigation, which found the blame to be so evenly distributed among so many officers that nobody was punished. One of the findings revealed that Fletcher's carrier force had plenty of fuel on board, prompting the eminent historian Samuel Eliot Morison to quip that "[Fletcher's] force could have remained in the area with no more severe consequences than sunburn."[22]

Morison agreed, however, that it would be unfair to censure any particular officer in this sad affair, rightfully pointing out that the Allies were also victimized by fate, or "luck" as he called it.

The Savo Island debacle shocked Americans on the scene and in Washington. What had appeared likely to be a quick and not too painful surgical operation on Guadalcanal would become a desperate struggle to survive. What started as a limited campaign in the Solomons would grow into an engagement of vast proportions, involving large numbers of men, ships and aircraft. Japan's plan to isolate Australia teetered on the brink of success. Doubts were planted in the minds of high-ranking American officials, including Vice Admiral Ghormley, that perhaps Guadalcanal could not be held after all.

Admiral King refused to indulge such thoughts. The Navy chief, never one to mince words, refused to comment on the exaggerated Japanese claims at Savo. When asked repeatedly by an aide what to tell a bunch of inquiring reporters gathered in his outer office, King snapped at the officer: "Tell them nothing! When it's over—tell them who won!"[23]

It was next to impossible to get any news out of Admiral King's office. Only grudgingly, and under orders from President Roosevelt, did King even admit to the American people that there were combat operations going on in the Solomon Islands. On August 10, his office issued a written statement that consisted of the following six paragraphs:

"Offensive operations by the United States naval and other forces, looking to the occupation of islands in the Tulagi area in the southeasterly Solomon Islands, have now been under way for about three days.

"The operations are under the immediate command of Vice Admiral Ghormley and under the general control of Admiral Nimitz. Certain of the forces under General MacArthur are cooperating.

"The objective of the current operations is to expel the

Japanese from the Tulagi area and to make use of that area for our own purposes. The enemy have been in [the] process of consolidating their positions, in which their purpose has been not only to deny them to us but to use them as a base of offensive operations against our positions which cover the line of communications to Australia and New Zealand.

"An initial surprise was effected and planned landings accomplished. The enemy has counter-attacked with rapidity and vigor. Heavy fighting is still in progress. Our operating forces are employing all available communications in the conduct of the operations, so that our information is incomplete but it appears that we have had at least one cruiser sunk and two cruisers, two destroyers and one transport damaged. Likewise, information as to the extent of damage inflicted on the enemy is incomplete, but includes a large number of enemy planes that have been destroyed and surface units put out of action.

"This operation in the Tulagi area is significant in that it marks our first assumption of the initiative and of the offensive. All of the previous operations in the Pacific, however successful, have been essentially defensive in character.

"It should be understood that the operation now under way is one of the most complicated and difficult in warfare. Considerable losses, such as are inherent in any offensive operation, must be expected as the price to be paid for the hard-won experience which is essential to the attainment of far-reaching results."

Within a few days of the Savo Island defeat it became very clear that the Japanese viewed the waters between Guadalcanal and Tulagi as their own private lake. No longer fearing any threat from the U.S. Navy, Japanese cruisers, destroyers and submarines patrolled the area in broad daylight and at night, shelling Marine positions and landing reinforcements at will. Without air cover, any life-line between the two strongholds was severed.

10

Time Out

Over on Tulagi, the Raiders continued to look for and eliminate enemy soldiers holding out in caves but all they found were dead bodies. The men enjoyed the spoils of war, liberating such items as food, drink and clothing from the many buildings on the island. Souvenir hunting was a full-time activity for many of the Raiders.

All hands smoked Japanese cigarettes, drank Japanese beer and listened to Tokyo Rose. The men got used to smoking captured cigarettes. Many of them supplemented their emergency rations with canned Japanese seaweed, tinned crabmeat and sliced beef packaged in soy sauce, which they found delicious. Some of the men tried their hand at using chopsticks, with hilarious consequences.

Defensive positions were set up throughout the island and patrols were sent over to nearby Florida Island to gather intelligence and track down any Japanese soldiers who might have escaped from Tulagi. Edson fully expected the Japanese to try and retake Tulagi as soon as they could.

The closest they came to repelling an invasion, however, was when an enemy submarine tried to enter port, obviously thinking it was still under Japanese control.

"We looked out and saw this sub headed our way. It was flying a Japanese flag and the crew was in white uniforms. I guess they thought they were coming home," said Capt. John Sweeney. "We quickly trained a gun on the sub but it got away."[1]

Edson set up his headquarters in the Residency. He spent a few hours daily reading an English translation of a short history of Japan. A Victrola had been liberated along with a collection of Japanese records from a warehouse on Carpenter's Wharf. It provided dinner music for the colonel's mess.

For the most part, duty on Tulagi over the next three weeks was uneventful.

"Rumors were rampant, from being relieved by Army troops, going to New Caledonia for a rest, another attack somewhere else and joining the division on Guadalcanal," Sergeant Guidone remembered.

"We were pleased about defeating the Japanese. We had measured up to and bettered their claim as the best fighting man. Their vast fighting experience did them no good against our forces. I believe we did pride ourselves on the job we had done to the point of cockiness."[2]

While the Raiders on Tulagi settled into a relatively quiet and boring regimen, it was different twenty miles away on Guadalcanal where the Marines had to cope with sporadic bombing runs from Japanese aircraft and nightly bombardments from enemy ships.

"Of all the shortages the isolated landing force faced during the early days," wrote 1st Division historian and press officer Lt. Herbert Merillat, "the most dangerous was the complete lack of air cover, beginning at sunset on August 8, ending only late in the afternoon of the 20th."

Merillat, Oxford educated and a lawyer by trade, joined the Marine Corps in the spring of 1942 as a public relations officer (PRO) and was assigned to the 1st Division throughout the Guadalcanal campaign. His mission was to assist the civilian press in the field and to supplement and censor their reporting. He was a facilitator, providing the press with more detailed descriptions of what individual units were doing and, above all, what individual Marines were doing. This latter reporting came under the heading of "Joe Blow" stories.

Assigned to the Personnel Section (D-1), Merillat had free access to roam the battlefield, taking many notes that would later provide the basis of a division history. Interestingly, this writer had a similar mission during a tour of duty in Vietnam twenty-five years later when I was an information advisor to the 1st Vietnamese Infantry Division in I Corps.

Most of the high-ranking officers in the Pacific had public relations staffs. The man who held the job on Admiral Ghormley's staff was known to many of his contemporaries as Mr. Lamarr because he was married to the popular film star Hedy Lamarr.

As the days passed, the scuttlebutt machines worked overtime on both sides of Sealark Channel. The men began to think of being replaced by Army garrison forces while they sailed away as heroes to rest and rehabilitation ports in New Zealand. It was purely wishful thinking.

With no enemy forces available to absorb their aggravation and frustration, some of the Marines turned to bad-mouthing their own forces, particularly the "swab-jockeys" who had "hauled ass" and left them stranded and the Army troops, "the dog-faces sitting on their butts in New Caledonia." They even made up verses deriding "Dug-out Doug" MacArthur.

Laxness in sanitary discipline had led to the rapid spread of an acute form of dysentery that sapped the strength of the men. Hundreds of sufferers visited latrines twenty to thirty times a day, and by mid-August one man in five was so weak he could scarcely drag himself to these stinking boxes. Many had to be assisted to take their trousers down and to pull them up. There was no toilet paper.[3]

A boring diet of captured Japanese rice also contributed to intestinal difficulties. Reduced to two meals a day to conserve dwindling food stores, the men often received a cup of rice or oatmeal in the morning and the same meal late in the afternoon. It had little or no nutritional value and it gave the men "the trots."

Another problem was fungus infections, particularly to the feet. When the half-loaded transports departed on the third day, they took with them many personal items, including spare socks.

It was much worse in the jungle climate of Guadalcanal where the men were admonished to pull their socks up or keep their leggings on as a means of keeping insects from the skin, which could, and did, cause typhus.

The Marines were also attacked by swarms of malaria-carrying mosquitoes, which seemingly could penetrate any barrier to inflict their deadly bite. Flies and mosquitoes were so thick the men had to master a special technique to eat. After spearing a forkful of food from their K-ration cans, they shook the fork vigorously to drive away the flies and then quickly plunged the forkful into their mouths. Before chewing and swallowing, they still had to spit out a few flies.

Numerous swamps, streams, lagoons and rain-filled bomb craters and foxholes proved to be ideal breeding grounds for the disease-carrying mosquitoes. Malaria produced teeth-chattering chills, high fever, weakness and profuse amounts of sweating.

The early spread of the disease was helped by a reluctance by the Marines to take their medicine, notably Atabrine, a bitter little yellow pill that produced nausea and made your ears ring. A rumor went around that taking the pills, which were a substitute for quinine, would make you impotent. When taken daily, however, the Atabrine pills did help in suppressing the disease but it never did prevent it. It was estimated that at least 90 percent of the original force to land on Guadalcanal came down with some form of malaria.

"It was part of doing business on the Canal," Colonel Twining wrote.

The Atabrine pills had a peculiar side effect on many. It turned their skin, particularly the eyeballs, a sickly shade of yellow.

"I can't send you out on patrol," more than a few Marines were told by a grizzled gunny. "You're yellower than a Jap."[4]

The Raiders on Tulagi were also bitten hard by the malaria bug. Major Walt and one of his platoon leaders, Lt. Tom Mullahey, each contracted a severe form of the disease, one that kept them hospitalized for over a month. Walt became the third company commander lost to Edson in the span of a week.

On Guadalcanal, Vandegrift had assigned two battalions of the 1st Marines to guard the right, or east, flank of the beachhead along Alligator Creek and two battalions of the 5th Marines to protect the left, or west, flank. These four battalions also provided troops to secure the beaches on the north. A fifth battalion (1/1) was held in reserve while his artillery set up positions within the perimeter to cover both flanks.

The 105mm howitzers would become the workhorses of the division, just as they would later in Korea and Vietnam. Weighing some 4,980 pounds and requiring a crew of nine, the "105" could throw a thirty-three-pound shell some 12,000 yards. The shell burst was considered 50 percent lethal within a radius of twenty meters.

Concerned about an attack from the sea, Vandegrift deployed most of his .30-caliber machine guns and 37mm antitank weapons to cover the beach areas. Other artillery, including the 105s and 90mm antiaircraft guns, were positioned near the edge of the airfield.

There was little Vandegrift could do but send out a few patrols and wait to see what the enemy would do. Completing the airstrip had first priority and was the key to his division's long-term survival. Those not involved with the airfield construction dug in and waited for action.

No Japanese planes appeared on August 9 and those that flew over the island the next day did not drop any bombs. Six Zeros flew a strafing mission on August 11 and only three bombers showed up on the 12th, inflicting little damage.

Quartermasters and their troops began the dual task of moving supply dumps to dispersed locations within the perimeter and taking inventory. It was determined that there were seventeen days' supply of food on hand. This included a limited amount of food captured from the former garrison. The booty was especially prized because it was so tasty—sliced beef in soy sauce, tins of fruit, crabmeat, candy and, of course, rice. The food situation and realization that resupply was doubtful in the immediate future caused a two-meals-a-day schedule to be in effect beginning on August 12.

Also on the 12th, a seagoing communications and mail service was established between Guadalcanal and Tulagi. The first convoy, which consisted of two Higgins boats left behind when Admiral Turner pulled out his transports and a tank lighter loaded with fuel drums for the Tulagi boat pool, almost ended in disaster. Lieutenant

Merillat was aboard one of the Higgins boats on that first run while correspondents Richard Tregaskis of International News Service and Robert Miller of United Press were on the other.

The convoy, originally scheduled to depart at dawn, left Guadalcanal around 0900, chugging along on its two-hour trip as a school of dolphins provided a friendly escort. Midway, a low-flying plane was spotted coming up the channel from the southeast. The crews stood by on the machine guns. As it neared, the men could see it was an American Catalina. Later, they found out it was piloted by Admiral McCain's aide, who, minutes later, became the first pilot to land on Henderson Field.

A half hour later, a Japanese submarine surfaced between the boats and Tulagi about two miles from their destination. Several white-uniformed crew members emerged from the sub's conning tower, uncovered a deck-mounted gun and began firing shells at the boats in full view of Raiders stationed on Tulagi.

A decision had to be made quickly, whether to turn back, race toward the open sea or continue on at full speed for Tulagi. Lieutenant Merillat's boat made a sharp right turn and headed back toward Guadalcanal. Then the boat began to sputter.

"The desperate burst of speed was too much for our creaky engine," Merillat wrote. "It clanked and groaned and hissed, as clouds of steam and smoke poured from the housing. We decided to abandon our boat and move to another, if we could. Our coxswain signaled frantically to the others."[5]

Meanwhile, the submarine continued to gain ground on the boats.

"It was a horrifying sight to see geysers of water leaping up between us and the submarine for we knew then that he was ranging in on us," Tregaskis wrote of the crossing. "We heard the sharp bang of the shells exploding, and knew they would soon be coming dangerously close.

"Then there were more geysers, closer to the submarine, and we were mystified for a moment, until we heard the booming of gunfire coming from Tulagi shore. We knew then, and were thankful, that a shore battery was opening up on the submarine."[6]

Just then, the coxswain in Tregaskis' boat saw the other boat belching smoke and thought it had been hit.

"I crouched behind the gunwale, watching the sub coming toward us and thinking that there were only two possible outcomes: we would be hit and sunk, or we would be taken prisoner," Merillat said. "I don't recall having a preference."[7]

In an instant, the helmsman of Tregaskis' boat turned and raced to Merillat's rescue.

"Our boat swung over next to the crippled one and we bumped gunwales, pulled apart, and smashed together again as the two boats, running at high speed, ran parallel courses," Tregaskis said. "The crew of the other craft fell, slid and vaulted into our boat. Lt. Herb Merillat, Marine public relations officer and ordinarily quite a dignified young man, jumped over from the other boat and landed, a disordered collection of arms and legs, on the bottom of our boat. He was wearing white socks. In the haste of the moment, he had left his shoes behind. Even in that moment, the sight of his descent was humorous."[8]

The delay allowed the submarine to narrow the gap substantially, causing much alarm from Tregaskis and his crewmates.

"I told myself that this was my last day of existence, as it seemed certain to be," the correspondent wrote.

Above the noise of the engine Tregaskis and Merillat swore they could hear the Marine gunners on Tulagi whistling and cheering as if they were at a football game as their artillery fire began dropping near the submarine. Moments later the sub captain abandoned the chase and submerged. The tank lighter and surviving Higgins boat pulled into Carpenter's Wharf a short time later.

"At noon, we arrived on Tulagi, feeling lucky to be alive," Merillat said.

That afternoon, Merillat and the two civilian correspondents, Tregaskis and Miller, conducted interviews with Colonel Edson and several Raiders as they toured the former battlefield. Tregaskis explored the caves overlooking the cricket field, noting that the "stink of rotting bodies was very noticeable."

The day had another lasting memory for Merillat.

"Among other things I saw my first dead Japanese," he wrote, "his corpse enormously bloated under the tropical sun, like a grotesque balloon in a Macy's parade."[9]

Later that day, Tregaskis and Miller visited the Gavutu and Tanambogo battle grounds by launch, landing on the concrete-shattered docks of the former.

"From the dock we had a good view of the two hills, for in fact they seemed to occupy practically all of the land space on the two small islands," Tregaskis wrote. "It was as if an overgrown beehive or anthill had been planted on each island. The two land bodies are connected by a long, narrow causeway apparently built of sea shells. We passed several concrete-walled, metal-roofed buildings as we left the dock . . . Now the walls and roofs had been riddled by bullets and shell fragments.[10]

"Climbing down the steep Gavutu Hill, I wondered how the troops had ever succeeded in taking this island. Looking down from that precipitous hill to the strip of docks where the Marines had landed gave one the commanding feeling of looking into the palm of one's own hand. I thought then: If I did not know that the Marines had taken this island hill, I would have said that the job, especially against a well-armed, numerically superior force, was impossible."[11]

Crossing by launch to Tanambogo, the writers were shown two burned-out Marine tanks. The Japanese had swarmed over the tanks shortly after landing, jammed metal bars in their treads and set them afire with rags soaked in gasoline. The enemy had actually beat on the tanks with their fists and bayonets, they were told, screaming slogans in a furious rage.

The visitors were ferried back to Tulagi just before nightfall and then left the next morning for Guadalcanal.

Merillat made the return trip in the company of a few Japanese prisoners who were captured on Tulagi during the past few days.

"[The prisoners] huddled against the ramp in the bow of the craft, while MPs in the stern kept weapons trained on them," Merillat wrote. "I wondered whether the prisoners expected to be shot at sea and dumped over the side."[12]

Vandegrift took time out from his hectic schedule on August 12 to send his wife a brief note to assure her that all was well.

"The weather here is really ideal," he wrote. "We sleep under a blanket every night. And the days are not too hot. We have a portable radio and every night at 7 P.M., when time permits, we hear the broadcasts from San Francisco."

Vandegrift's first lapse of judgment came on August 12 when he grudgingly approved a hastily assembled patrol to the west to be led by his division intelligence officer,

Lt. Col. Frank Goettge. Accepting the word of a captured Japanese sailor that others in his unit might want to surrender, Goettge put together a twenty-five-man patrol that included many key personnel from both his intelligence staff and that of the 5th Marines. The patrol would also include the chief interpreter and the head surgeon of the 5th Marines.

The ill-fated patrol was transported by a Higgins boat to a promontory just west of the division perimeter. Goettge and a few others, who were leading the Japanese sailor by a rope around his neck, slowly went forward to reconnoiter. They were met by machine-gun fire. Goettge was one of the first men killed. Only three men escaped the slaughter, jumping into the sea and swimming to safety. One of the three enlisted men who escaped, Sergeant Frank L. Few, told Tregaskis that he saw the patrol hacked to death by swords and bayonets.

"They got Col. Goettge in the chest right quick," Sgt. Few said. "I went up to him, but when I put a hand on him I knew he was dead. Just then I saw somebody close by. I challenged him, and he let out a war whoop and came at me. My sub-machine gun jammed. I was struck in the arm and chest with his bayonet, but I knocked his rifle away. I choked him and stabbed him with his own bayonet."[13]

Sergeant Few turned back to join the rest of the landing party, which was digging in on the beach. The Japanese had stayed in the tree line where they could systematically pick off the Marines one by one. The men began to look for a way out.

"The Japs were closing in for the kill when the sky began to grow light with a pre-dawn glow," Tregaskis wrote. "[Corp. Joe] Spaulding had earlier made a break for the beach, started to swim for Kukum. [Sgt. Charles]

Arndt followed. And then Few, stripping down to his underclothes, made a dash for the water.

"It was the end of the rest on the beach," Sergeant Few told Tregaskis. "The Japs closed in and hacked up our people. I could see swords flashing in the sun."[14]

All three swam about four miles back to the Marine perimeter, dodging bullets and sharp coral. The men killed on the raid are still listed as missing.

The intelligence capabilities of the division in the coming months were severely affected by the loss of such valuable personnel and Vandegrift second-guessed himself for allowing the mission in the first place. The incident also inflamed feelings toward the Japanese as Marines were loath to take prisoners after that.

"I write this with a heavy heart. We lost Frank Goettge," Vandegrift said in a letter to his wife on August 14. "In addition to being a splendid and brave officer, Frank was a fine shipmate."

Three days later, Vandegrift's weakened intelligence staff was bolstered by the sudden appearance of coast-watcher Martin Clemens, the official representative of His Majesty's Government, and his band of native scouts. Dressed in a tattered shirt and shorts, wearing a brand-new pair of black dress oxfords that were much too small for him and accompanied by a little dog, Clemens led a group of about two dozen scouts down the beach in a column of twos right into a startled Marine sentry.

Clemens and his natives, who had been dodging Japanese patrols the past two days, were nearly shot. He had no identification and, of course, didn't know the password. He had earlier decided that his safest course of action would be to put on a bit of a British show and hope for the best. Adjusting the pistol on his hip and making sure his rifle-bearer had the weapon at port arms, he and his band stepped smartly toward the Marine lines. The pomp and circumstance worked.

The sentry, who obviously hadn't seen anything quite like this, lowered his rifle and waved Clemens and his men into the perimeter. Other Marines gathered around, passing out cigarettes and pieces of chocolate.

One of the Marines kept staring at one of the natives who had mottled scars on his shoulders showing bright pink on his dark skin. The native had obtained these wounds recently when he had nearly been buried alive during a Japanese air attack.

"What disease has this native got?" a curious Marine asked Clemens.

Before Clemens could explain, the native's eyes lit up and a grin spread over his face.

"That's bomb-bomb disease," he said, smiling broadly and pointing toward the sky. "You will soon find out."[15]

If some Marines did not like or trust the natives, Colonel Thomas had no such reservations, for he quickly decided that only Clemens knew Guadalcanal well enough to be a trusted advisor on Japanese movements and the nature of the terrain.[16]

Clemens and his native scouts would prove to be of immeasurable help in the coming days, and one of them, Sgt. Maj. Jacob Vouza, would become a legendary figure in Marine Corps history. Vouza, an ex-constable of the Guadalcanal police force, was an old hand at tracking murderers, pig rustlers, chicken thieves and disturbers of the peace. He had retired three years earlier after twenty-five years of service but returned to duty when the Japanese came to his island.

Vouza first displayed his value on D-day when he rescued a downed naval pilot from the USS *Wasp*, who had been shot down over Guadalcanal, and guided him to friendly lines.

It was Vouza who provided critical intelligence on the coming attack against the Marine east flank along Alligator Creek after being tortured and left for dead. The Japanese had apprehended Vouza in his native village of Tasimboko to the east of the Marine perimeter after discovering a small American flag tucked into his loincloth. He was tied to a tree and interrogated for hours but he refused to talk. He was beaten with rifle butts and bayoneted several times in his chest, face and stomach. Before leaving, a Japanese officer slashed his throat with a sword.

When the Japanese left, Vouza regained consciousness, chewed through the grass ropes tying him to the tree and stumbled toward the American lines. Covered in blood and near death, Vouza still managed to describe the size and armament of the force he had seen before losing consciousness.

"He was in an awful mess, not able to sit up," Clemens wrote. "I could hardly bear to look at him. We dragged him behind a jeep, and he told me his story as best he could in spite of the gaping wound in his throat . . . He fully expected to die and before he passed out again he gave me a long dying message for his wife and children. Once he had done his duty, the terrific strain told, and he collapsed. We carried him back and got the doctors working on him. He was operated on, pumped full of new blood, and it was expected that he would live, that was, if the hospital was not disturbed by air-raids. What loyalty the man had, and what amazing vitality. I felt immensely proud."[17]

Vouza, then forty-two, made a remarkable recovery. He was back on his feet in a little over a week and out on patrols within two weeks. Vandegrift was so appreciative of his efforts that he awarded him a Silver Star. Later, he was awarded a Legion of Merit for his role as chief scout with the 2nd Marine Raider Battalion on their famed "long patrol" behind enemy lines in November. In addition, Vouza received the special honor of being named an "honorary" sergeant major of the U.S. Marine Corps. In 1979, the old man was knighted by Queen Elizabeth II for his efforts on Guadalcanal. He died in 1984 at the age of eighty-four.

It is difficult to overestimate the value of the coastwatchers and their native guides to the overall success at Guadalcanal. Organized by the Australian Navy well before the outbreak of hostilities with Japan, it was put into operations as a part of the Allied Intelligence Bureau in March 1942. Their mission was to convey intelligence of Japanese aircraft and ship movements in the Bismarck and Solomons archipelagoes. Men like Martin Clemens, Kenneth Hay, Donald Macfarland and F. Ashton "Snowy" Rhoades on Guadalcanal and Paul Mason and Jack Read on Bougainville were a special breed of individuals.

General MacArthur would later write that "the enormous contribution of the Australian Commonwealth to the Allied war effort contains no brighter segment than this comparatively unknown unit."

There had been a loosely knit group of coastwatchers since World War I, but in 1939, with the British and Australian fleets occupied in European waters, its membership was tightened under the leadership of Australian Navy Lt. Comdr. Eric Feldt. By 1941, some 100 coastwatchers covered a half million miles of land, sea and air.

It was a coastwatcher who alerted the Americans to the construction of an airfield on Guadalcanal in early July of 1942, leading the allies to seize the island and do it quickly. More than a year later, another coastwatcher, Australian Navy Sub-Lt. Austin Reginald Evans, hid U.S.

Navy Lt. John F. Kennedy near Kolombangara from the Japanese after his PT-109 was rammed and sunk by an enemy destroyer.

For the most part, coastwatchers were rugged adventurers who prized the independence they enjoyed.

"They were planters, ship captains, goldminers or unmitigated scamps with here and there a blackbirder or slavetrader," said historian Robert Leckie. "They drank hard, loved wildly and freely, looking down upon the natives they exploited and spoke a language which, bristling with 'bleddy' this and 'baastid' that, was unprintable in the extreme, especially when it relied upon that famous four-letter word to modify the nouns of the pidgin English they taught the Melanesians. Missionaries were always shocked to discover that pidgin English was studded with scatology. Ashes, for example, were 'shit-belong fire,' and an enemy air raid was described as 'Japan he shit along sky.' "[18]

Operating singly or in pairs and accompanied by a few trustworthy natives, these unique men braved months of solitude and anxiety in some of the most inhospitable territory on earth, surrounded by the enemy and an equally hostile force of savage tribesmen who owed loyalty to neither side.

They lived constantly in fear of being captured and the torture and death that would bring. It took a special kind of courage just to endure the possibilities.

One of the most feared Japanese officers on the island was a man named Ishimoto. Prior to the invasion, he had worked as a carpenter on Tulagi where he also spied for the Japanese. When the Americans came, Ishimoto led a band of about forty men who were charged with gathering intelligence from the natives. He and his men were responsible for killing two priests and several nuns, leaving their bodies on display as a warning. They would have done the same to any coastwatchers had they been able to catch up with them.

The coastwatchers' code name was "Ferdinand" and it was chosen as a reminder that, like Munro Leaf's famous bull, they were to sit quietly under the jungle and to fight only if they were stung.

Part of their mission was to draw as little attention to themselves as possible and while the Japanese occasionally made concerted drives to find them and destroy their camps and equipment, they seldom succeeded in doing more than chasing them out of one hideout into one even more remote.

They were to take overt action only when the security of their positions was directly threatened. When they did, it was usually brief and bloody. More than one small Japanese patrol that had inadvertently stumbled upon a coastwatcher's hideaway was wiped out to the last man by a well-trained native force.

Natives were much more than carriers. They would mix with Japanese-gathered working parties, collect precious details on supplies, count heads, ships, airplanes and report on people who had grossly underestimated them.

All of the coastwatchers were equipped with cumbersome communications gear called teleradios. Though highly efficient, the speakers, receivers and transmitters weighed between seventy-five and 100 pounds apiece. It often took a native crew of a dozen or more to transport a teleradio, along with the batteries and antenna, to a new location.

"The intelligence signaled from Bougainville by Read and Mason saved Guadalcanal, and Guadalcanal saved the South Pacific," Adm. "Bull" Halsey would later write.

Not all of the natives were friendly, however. They often attached themselves to what they perceived to be the most powerful force. It did not pay to insult their dignity or family, a fact the Japanese took lightly or not at all. The Japanese lost many converts by their policies of flogging for perceived disrespect, minor infractions or drinking. Villages of the disloyal were burned.

For the most part, the natives proved to be brave and resourceful allies of the Americans. They hated the Japanese. And, despite the treatment they often received from the coastwatchers, the natives also proved to be very loyal. Not a single coastwatcher was betrayed to the Japanese during the Pacific War.[19]

Vandegrift knew that the Japanese were landing troops on Guadalcanal in nightly operations that had come to be called the "Tokyo Express," but there was little he could do about it. Destroyers appeared almost every night off Lunga Point starting in mid-August and shelled the Marines while other ships quietly dropped off troops to the east and west.

The Japanese were anxious to dislodge the Marines before the airstrip was finished and selected one of its finest units, the elite 28th Infantry Regiment, to do the job. The 28th was actually a hybrid unit, consisting of only two infantry battalions, but it was augmented by several support companies. Its commander, Col. Kiyoano Ichiki, was a headstrong and fearless leader with extensive experience in China. He had been an instructor at the Imperial Army's Infantry School for many years and had been handpicked to command the 28th when it was chosen to spearhead landings on Midway before the Americans turned away the Japanese invasion force in June of 1942.

The initial consensus within the Japanese intelligence

community was that the American invasion of Guadalcanal was nothing more than a reconnaissance in force.
At most, the Marine force consisted of a few thousand
troops whose mission was only to destroy the airfield and
withdraw. In addition, morale of the American force was
believed to be very low because of the Savo Island defeat.

The Japanese high command didn't believe the United
States was capable of launching a full-scale counteroffen-
sive until 1943. They had downgraded the number of
Marines on Guadalcanal from 5,000–6,000 to only 2,000–
3,000 because of their losses at Savo Island and the withdrawal of the transports. Higher headquarters felt that
Ichiki's 900-man initial detachment, which was to be augmented five days later with the other 1,100 men of his
brigade, could do the job.

Ichiki was told that if his attack failed he was to take
up a position near the airfield and wait for reinforcements. So confident was Ichiki of success, he had asked if
he could also retake Tulagi the next day. The request was
denied.

Based on the available intelligence, Ichiki believed he
could easily overpower the Americans and retake the airfield. Underestimating the Marine strength and their grit
was a fatal error, one the Japanese would commit several
more times during the Guadalcanal campaign.

Ichiki's detachment landed at Taivu Point twenty-two
miles east of the Marine perimeter at 0100 on August 19.
After leaving a token force of about 100 men to secure
the beachhead, Ichiki immediately headed west with
about 800 men before resting at daylight. Across Sealark
Channel, three enemy destroyers shelled Tulagi as a
diversion.

Around noon that day, a sixty-man Marine patrol under
Capt. Charles H. Brush, which included three native

guides, ran head-on into one of Ichiki's patrols about ten miles from the Marine perimeter, killing all but five of the forty-man party. The helmets of the dead Japanese bore the star of the Imperial Army, not the chrysanthemum of the Navy. Four of the dead were officers carrying swords and field glasses. They were wearing polished boots and dressed in pressed uniforms complete with rows of varicolored ribbons. As Brush went to search one of the "dead" officers the officer pulled out a pistol and shot himself in the head. The Marines would see more of this in the weeks to come.

Brush quickly gathered up all the intelligence he could find and returned to division headquarters. Among the booty were several maps and recent low-level aerial photographs that detailed the Marine defensive positions and pinpointed the placement of artillery positions around the airfield. Colonel Thomas found the accuracy of the enemy maps to be "chilling."

Based on the evidence, Vandegrift knew the enemy might attack as early as the next night. What Vandegrift didn't know was exactly how many or where they would strike. It appeared the enemy force was headed straight for Alligator Creek, which was manned by units of the 2nd Battalion, 1st Marines. But, rather than plug in his reserve battalion (1/1), Vandegrift decided to keep it available as a reaction force—just in case the Japanese decided to attack from another direction.

11

Smitty

Pvt. Al Schmid was typical of the men who enlisted in the Marines after Pearl Harbor. Called "Pearl Harbor Avengers," Schmid and many of the young recruits didn't even know where Pearl Harbor was, nor did they care. What they all had in common, however, was a bitterness against all things Japanese. They all wanted to get some payback for the Japanese treachery on December 7, the sooner the better.

Schmid, twenty-one, landed on Guadalcanal on August 7 as a machine gunner with H Company, 2nd Battalion, 1st Marines. A native of Philadelphia, he was called "Smitty" by the boys in his outfit. When he was carried off the island on August 21, more dead than alive, he was cheered and saluted by his entire unit as a full-fledged hero.

"[I was] just one of the gophers of Guadalcanal," Schmid would tell his biographer, Roger Butterfield, later after being awarded the Navy Cross. "That's what the Marines in our outfit called each other, and it was a pretty good name for us, the way we were always ducking in and out of our holes. We were a pretty crazy bunch, and we didn't care for anything but killing Japs.

"We were scared as hell. But you'd never know it from the way we acted. We used to carry our .45s tied on a string around our waists, like a gang of cowpunchers. We'd walk along and when we'd meet some guy from our own outfit we'd say, 'Halt, pardner, and draw your weapon,' and then we'd pull our guns."

When their lieutenant would yell at them to knock it off and asked if they wanted to kill somebody, Schmid would laugh and say, "Sure we want to kill somebody."[1]

Schmid's outfit was assigned a section of front along the western bank of Alligator Creek, which was a complete misnomer. It wasn't a creek at all, but rather a lagoon that was cut off from the sea by a sandbar. Second, there were no alligators on Guadalcanal. There were crocodiles, however.

Schmid's foxhole was about 100 yards from the sea and overlooked the sandbar. He and the other two members of his machine gun crew, Pvt. Johnny Rivers and Corp. Leroy Diamond, dug a semicircular trench about four feet deep and two feet wide. It was just deep enough so that when they stood in it the stock of the .30-caliber gun came about up to their chests.

They stacked sandbags up in front and all around the outside of the trench and plastered the bags inside and out with river mud. They also put two big coconut tree logs across the top as a protection against mortar fire. They camouflaged the whole thing with palm fronds and green leaves until it was practically invisible from ten yards away. It took nearly five days to build the nest.

"It was a thing of beauty," Schmid said.

The next machine gun position was 100 yards to the right near a little bend in the lagoon. There were coconut trees on both sides of the lagoon, coming down almost to the water. When the time came to use the gun, Rivers would do the firing and Schmid would load. If one of them became incapacitated, somebody else from the squad was supposed to take his place—whichever one could get there fastest. They practiced the procedure daily.

The gun was the most important member of the squad and Schmid knew it. He greased it and petted it. He even painted a shamrock on it. The rest of the squad would laugh when Schmid put his cheek near the steel barrel, patting it while he said: "Well, baby, are you gonna speak your piece tonight?"

Colonel Ichiki, giving no thought to waiting for the rest of his regiment, called his commanders together at noon on August 20 to give them his attack plan. It was a pretty straightforward scheme, one that Ichiki and other Japanese commanders had used often in China and other areas of the Pacific rim. They would attack head-on in the middle of the night, brandishing swords and bayonets and screaming their heads off. The Americans, they firmly believed, would scatter like so many autumn leaves.

Ichiki was a devotee of the Bushido Code (the way of the warrior). The Japanese soldier placed much more emphasis on individual ability and bravery than upon numbers and material power. That philosophy was developed centuries earlier by Japan's samurai caste in connection with the Shinto religion. The code stressed aggressiveness, courage, honor, loyalty, self-sacrifice and stoicism during suffering and pain, and a contempt for death. Commonly, you either won a battle or you died—if not at the enemy's hands, then by your own. It was a terrible disgrace to become a prisoner of war. Suicide was infinitely preferable. The Emperor was venerated and it was a privilege to die for him.

The detachment would be marching to war under the revered colors of the 28th Regiment, carrying the same flag that flew atop 203-Meter Height during the siege of Port Arthur in the Russo-Japanese War of 1904–1905. The flag was the symbol of honor and esprit de corps within the Imperial Japanese Army and its capture would be a disgrace.

The main weapon of the infantrymen was the Arisaka rifle. It was comparable to the Marine Springfield as both were reliable, bolt-action rifles. The most important weapon, however, was the bayonet. In training, Japanese soldiers were constantly reminded not to "rely on your bullets, rely on your bayonet."

The Japanese belittled the American fighting man, believing he lacked all the qualities of a warrior. A pamphlet issued to Japanese soldiers early in the war described Americans and other westerners as "being very haughty, effeminate and cowardly" and who "intensely dislike fighting in the rain or mist or in the dark. They cannot conceive night to be a proper time for battle—though it is excellent for dancing."[2]

As the sun began to set behind them through a grove of coconut palms, the Marines grew quiet. "Across the creek the trunks of trees and leaves and underbrush slowly slid together in a black mass against the dark blue sky," wrote historian John Foster. "The night was hot, sticky, and singing with thirsty mosquitoes. The Marines waited, sweat crawling like worms down their back. Some, somehow, managed to snooze."[3]

Soon after dark, an enemy patrol of engineers moved out to try and locate a good crossing point on Alligator Creek. The main body got underway about 2000. Around midnight, Marine outposts on the east side of the lagoon began to hear high-pitched voices and noises of men on the march. The outposts were withdrawn to the west bank of the creek where they occupied prepared defensive positions.

Ichiki paused when he reached the east bank to consult with his unit commanders. It was pitch-black, which only highlighted the countless blips of fireflies hovering over the lagoon. The men began working themselves into a frenzy, sounding to one Marine "like a flock of turkeys." Other chants were clear and cold.

"U.S. Madeen, tonight you die" and "Japanese boy drink American boy's blood" could be heard clearly across the placid lagoon.

One private from G Company, who was standing guard on the west bank, thought he saw a disturbance in the water right in front of him. As he continued to stare at the sight, the dark form of a helmeted soldier with a rifle strapped to his back silently rose up out of the water and crawled right at him. Rather than give his position away by firing his rifle, he turned his rifle around and butt-stroked the infiltrator square in the face, causing him to slide silently back into the water.

Other movements could be heard and seen.

"We could hear them walking along the beach toward us and jabbering away," said seventeen-year-old Pvt. Richard W. Harding. "They didn't even have scouts out."

At about 0200, a green flare drifted over the mouth of the lagoon illuminating more than a hundred Japanese soldiers, shrieking their battle slogans and racing for the sandbar. As they ran, they worked the bolts of their rifles and fired from the hip. Their bayonets glistened in the light from the flare.

At the same time, an explosion of enemy machine gun fire sent a rain of tracer bullets across the lagoon, slamming into the coconut trees and the foxholes of the Marine defenders. The attack was on.

Schmid's orders were to hold fire until the enemy started to cross the lagoon. If they opened up too early, they were told, it would give away their positions and the enemy would try to knock them out with mortars.

The Japanese were screaming in high-pitched voices, screeching what sounded like "EEEE-YI." Schmid could see the little white lights of Japanese gunfire winking like fireflies across the lagoon. Soon, the bullets began slamming into the sandbags placed around the nest. Then he could see bodies advancing across the lagoon and sandbar. He thought they looked like a bunch of cows coming down to the river for a drink.[4]

Finally, the order was given to fire. Rivers swept the area to his front while Schmid acted as the loader. To the left, a Marine 37mm antitank gun took aim down the beach and belched mouthfuls of ball bearings that cut the Japanese infantry to pieces.

The machine gun to Schmid's right suddenly stopped firing and then a burst hit Rivers square in the face. Blood spurted everywhere. Rivers, mortally wounded, fell back without making a sound. He had been killed instantly. Corporal Diamond, covered with Rivers' blood, moved up to man the gun before he, too, was wounded in the arm.

Schmid, also covered in Rivers' blood, took over in a rage, firing and loading like a madman. The barrel of the water-cooled gun grew red hot and started to crackle and sputter like an empty kettle on a stove. Schmid could hear his bullets banging into Japanese helmets. He could also hear the screaming and sobbing of the enemy, who, nonetheless, kept on coming.

When the enemy column reached the west bank of the lagoon they were held up by a makeshift barbed-wire fence just thirty yards from the Marine positions. As the bodies began piling up, a few intrepid souls broke free and rushed the Marine foxholes with bayonets and swords where a series of fierce hand-to-hand combat encounters took place.

Not long before dawn, a Japanese survivor managed to

crawl near Schmid's machine gun position and lobbed a grenade. It exploded only a few inches from the left side of Schmid's face. Schmid was blown to the back of the trench and fell on top of Diamond. Dazed and blinded by the grenade, Schmid still managed to pull out his .45-caliber pistol, according to Butterfield, who wrote the following narrative.

"Don't do it, Smitty, don't shoot yourself," Diamond said.

"Hell, don't worry about that. I'm going to get the first Jap that tries to come in here," Schmid responded.

"But you can't see," Diamond told him.

"That's all right," Schmid answered. "Just tell me which way he's coming and I'll get him. I can smell the rotten buggers."[5]

Not a single enemy soldier entered Schmid's foxhole but other Marines had to expel the enemy in fierce hand-to-hand fighting that included bayonets, swords and even machetes.

Shortly after dawn and still under sniper fire, Schmid was carried from his foxhole in a blanket. His fellow Marines were cheering. He heard his lieutenant say, "Hey, Smitty," and he responded quickly with "Whaddya say, boss?"

He still had his .45 in his hand. "I guess I won't need this any more," Schmid said as he reached out and gave the pistol to the lieutenant. Then, he passed out.[6]

Vandegrift was determined not to let the enemy "lay around" in the coconut grove. He sent his reserve battalion (1/1) on a sweep to Ichiki's rear to envelop the enemy and cut off any retreat. The battalion compressed the remnants of Ichiki's force into a triangle by the mouth of the lagoon. Frenzied Japanese began racing out of the coconut palms into the waiting guns of Marines on the west back of the lagoon.

The Marines also committed a platoon of light tanks to the mop-up, sending them across the sandbar, which had been named "Hell's Point," and into the coconut grove on the east bank of the lagoon.

"The tanks halted for a few moments, then plunged on across the sandspit, their treads rattling industriously," Tregaskis wrote. "We watched these awful machines as they plunged across the spit and into the edge of the grove. It was fascinating to see them bustling amongst the trees, pivoting, turning, spitting sheets of yellow flame. It was like a comedy of toys, something unbelievable, to see them knocking over palm trees which fell slowly, flushing the running figures of men from underneath their treads, following and firing at the fugitives . . . We had not realized there were so many Japs in the grove. Group after group was flushed out and shot down by the tanks' canister shells."[7]

United Press correspondent Robert C. Miller also witnessed the final destruction of the Japanese force.

"It was almost pitiful to watch them lie in a coconut grove near the beach and fire their rifles and machine guns at the armor plating of our tanks," Miller wrote. "The tanks shed off these bullets with harmless 'pings' and did a thorough mopping-up job.

"Every Marine in our outfit let out a yell when the tanks came and the whole American side of the [river] front sounded like the bleachers at Ebbets Field when the Dodgers win a close one. The tanks rumbled down in single file toward the palms where the Japanese were hiding among the trees and brush.

"There were only two things the Japanese could do. They could scramble and run—and be mowed down by machine guns. Or they could lie low in hope the tanks would miss them as they raced back and forth blasting everything on the ground that moved.

"From a point on the Marines' front lines I could watch the ring drawn tighter around the enemy. Although they were being pounded to pieces, the Japanese made no attempt to surrender en masse. Individual groups of prisoners, however, ran out with their hands raised."[8]

Also watching the destruction was Vandegrift, who would later write that "the rear of the tanks looked like meat grinders."

Ichiki, who must have realized the end was near, burned the regimental colors and committed suicide at about 1630. Conflicting reports claim he either shot himself with a pistol or committed hara-kiri with a ceremonial knife. Some of the Japanese survivors claim that Ichiki was killed on the sandspit.

The remaining survivors desperately looked for an escape route. The only one available was toward the sea where they were systematically picked off on the beach or in the water by Marine sharpshooters. One rifleman, Pfc. Andy Poliny, later claimed that one of the Japanese soldiers he shot and killed with his BAR on the beach was none other than Colonel Ichiki himself.

Poliny was part of the enveloping force (1/1) that outflanked the remaining pockets of Japanese, an experience he never forgot.

"As we came to a slight depression in the coconut grove terrain, there lay two Japs who seemed to be playing dead," Poliny said. "Our battalion commander [Lt. Col. Lenard Cresswell] was present, and he ordered the pair bayoneted. As a Marine approached to do the job, one of the Japs rolled over with a pistol in his hand and shot him in the face, just above the right eye. Seeing this, I opened up on both Japs with my BAR on full automatic, and that was the end of that."[9]

Dozens of little bobbing heads could be seen just offshore, presenting inviting targets for the Marines, who had hunkered down behind some sandbags and methodically lined up their targets and squeezed off their shots just like they were back on the rifle range at Quantico.

Japanese bodies were piled up on the beach, half covered with sand and bloated to near twice their original size. Many had been washed ashore during an escape attempt hours earlier. They looked "puffed and glossy, like shiny sausages," Tregaskis wrote.

The smell was overwhelming. The men used handkerchiefs or other pieces of clothing to cover their noses while they frisked the dead Japanese for bits of intelligence, as well as souvenirs. Then a trench was dug nearby to bury the bodies.

The Marines still had one hard lesson to learn, however. A few of the wounded Japanese among the dead chose to use their last breath to take a Marine with him. Some committed suicide right in front of Marines searching their ranks for souvenirs. Then and there, Marines adopted a policy of shoot first and search later.

"I watched our men standing in a shooting-gallery line, thumping bullets into the piles of Japanese carcasses," Tregaskis wrote. "The edge of the water grew brown and muddy. Some said the blood of the Japanese carcasses was staining the ocean."[10]

Though the actual fighting had calmed down, Japanese snipers were still at work picking off unsuspecting Marines who dallied too long in the open. Most of the Marine casualties, in fact, were inflicted by snipers who had to be routed out one by one. The crack of their rifles could be heard all along the beach.

Even Vandegrift was stunned by the enemy's willingness to die as he communicated in a letter to his boss, General Holcomb, a few days later.

"I have never heard or read of this kind of fighting. These people refuse to surrender. The wounded wait until men come up to examine them and blow themselves and the other fellow to pieces with a hand grenade," he wrote.[11]

One of those on the scene that day was Raider Robert Youngdeer, who had come over from Tulagi a week earlier to help guard some Japanese prisoners. Corporal Youngdeer, a full-blooded Cherokee Indian, had been assigned temporary duty at the small POW compound on Guadalcanal when the Alligator Creek battle began.

"I was put on guard duty at one corner of the compound and armed with a Thompson submachine gun," Youngdeer later wrote. "The firing and the battle raged all night; too close for comfort. The next day we took prisoners to the scene and helped bury some 700 enemy dead—the figure I remember."

Policing the battlefield over the next few days was a gruesome task. A lot of boys became men overnight.

Tregaskis, a twenty-five-year-old civilian, made a complete tour of the killing ground and came away hardened by the experience.

"There is no horror to these things," he wrote. "The first one you see is the only shock. The rest are simple repetition."[12]

The Marines, too, came away hardened.

"I will never forget the speech our battalion commander [Colonel Cresswell] made that evening," recalled Pfc. Poliny. "He told us we were now real men and good Marines, and that we were going to kick the Japs' asses all the way back to Tokyo. After a hot meal of canned red beans and beef stew we crawled into our foxholes for a little rest. It's true that many of the men had no stomach for food that night even though they hadn't eaten all day.

The adjustment to this kind of combat would take some time."[13]

Schmid arrived at the field hospital about eight o'clock. His face and eyes were riddled with shrapnel and puffed up with blood and bruises. His left eye was swollen as big as a golf ball and Schmid could feel it hanging down over his cheek. The shrapnel had clipped off a piece of one ear and cut into his neck, shoulder, left arm and hand. One piece gouged a big chunk of knuckle off his left thumb. He had suffered a concussion and hemorrhage to the head and powder burns to the chest.[14]

He was coming to and passing out every few minutes. When he was loaded aboard a ship he heard someone say, "Jeez, it ain't no use taking him down—he's dead." Schmid knew the sailor was talking about him. For a minute he thought they were going to throw him overboard. That's how they buried people at sea, he told himself before passing out once again.[15]

As they left the harbor a few minutes later, the ship barely managed to evade an enemy torpedo.

Schmid reached the Naval hospital at San Diego on October 23 and finally went home to Philadelphia on January 19 where he slowly regained partial sight in his right eye. He received his Navy Cross on March 11, 1943. Two years later a movie, starring John Garfield, was made of his life. It was titled simply, but eloquently: *Pride of the Marines*.

Of the 800 or so Japanese who tried to cross Alligator Creek on the early morning of August 21, twelve were picked up wounded after the battle, including one officer, and two who were captured unhurt. The official Japanese body count was at least 777 killed. They were crack Japanese infantrymen, with new uniforms and medals on their chests—the best the enemy had to offer. Marine losses totaled forty-four dead, including three on Capt. Brush's patrol the day before, and about seventy-one wounded.[16]

The Japanese had assumed the untested Marines would panic and run at the sight of bayonets and swords. That's what happened on dozen of fronts in the Philippines, China, Borneo, Indonesia, Manchuria and Malaya. Japanese tactics had proven infallible.

Not this night, however. The Marines did more than annihilate a highly decorated shock force, they shattered the myth of Japanese invincibility.

"Ichiki was a firebrand. Luckily for us he was also a fool," wrote Lieutenant Whyte. "If you had to devise a way to get a lot of people killed very quickly, you couldn't think of a better way than a banzai charge. The carnage was terrible.

"The Ichiki attack was just plain dumb. Though the Imperial Army's staff had never actually authorized it, they hadn't discouraged it either. The fact that eight hundred of Japan's most skilled fighting men were slaughtered in a matter of two hours speaks for itself."[17]

The Japanese were stunned. Years later, Admiral Tanaka tried to explain what had happened, lamenting the fact that very little was done to change Japanese tactics over the course of the war.

"I knew Colonel Ichiki from the Midway operation and was well aware of his magnificent leadership and indomitable fighting spirit," Tanaka wrote. "But this episode made it abundantly clear that infantrymen armed with rifles and bayonets had no chance against an enemy equipped with modern heavy arms. This tragedy should have taught the hopelessness of 'bamboo spear' tactics."[18]

The number of bodies counted within range of Schmid's

machine gun ran into the hundreds. Marines who were there that night credited him with killing at least two hundred of them. He never got a chance to count them himself.

Newspapers back home got word of the victory over Ichiki's forces in a communiqué from Admiral Nimitz' headquarters in Hawaii. Nimitz had sent a message to General Vandegrift saying how "proud" he was of him and his "gallant Marines" but offered the public little else in the way of details.

"The Navy declined to reveal additional information about the progress of operations in the Solomons," said the lead story in the *New York Times* on August 23. "Considerable speculation was aroused, however, by the communiqué issued at Pearl Harbor by Adm. Nimitz relating how 700 Japanese soldiers were landed with speedboats on islands occupied by the Marines.

"That announcement, unofficial naval sources remarked, suggested that the American naval forces that covered the landings on at least three Solomon Islands may have retired after the successful landing operations or the capture of the islands. This would have permitted the enemy to bring in reinforcements by water."

In the same edition, a columnist wondered out loud why the country was not being better informed of the fighting taking place in the Solomons.

"The sum total of Washington communiqués in the nearly two weeks of that action reaches a total of about 1,500 words. That is not enough and the official declarations that nothing else is known are not impressive," the writer stated. "It must be possible to put out statements regarding that engagement without giving information to the enemy. That this could be done is illustrated by the circumstance that a good deal of material on the operation has come from

Gen. MacArthur's headquarters in Australia. He is not conducting the fight, but some units under his command are involved. It is apparent that he thinks it wise to put out information for the public. And there has been no complaint that he has given any information to the Japanese."

All that would change six days later when the first reports from civilian correspondents were cleared by the military censors. Many readers of the *New York Times* must have scratched their heads in wonderment when they read Robert C. Miller's lead story on August 29, which was actually written on August 8, that stated:

"The Marines have landed and Old Glory is flying today over the first Japanese-conquered territory retaken by the United Nations in the Pacific War."

Miller wrote almost fifty inches, describing the unopposed landing on Guadalcanal and the fierce fighting on Tulagi and the twin islands of Tanambogo and Gavutu. Miller was able to get to all four locations for interviews. Amid all the chaos of the first few days, he also managed to claim credit for apprehending a Japanese prisoner.

"The press captured the first Japanese prisoner on Guadalcanal Island today, and was scared out of ten years' growth doing it," the excited Miller wrote. "Accompanied by Sherman Montrose of Acme Newspictures, this correspondent discovered the first Japanese hiding in a tent and a few minutes later a second was found. Both were rounded up by a Marine patrol and taken to the rear for questioning."

At least a couple of enemy soldiers had fallen victim to the power of the press, it would seem.

12

Adding Muscle

Vandegrift and his staff were feeling pretty good on August 21 but there was no time to celebrate the destruction of Ichiki's battalion. The victory only exposed how thin Vandegrift's forces were should the Japanese mount another attack. He needed reinforcements if the Marines had any intention of holding on to their beachhead.

Vandegrift had asked repeatedly for the 7th Marines, who were still languishing on Samoa. And he wanted to bring over some units from Tulagi, which appeared out of danger of an invasion. He could get neither because there was no air cover. All that changed on the afternoon of August 20 when a total of thirty-one American planes landed at Henderson Field—twelve SBD3 Dauntless dive bombers under Lt. Col. Dick Mangram and nineteen F4F Wildcat fighters under Capt. John Smith. The Wildcats had been catapulted off the deck of the auxiliary escort carrier *Long Island,* a first for most of the young pilots.

"I was close to tears and I was not alone when the first SBD taxied up and this handsome and dashing aviator jumped to the ground," Vandegrift later wrote. "Thank God you have come, I told him."[1]

Two of the dive bombers deliberately circled Henderson Field and the Marine perimeter for all of the foot Marines to see. The men ran whooping and cheering along the beaches and through the jungles throwing their helmets in the air in a wild celebration.

"During the months on Guadalcanal there were few moments of unalloyed general joy. This was one of them," Colonel Thomas would later write.

Vandegrift shook hands with every pilot. The general also reveled in the fact that the island now had air power, a "Cactus Air Force," as it would be called. It would grow a little more two days later when the Army sent in five P-400s, which provided the Marines with close ground support on the island by strafing enemy positions.

There was a new bounce in Vandegrift's step.

"That evening I joined my Marines for a bath in the [Tenaru] River," Vandegrift wrote. "From the brown water I looked up at a young Marine positioned behind a .30-caliber machine gun guarding our relaxation. Somehow he epitomized everything that all of us were working for. Somehow he caused me to face the future with sublime confidence."[2]

August 21 was an especially busy day on Guadalcanal. While some of the newly arrived aircraft participated in the mop-up of Ichiki's forces to the east, all six APDs (*Manley, McKean, Stringham, Little, Gregory and Colhoun*) arrived off Lunga Point early in the afternoon with 240 tons of badly needed food and supplies. This was the second run to the island these "elderly" converted destroyer transports had made in the last week. The small, lightly armed APDs, along with a few escorting destroyers, were the only U.S. Navy ships to be seen anywhere near Guadalcanal since Admiral Fletcher pulled his forces away on August 9.

Now that he had some air cover, Vandegrift sent three of the APDs over to Tulagi to shuttle the reinforced 2nd

Battalion, 5th Marines to Guadalcanal where they would become his division reserve. Attached to 2/5 was a 142-man battery of 105mm guns, a platoon of engineers, a platoon from the 1st Amphibian Tractor Battalion and a forty-nine-man medical detachment.

Vandegrift now had six rifle battalions and 12,000 men on Guadalcanal.

He wanted more, however. He needed an offensive force to act as his eyes and ears, a sort of fire brigade to probe and upset the enemy's future plans. He issued orders for the 1st Raider Battalion, along with the remnants of the 1st Parachute Battalion, to prepare to embark for Guadalcanal. It would take ten days to get these units to Guadalcanal because of a lack of shipping and sufficient air cover. Half the contingent arrived on August 30 and the other half came over on the 31st.

One of the APDs, the *Colhoun,* had a special delivery for the Raiders—a trio of "wandering cooks." It seems that when Admiral Turner was forced to quickly withdraw his transports from Sealark Channel back on August 9, three cooks from the 1st Raider Battalion were still aboard the *Colhoun.*

In subsequent trips back to Guadalcanal, the *Colhoun* had no opportunity to visit Tulagi and drop off the cooks. This time was different. The Raiders, who had to endure the concoctions of "amateur" chefs for three weeks, greeted their long-lost comrades with wild applause, doubly so because they brought along with them some food, "pogey bait" and a good supply of cigarettes.

The three cooks had helped out in the *Colhoun's* galley during their stay aboard and made many friends among the crew, a fact that caused much personal pain the next day when the ship was sunk following a successful delivery of Raiders to Guadalcanal.

En route to Guadalcanal, Rear Adm. Richmond Kelly Turner, commander of the Amphibious Force, and Maj. Gen. Alexander A. Vandegrift, 1st Marine Division commander, review the Operation Watchtower plan.

Vandegrift confers with his staff on board the transport USS *McCawley* en route to Guadalcanal. From left: General Vandegrift; Lt. Col. Gerald C. Thomas, operations officer; Lt. Col. Randolph McC. Pate, logistics officer; Lt. Col. Frank B. Goettge, intelligence officer; and Col. William Capers James, chief of staff.

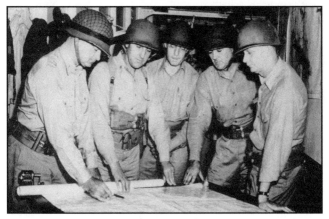

(*above*) APD 3—USS *Gregory* in convoy en route to Tulagi-Guadalcanal in early August 1942.

(*right*) Lt. Frank Guidone, one of the many young NCOs who rose through the ranks of the 1st Raiders to receive meritorious field commissions.

(*below*) More than 200 Japanese soldiers were killed in the sandspit where the Tenaru River flows into Ironbottom Sound (Sealark Channel).

Japanese soldiers killed on the beach in front of Marine positions west of Alligator Creek during Ichiki's assault.

A prelanding strike by USS *Enterprise* aircraft flown by Navy pilots. Tanambogo and Gavutu Islands lie in ruins in the morning sun. Gavutu is on the left.

The Pagoda at Henderson Field served as headquarters for Cactus Air Force throughout the first months of air operations on Guadalcanal.

Edson's Ridge after the valiant and bloody fighting on the nights of September 12–13 and 13–14, which proved crucial to maintaining Henderson Field and the Marine perimeter on Guadalcanal. Henderson Field lies beyond the trees in the background.

(top) Left to right: Maj. John L. Smith, Maj. Robert E. Galer and Capt Marion E. Carl received the Navy Cross from Adm. Chester Nimitz on October 1, 1942. Smith and Galer later received the Medal of Honor.

(middle) Lt. Gen. Thomas A. Holcomb, left, listens to Colonel Edson describe the fighting that took place while protecting Henderson Field. On the right, Major General Vandegrift listens.

(left) Col. Merritt A. Edson receives the Medal of Honor from Brig. Gen. William H. Rupertus for intrepid leadership in action on Guadalcanal.

The Survivors. First row, from left: Maj. Ira Irwin, Capt. John Salmon, Capt. Robert Neufer, Capt. Ed Wheeler, Capt. Rex Crockett and Capt. Ed Dupras. Second row, from left: Capt. John Sweeney, Lt. John Erskine, Capt. George Herring, Lt. James Blessing and

Lt. Astle Ryder. Third row, from left: Lt. Robert Skinner (asst. surgeon), Capt. William Stevenson, Gunny Elwood Gebhart, Lt. Richard Sullivan, Lt. Jack Goulding and Lt. Ray Schneider.

Taken on Guadalcanal in 1942, this photo pictures three of the main players in the brief history of the Raiders. Left to right: Lieutenant General Holcomb, Colonel Edson and Major General Vandegrift.

President Franklin D. Roosevelt presents Gen Vandegrift the Medal of Honor. On the left is Maj Alexander A. Vandegrift, Jr., and on the right Gen Vandegrift's wife.

The cloudy weather also allowed the transport *Betelgeuse* to sneak into Kukum Landing on September 1 with 393 members of the 6th Naval Construction Battalion. The "Seabees," as they were called, went right to work improving Henderson Field. At the same time, they began construction of a nearby field called Fighter One. Two days later, Brig. Gen. Roy S. Geiger, a legendary fighter pilot during World War I, flew in to take charge of the "Cactus Air Force" on Guadalcanal.

The Leathernecks had a little fun with the "Seabees," whose average age of thirty-five was nearly twice that of the young Marine infantrymen.

"Hey pop—you get your wars mixed up or somethin?" shouted one of the hardened teenaged veterans.

"Hang onto yer false teeth, grandad—the Japs are dropping sandwiches," said another as an old-timer came ashore.[3]

The "Seabees" brought a wealth of experience and knowledge about building and repairing airfields. Their energy and work rate was impressive. Seldom would a runway be out of action for more than a couple of hours when the "Seabees" were around.

Geiger and his staff flew in an hour after sunset on September 3, landing in the glare of jeep headlights. The next morning, he made a call on his old friend and classmate, General Vandegrift, bringing along a package for him from Nimitz, marked "fan mail." It was a case of scotch.

Knowing that Vandegrift, being the Southern gentleman he was, was partial to bourbon, not scotch, Geiger is reported to have said: "Archer, I have a case of bourbon, and I'll trade you level—even though mine are quarts."[4]

Vandegrift was delighted to accept the offer. The two generals then hopped into a jeep and drove off to Geiger's quarters to consummate the deal. Geiger, a rotund figure of a man, looked all over his tent for the bourbon and couldn't find it, sending him into a cold rage.

Suspecting that one of his fliers had committed the theft, Geiger would make all of his men pay for this act of larceny by increasing the workload over the coming weeks.

The heavyset Geiger, who detested paperwork, arrived determined to squeeze the last ounce of performance from his air crews and machines. He quickly injected a new spirit among the men. Much work still needed to be done on the airfield. Only 1,000 feet of runway was covered with steel matting and after each heavy rain, the remainder became a rutted, muddy swamp that even jeeps found difficult to negotiate. Each takeoff and landing was an adventure.

Geiger hit the island running, leaving no time for the tired and grumpy air crews to feel sorry for themselves. Instead, a new pride developed. A chalkboard was put up at the air operations center so the men could see how their planes were doing in dogfights with the enemy. The infantry Marines, who were proud of "their" fliers, would march by and cry out: "What's the score?" just as if they were at a ball game.

Colonel Edson, who had become decidedly edgy with the recent inactivity, arrived on Guadalcanal on August 29 for a briefing. After spending a boring and relatively uneventful three weeks on Tulagi organizing patrols in search of Japanese stragglers, Edson was raring to go. His energy was infectious. He and Colonel Thomas, Vandegrift's operations officer, quickly became close allies. The handsome, bushy-eyed Thomas, who won a field commission during World War I, had only known Edson by reputation. He did know Edson's executive officer, Sam Griffith, very well, however. The two men had served together in China. Thomas greatly respected Griffith's judgment and when Griffith told him there was no finer tactician than Edson in the Marine Corps, it was good enough for him.

Thomas and his deputy, Lieutenant Colonel Twining, held enormous power within the 1st Division and Vandegrift swore by their judgment. Edson knew this instinctively as he and Thomas hit it off immediately. It was the beginning of a long and fruitful relationship.

Vandegrift was extremely impressed with Edson's performance on Tulagi where he pretty much ran the whole show. He and Thomas were less enthusiastic about the leadership exhibited thus far by some of the regimental and battalion-level officers on Guadalcanal. Perhaps softened by twenty years of garrison life, they had proven much too cautious and hesitant for Vandegrift's liking. Edson, on the other hand, had been aggressive and decisive. He took charge on Tulagi, a job that should have been performed by the campaign commander, Brigadier General Rupertus.

According to Edson's biographer, Jon Hoffman, Rupertus had developed a propensity to follow operations "from a distance." He waited, for example, until the night of D-day to head for Tulagi, a difficult time to set up a functioning command post and get the lay of the land.

"The misplaced priorities of the group commander were apparent when [Rupertus] made a visit to the Raider CP on the morning of the ninth, just after the island was secured, but with a counterlanding apparently imminent. His first reaction was to take the acting sergeant major to task for the 'careless policing of the area,' a place the Raiders had defended in hand-to-hand fighting not many hours previously," Hoffman wrote.[5]

Griffith "had practically no confidence in General Rupertus" and he was "sure Edson felt this way about him . . . [Rupertus] relied almost entirely on Edson for recommendations, suggestions, this sort of thing."

Edson's Navy Cross citation left little doubt who took charge on Tulagi, stating: "Colonel Edson advanced the attack of his battalion and its supporting units with such skill, courage, and aggressiveness that he was an inspiration to the entire Combat Group and was directly responsible for the capture of Tulagi Island." (Rupertus also received a Navy Cross for the Tulagi operation).[6]

Vandegrift needed a man of Edson's ability on Guadalcanal—the sooner the better.

Getting the Raiders to Guadalcanal proved to be a tougher-than-expected chore because of the presence of enemy submarines and aircraft. The first ship to dash across Sealark Channel on the morning of August 30 was a small auxiliary cargo vessel, the *Kopara,* which took most of Baker Company.

"It was loaded with bombs and fuel but I didn't really care," John Sweeney remembered. "I was just happy to make it a fast trip and do it early."[7] Other ships were not so lucky.

The USS *Little* shuttled across Able Company around noon and the USS *Colhoun* followed next with Dog Company. Just after discharging its cargo near the Kukum landing, the *Colhoun* heard an air raid alert and began making preparations to leave for the relative safety of Tulagi harbor. She didn't make it. Japanese bombs found her just off Kukum and she sank in two minutes, taking with her fifty-one of her crew. Had it happened an hour earlier, many Raiders of D Company would have been killed.

The transfer of the Raiders and 1st Parachute Battalion was completed the next day as the two units set up a bivouac in a large coconut grove just west of the Lunga River, about 1,500 yards inland from Kukum landing. The men seemed pleased. It beat the heck out of setting up camp in the jungle.

The palm groves, the men found out, were part of the world's largest coconut plantation, owned by the Lever Brothers company. The trees provided the copra for the Palmolive soap products that were sold all over the world.

Most of the men set up pup tents right next to their foxholes, making it easy for them to find shelter during a bombardment. Many strung hammocks between the trees so they could sleep off the ground. Others constructed sleeping quarters of wood and tin found lying around the island.

Other than the noontime bombings and nightly shelling, the other constant was the rain, a dripping and soaking wetness that permeated every part of their bodies no matter how hard they tried to keep it away. The puddles, of course, proved perfect breeding grounds for the malaria-carrying mosquitoes.

A source of welcomed relief during the daytime was a swim in the sea or the Lunga River, which ran directly through the Marine perimeter. Cool, clean and swift, the Lunga was an ever-ready shower. Men would drive their muddy trucks and jeeps into the shallow stream and wash themselves, their vehicles and their clothes all in one session.

Swimming in the waters off Kukum Beach took a little more work. You first had to negotiate the barbed wire and booby traps and then be on the lookout for sharks once in the water. Also, much of the coastline was filled with flotsam and oil slicks from all the ships that had been sunk over the past few weeks. Most of the men preferred the

Lunga River, even though it was said to be a habitat for crocodiles.

"I never saw a crocodile or heard of one in all my time on Guadalcanal," Sweeney said. Neither did anyone else.

Lieutenant Whyte also enjoyed using the Lunga to wash away much of the residue of living on the Canal.

"I would sometimes show up . . . to launder two or more of the several muslin sheets I had managed to sneak ashore when we came to the island," he wrote. "They were the subject of some derision, but I had the last laugh. No matter where headquarters moved our tents, I slept on clean sheets every night. I'm not sure anyone else who served on Guadalcanal can make the same boast.

"Evening was the best time. The sun had set and the blazing temperatures had receded. A light breeze would be coming in from offshore. Now was the cocktail hour. We used canned grapefruit juice as the base, to which we would add several squeezes of toothpaste. Doc Keyserling, the battalion surgeon, supplied us with medicinal alcohol. I found Pepsodent, grapefruit juice, and medicinal alcohol quite tolerable."[8]

Whyte and other officers of the 3rd Battalion, 1st Marines conducted their social rituals right under the nose of their commanding officer, Lieutenant Colonel McKelvy, who was a bit of a "character" or "nutty as a fruitcake" to some.

"McKelvy avoided us most of the time—he had his own booze supply, which he never shared with anyone. We would rattle the ice—courtesy of the Tojo Ice Company, of course—in our cups to taunt him," Whyte said.

"McKelvy got his own revenge. He had this sergeant who used to toady up to him all the time, and he played the harmonica. He and the sergeant would get together, night after night, and sing the same three songs over and over again. McKelvy's favorite was, 'Come, Josephine, in My Flying Machine.' We heard it so many times we thought we would all go mad."[9]

Colonel Thomas knew that McKelvy had a tendency toward depression, exacerbated by drinking, and he made it a point to see McKelvy often for a pep talk and one carefully rationed drink. In turn, McKelvy would have stormed hell with his battalion if Thomas had ordered the attack.[10]

Despite being "just a little intoxicated, just a little confused" and "always impossibly difficult," Whyte wrote, "McKelvy achieved results when he had to. We didn't miss him when he went home, but we will always remember him."[11] (After leaving Guadalcanal, McKelvy never commanded troops in battle again. He retired in 1948 as a brigadier general.)

This conviviality wasn't encouraged or practiced by the Raiders. Edson, who was given operational command of the Parachutists, let his troops know the day they arrived on Guadalcanal that they weren't there for a rest. He had no intention of letting the men lie around in any coconut grove drinking booze and singing songs.

"[Edson] straightened us out soon after we got to Guadalcanal," Sergeant Guidone said. "He gave us a little speech that deflated our balloon. We were not going anywhere, he said. There was a lot of work to be done here. The Japanese will fight to the death. He is good and determined. It is back to work and it will be a long road to victory and other words to that effect. Our morale sank to a low ebb—for the time being."[12]

The Raiders were also introduced to a new distraction their first night on the island, a couple of bothersome Japanese aircraft dubbed "Louie the Louse" and "Washing Machine Charlie." The former would drop parachute flares to illuminate the area for the latter, also known as "Maytag Moe" because of the clanking rhythm of its motors, to drop a few bombs. Also appearing nightly were enemy submarines—called "Oscar" by the men—that would pop up offshore and throw a few shells at the Marines. The mission of these deadly pests wasn't so much to cause bomb damage as it was to keep the Marines on edge and deprive them of sleep. It worked very well. Combined with a steady rain, the enemy shelling allowed the Marines very little in the way of rest after the sun went down.

Some of the men gathered up pieces of metal and shell casings that had come from the low-flying Japanese aircraft and treated them as souvenirs.

"One corporal claimed he recognized Eleanor Roosevelt's false teeth," Manchester wrote. "Nobody laughed. Louis and Charlie weren't funny. Nights were feared on the Canal. You watched the beautiful tropical sunsets with dread."[13]

The Raiders, who were seldom bombarded on Tulagi, also had to get used to life in bomb shelters, often just a shallow slit trench with little if any overhead cover. More than one Marine, hearing the call of "Condition Red," scrambled for the nearest shelter only to land in a latrine trench by mistake, acquiring long-lasting nicknames, the least offensive of which was "shithead."

Admiral McCain, the commander of land-based Marine Air in the South Pacific, flew in for an overnight visit on August 30 and, after meeting with General Vandegrift and touring the air facilities, issued a strong plea to his superiors for more fighters and dive-bombers.

Noting that of the nineteen Wildcats flown in on August 20, only five were still operational, he urged that two full squadrons of the Army's new P-38s, a high-flying, long-range fighter, and some more Wildcats be sent to Guadalcanal as soon as possible.

McCain pulled no punches in his report, saying that "the situation admits of no delay whatever."

"With substantially the reinforcement requested, Guadalcanal can be a sinkhole for enemy air power and can be consolidated, expanded, and exploited to the enemy's mortal hurt," McCain wrote. "The reverse is true if we lose Guadalcanal. If the reinforcement requested is not made available Guadalcanal cannot be supplied and hence cannot be held."[14]

Edson had been at division headquarters every day since his battalion landed on Guadalcanal, looking for a mission. He finally got one. Intelligence had received word that enemy troops may have landed a small party on Savo Island. One pilot had claimed he had been fired on as he flew over the island. Smoke that might have come from Japanese cooking fires also had been seen on the island, which was in a perfect spot to observe movements on Guadalcanal and Tulagi. Thomas and Edson worked out a plan to send two Raider companies (A and B) on a reconnaissance under the command of Lieutenant Colonel Griffith. Coastwatcher Dick Horton and correspondents Tregaskis and Miller would also go along.

About 300 men embarked aboard familiar APDs *Little* and *Gregory* early on the morning of September 4 for a one-day, hit-and-run operation. The plan was to land at the northern tip and scout each side of the island, Baker Company taking the west side and Able Company the east. The two companies would meet some ten hours later at the southern tip for reembarkation.

After a submarine false alarm, the two ships approached

the island with the same heightened anxiety they felt during the landings on Tulagi.

"The movements were the same—our sitting low in the boat, our strung-out lines of landing craft streaking in toward the beach, and even the growing distinctness of the island, as palms began to stand out against the sky and thatch huts became visible, seemed something like routine," Tregaskis wrote. "But there remained the breathless suspense, wondering when and if machine guns would open up on us from the shore, and in those moments of wondering, as usual, one imagined the arrival of bullets and the prospect of men being hit in the boat."[15]

The landing proved uneventful. They had come ashore near a small village and were greeted by friendly natives, who were wearing only brightly colored loincloths. The Raiders spread out, weapons at the ready, to guard against any ambush.

Horton went up to one of the older natives and, speaking in pidgin English, said something like: "Me fella lookum Japanese man." All of the natives said there were no Japanese on the island, promising to kill them if they found any. Horton said the Marines wanted to see for themselves.

Furnished with native guides, the two prongs of the patrol started out, making brief forays inland from time to time to investigate possible traces of enemy occupation. None was found. The patrol did find that much of the eighteen-mile coastline was covered with oil from ships sunk nearby during the past few weeks. In addition, some of the beaches were littered with flotsam, including rubber boats, life rafts, life jackets and broken crates, much of it residue from the Savo Island naval battle on August 9. Some fresh graves were also found, including that of the captain of the USS *Quincy*, according to Lieutenant Colonel Griffith.

"Apparently the Japanese had been there but had left," said Captain Sweeney, who went on the patrol. "The natives were very friendly. Some corpses had washed ashore and we helped the natives bury them. We saw some graves of U.S. sailors but not a single Japanese."[16]

Once again the Raider timing had been just right or just wrong, depending on how you viewed it. Ten hours later, a floundering barge flotilla that was towing some 400 or so Japanese soldiers to Guadalcanal had to put in on the north shore of Savo Island to make repairs. Had the Japanese landed earlier and met up with the Raiders there would have been one hell of a reception awaiting them.

After experiencing some trouble getting back aboard the APDs (one of the Higgins boats capsized and had to be abandoned), the *Little* and *Gregory* returned to Kukum landing, arriving just after dark, and began disembarking. As the unloading was nearing completion, Griffith received orders from Edson to have the men remain aboard for the night for an early-morning reconnaissance mission the next day. It was too late. By then, most of the two companies were halfway through disembarking so Edson allowed the process to continue. The men set up camp near the beach.

Because of the late hour, the two APDs took up patrol stations offshore rather than return to their berths at Tulagi. Just after 0100, the two ships were mistakenly illuminated by friendly aircraft flares and became sitting ducks for several enemy destroyers that were cruising off the coast.

"It was like one of those bad dreams where you find yourself naked on Broadway," Morison wrote.[17]

With only three four-inch guns, *Little* and *Gregory* were no match for Japanese destroyers. The enemy ships trained their searchlights on the two APDs and sank both of them. The *Gregory* remained afloat for about forty minutes and the *Little* for about two hours. As the survivors struggled for their lives in the water, the Japanese destroyers steamed at high speed between the two ships, dropping depth charges and machine-gunning the helpless men.

The survivors spent a miserable and frightening night, floating in their tattered life jackets, treading water or clinging to shattered Higgins boats and overturned life rafts. Some of the men managed to swim to shore but most had to be rescued. A total of 226 men and a dozen officers were picked up the following morning. Losses came to 22 killed and 44 wounded on the *Little* and 11 killed and 26 wounded on the *Gregory*.[18]

Had the two Raider companies stayed onboard that night it could have been a whole lot worse. Counting the near-miss with the *Colhoun* on August 30 coming across from Tulagi, it was the second "lucky" break for the Raiders in one week.

The Raiders had grown quite close to the crewmen aboard the APDs. The loss of the ships was a bitter blow. These doughty little vessels had been carrying the Raiders for more than a year—up and down the Atlantic coast, into the Caribbean, then from New Caledonia to Tulagi, to Guadalcanal and to Savo. They had performed yeoman service bringing up food, ammunition and aviation gas from rear areas. They had become the workhorses of the American Navy during the first month of battle as they time and time again ran the Japanese gauntlet to deliver critically needed men and supplies to desperate Marines. Just the sight of them lifted the morale of all, prompting weary Marines to stand up and shout for joy.

"They brought us to Tulagi where they literally cheered us over the side to make that first assault," John Sweeney said. "They were part of us and we hurt for them."

Also critical to the survival of the Marines during this period was the growing number of brave crews of the "Cactus Air Force." Those men and machines were virtually the only offensive weapons available to contest the shelling and bombing by Japanese forces. Their most valuable contribution, however, may have been their role in blunting troop landings, which were growing in number. The Cactus pilots made the movement of Japanese landing craft in daylight so costly that they were forced to depend on only night landings.

The pilots and ground crews lived in tents in the strip of coconut grove between the airfield and the beach. They called the area "Mosquito Gulch." The tents had no flooring and until there were enough cots, some of the flyers had to sleep on the ground on Japanese straw mats. The daily rains turned the ground into stinking black mud, into which cots and mats alike sunk. The crews worked all night—in between air raids and naval bombardments—to repair, rearm and refuel the aircraft and the planes flew all day. It was a twenty-four-hour operation.

Most of the work was done by hand. There were no electric gas pumps or tankers, no bomb dollies or hoists, no machines to belt ammunition and there were few spare parts other than those cannibalized from one of the wrecks.

Food, such as there was, was prepared over open fires. Although the Marine cook who took care of all the flyers did his best, the only thing that was consistently good was the hot coffee. A steady diet of Spam, canned hash, sausage, captured Japanese rice and dehydrated potatoes often caused intestinal gas, which at high altitudes resulted in excruciating stomach cramps. Dysentery was rampant and there was no toilet paper.

The poor diet, lack of sleep, physical fatigue and emotional stress took their toll on pilots. Those who weren't wounded or infected with malaria were certain to be unfit to fly within thirty days and this became the maximum permissible combat tour for pilots on Guadalcanal.

Though they were always outnumbered, their skill in aerial dogfights became legendary. It was truly surprising how the Grumman Wildcats consistently outmaneuvered the faster, quicker Zeros. Of the eleven Medals of Honor awarded on Guadalcanal to Marines, five were earned by pilots—Harold W. Bauer, Jefferson J. DeBlanc, Joe Foss, Robert E. Galer and John L. Smith.

One of the more famous stories stemming from this period concerned the friendly rivalry among the pilots to see who could shoot down the most enemy planes. Capt. Marion Carl, who was forced to bail out of his plane deep in the jungle of Guadalcanal, had missed five days of flying before he was rescued by friendly natives. While he was away, his squadron commander, Major Smith, had raised his kill total to sixteen planes, four ahead of Carl.

General Geiger, the air boss on Guadalcanal, welcomed Carl home and told him the news about Smith's new total.

"What are we going to do about that?" Geiger asked Carl in a kidding manner.

Carl thought for a moment and then said: "Goddammit, General, ground him for five days."[19]

Achieving less recognition were the overworked ground crews, who dodged bombs and bullets every day and then worked all night to keep the planes in flying condition.

They more than made good on their promise to salvage everything except the bullet holes.

One ground crew member, writing in his diary, described vividly what it was like to endure a typical air raid.

"Almost daily, and almost always at the same time—noon, 'Tojo Time'—the bombers came," he wrote. "There would be 18 to 24 of them, high in the sun and in their perfect V-of-V's formation. They would be accompanied by 20 or more Zeros, cavorting in batches of three, nearby. Their bombing was accurate, and they would stay in formation and make their bombing run even as they knew the deadly fire from the Grummans would hit any minute.

"There was a routine of noises at Tojo Time. First the red and white flag [a captured Japanese rising sun] would go up at the pagoda [air control center]. That meant scramble. Every airplane that would fly would start up immediately and all would rush for the runway, dodging bomb craters. Often through the swirling dust the ground crews would see a wing drop. That meant another plane had taxied [into] a dud hole or a small crater, indistinct in the tall grass. The first planes to the runway took off first, and two at a time, whether . . . Grummans, dive-bombers or P-400s.

"The formations would join later in the air. The P-400s and dive-bombers would fly away to work over the Jap territory. The Grummans would climb for altitude, test-firing their guns on the way. The whining of engines at high r.p.m., the chatter of machine guns, and settling dust . . .

"On the ground the men would put in a few more minutes' work, watching the pagoda all the while. Then the black flag would go up. It was amazing how fast the tired and hungry men could sprint . . . In a moment the field would be deserted.

"Then the high, sing-song whine of the bombers would intrude as a new sound, separate from the noise of the climbing Grummans. Only a few moments now. The sing-song would grow louder. Then: swish, swish, swish. And the men would pull the chin straps of their helmets tighter and tense their muscles and press harder against the earth in their foxholes. And pray.

"Then: WHAM! (the first one hit) . . . WHAM! (closer) WHAM! (walking right up to your foxhole) . . . WHAAAMM! (Oh Christ!) WHAM! (Thank God, they missed us!) WHAM! (the bombs were walking away) WHAM! (they still shook the earth, and dirt trickled in). WHAM!

"It was over. The men jumped out to see if their buddies in the surrounding foxholes had been hit. The anti-aircraft still made a deafening racket. Grass fires were blazing. There was the pop-pop-pop of exploding ammunition in the burning airplanes on the ground. The reek of cordite. Overhead the Grummans dived with piercing screams. And the Jap bombers left smoke trails as they plummeted into the sea.

"In a little while the airplanes would return. The ground crews would count them as they landed. The ambulance would stand, engine running, ready for those who crashed, landed dead stick, or hit the bomb craters in the runway. Then the work of patching and repairing the battered fighters would start again."[20]

The Japanese Imperial Army and Navy had recovered from the shock of the near annihilation of Colonel Ichiki's forces back on August 21 and had begun making plans for a bigger commitment to retake Guadalcanal. By the end of August, it was clear that the Japanese had made the strategic decision to make the recapture of Guadalcanal its highest priority. All other campaigns, including the attack on Port Moresby, were put on hold while all available men and equipment were earmarked for Guadalcanal.

The Imperial Navy began increasing its nightly shelling of Henderson Field while systematically dropping off thousands of Army reinforcements and tons of supplies to both the east and west of the Marine beachhead.

The Japanese called these nightly reinforcement runs "Rat" operations and they proved virtually unstoppable. Almost every night, an enemy destroyer squadron would race into Sealark Channel and deposit 600 to 800 or more troops on a Guadalcanal beach and then shell the airfield on the way out. There was very little the Americans could do about it.

Without any surface ships to contest the landings of Japanese troops, the burden of blunting the enemy reinforcements fell to the small force of Marine and Army planes based at Henderson Field. Always outnumbered, this "Cactus Air Force" met the challenge head-on, strafing and bombing enemy troopships and barges headed for Guadalcanal in daylight and then gunning down troops who had made it ashore.

The new Japanese plan to recapture Guadalcanal called for a series of complex coordinated attacks on the Marine perimeter from the east, west and south, with a target date tentatively set for September 12.

The new commander would be Maj. Gen. Kiyotaki Kawaguchi, a short but muscular man with piercing eyes and a bushy mustache. His 35th Infantry Brigade had achieved great success in Borneo. Obstinate when it came to taking orders from the Navy, the forty-nine-year-old general often let his vanity interfere with his military good sense. Nonetheless, he was a professional in every way.

Kawaguchi stepped ashore at Taivu Point on Guadalcanal on September 1, not too far from where the ill-fated Ichiki detachment had landed two weeks earlier. He gathered his scattered forces, established a supply base and then began a gradual march to the west with his main body. On September 5, Kawaguchi turned down an offer of another infantry battalion, confident that the 6,200 or so men under his control would be more than enough to do the job. Besides, the new men wouldn't be available until the 11th, which would mean delaying the attack. His confidence was no doubt bolstered by the latest intelligence estimates that reported there were only 2,000 Marines guarding the perimeter, a figure that was one-sixth the actual total.

Heavy rain the next day halted Japanese movement as the men hunkered down in the mud. The weather had put them a day behind and Kawaguchi felt he had no choice but to delay the date of the attack to 2200 on the 13th.

Kawaguchi's new overall plan was formalized on September 7. It was a highly complicated scheme, one that required precise coordination from three different directions and a diversion by the Imperial Navy from the sea.

Like Ichiki, Kawaguchi had no information about the terrain he needed to traverse. His maps were inaccurate and the photos were fuzzy. There were no native guides available to him. They were all loyal to the Americans. Essentially, he would be leading four battalions of troops through unknown territory.

The plan called for Kawaguchi to drop off one of his battalions, the 1,200-man-strong Kuma Battalion (the other part of Ichiki's Regiment that never made it to Guadalcanal the previous month), on the way so they could make an assault from the east. On the west, a

1,000-man force under Col. Akinosuku Oka, which consisted of remnants of several units, which had arrived by barge the past few days, was to position itself to attack from the east. And Kawaguchi would take direct command of the remaining three battalions (1/124, 3/124 and 2/4), some 2,500 men, push on through the jungle and attack from the south. Because of the inherent difficulties of command and control in a night attack in thick jungle, there were no plans for a reserve force. Each unit would have to fend for itself once the attack began.

Kawaguchi was particularly pleased that the Kuma Battalion would have an opportunity to give "repose to the departed souls of the Ichiki Detachment commander and his men." It is also interesting to note that Kawaguchi had been given direct orders by his superiors to "isolate" the remnants of the Ichiki survivors from the coming battle because, having been defeated, they had "dishonored themselves and mustn't be allowed to infect others with their pessimism."

Many of these survivors were assigned rear-guard duty at base camps at Taivu Point and Tasimboko.

Just before midnight on the 7th, Kawaguchi received an urgent message that appeared to be asking him to speed up his attack plans. Kawaguchi, according to his memoirs, said he might be able to attack a day earlier, that is the night of the 12th. Somehow, the Imperial Navy got the message Kawaguchi would attack on the night of the 11th.

Meanwhile, late on the afternoon of September 7, word reached General Vandegrift by native scouts of a Japanese buildup of an estimated 200 to 300 men about eighteen miles to the east at the deserted coastal village of Tasimboko, but there were no other particulars. A scheme was quickly hatched to strike with a sufficient force to knock the gathering enemy off-balance. The plan called for sending Colonel Edson's 833-man unit (605 Raiders and 228 Parachutists) on an amphibious reconnaissance in force to Tasimboko. They would land some 3,000 yards behind the Japanese at Taivu Point where they could take them from the rear.

It was a risky proposition. The existing transports couldn't take the whole force. It would have to be done in two lifts. The objective was well out of range of any supporting artillery or reinforcements, for that matter. And, air support was only available if there were no air raids and the weather was good. Edson said his boys could do it. That's what they had been trained to do. They were Raiders.

Once again, intelligence was sketchy. Edson was told initially there was an ill-fed and poorly armed enemy force of no more than 300 in the target area

A few hours later, at 2000, Edson's force began loading aboard two APDs, the *McKean* and the *Manley*, which had been freshly painted in camouflage green, and two converted California tuna launches, called "Yippies" because of their nomenclature of YP 289 and YP 346. The latter boats, which varied in size from fifty to 175 tons' displacement, had loud engines and often belched bright-red sparks. They had made their troop-carrying debut a few days earlier by ferrying the 1st Parachute Battalion from Tulagi to Guadalcanal. Previously, these versatile boats were used as tugs, cargo haulers and rescue craft.

"The Yippies," Lt. Col. Sam Griffith said, "announced their presence to all but the blind and deaf."

Edson and his command group would go aboard the *McKean* with Baker Company and the *Manley* would take Charlie Company. Able Company would embark aboard the two "Yippies," along with Griffith's command group and the forty-six-man Dog Company. A, B and C companies were near full strength as Edson had practically gutted D Company to provide much-needed replacements. A total of 501 men were aboard on the first lift.

The plan called for Baker and Charlie companies to land abreast at Taivu Point in two waves of four boats each, establish a beachhead and wait for the Higgins boats to bring in A and D companies from the two "Yippies." The APDs would provide covering fire until all were ashore and then return to Kukum landing to embark the rest of the Raiders and the Parachutists. The entire party would cram themselves aboard the four boats for the return trip once the raid was over.

Captain Sweeney, Baker Company's 1st Platoon leader, nearly missed the embarkation. Fighting off an acute attack of diarrhea, he had to duck behind some palm trees en route to the ship to answer the urgent call of nature.

"I wasn't the only one," Sweeney said many years later.

Leadership would be a little thin on the raid and that was a source of concern for Edson. Among those who missed the raid because they were hospitalized were three company commanders, Maj. Lew Walt of A Company, who was battling a case of dysentery, Maj. Ken Bailey of C Company and Maj. Justice "Jumping Joe" Chambers of D Company. The latter two were hospitalized in New Caledonia recovering from wounds incurred on Tulagi. Also on the shelf was intelligence officer Capt. Hank Adams, who had malaria. Taking over Able Company was Capt. John W. Antonelli; Capt. Robert H. Thomas took command of Charlie Company and Capt. William Sperling took over Dog Company. All three had been the executive officer of their respective companies. Sgt. Pete Pettus was the acting intelligence chief.

Just before they shoved off, Edson received an intelligence update that said the enemy force at the landing site was now estimated at 2,000 to 3,000, a tenfold increase over the previous estimate. Edson never hesitated. He still wanted to go.

He had to convince his superiors, though. Colonel Thomas, who had coauthored the plan with Edson, was plagued by second thoughts. If Edson's men ran into trouble there was no way to support them or any way to rescue them. They would be well out of range of artillery fire and there were no more boats available to bring up reinforcements. Thomas felt the enterprise had all the makings of a disaster.

Vandegrift had the last word and though he was far from confident of its success, he had faith in Edson's leadership and resourcefulness. And, the Raiders were his "lucky" battalion, his fire brigade. With his fingers crossed behind his back, he gave the go-ahead.

13

Tasimboko

Around midnight, the four-ship convoy swung far out into Sealark Channel to avoid alerting any enemy forces along the coast or running into any enemy shipping hugging the shoreline. At around 0230, the convoy turned due south and headed directly toward Taivu Point, just east of Tasimboko. It was raining and visibility was poor. The men huddled against the steel bulkheads, shivering in the chill.

"That was a night of utmost suffering and misery," said Sgt. T. D. Smith of Able Company, who was aboard one of the "Yippies." "We were hungry, really hungry. The smoking lamp was out although the Yippie's stack poured sparks into the air all night. We were extremely crowded; there wasn't room on deck to lie down, so we huddled in a sitting position and attempted to brace ourselves for a catnap.

"The vessel rolled so badly that with every roll, waves came over the deck. As we counter-rolled, the water sloshed us again as it rushed toward the opposite scuppers. It was cold. The rolling made some of us seasick and as they heaved we were awash in cold sea water and vomit. I thought the morning would never come.

"Plt. Sgt. Joe Buntin and Sgt. Tom Pollard were quite loud about our predicament. Capt. Antonelli came up to say that there was nothing he could do to alleviate the situation. He was right, of course, but that didn't help any. I will always remember that night as the most miserable I ever spent. There were others, but nothing to touch that one."[1]

Tregaskis was aboard the same cramped "Yippee," which was skippered by a jovial Portuguese-American tuna fisherman, Capt. Joaquin Theodore, whom the correspondent quickly befriended.

"The ship was a tiny thing, with only limited supplies of stores," Tregaskis said. "But Captain Theodore passed out grub and all available cigarettes to the Raiders, and shared his little cabin with Col. Griffith."

Tregaskis got a big kick out of the efficient Captain Theodore when he announced in fractured English: "We'll have it coffee for everybody in the morning."

Getting through the night took some doing, however. Every square inch of space seemed to be taken.

A few hours earlier, unbeknownst to General Kawaguchi, the Tokyo Express had dropped off a battery of 75mm field guns, some ammunition and supplies at Taivu Point and quickly left. Because of the weather and perhaps another dose of luck, the Raiders never saw the convoy.

At 0500, the American ships anchored 1,000 yards offshore and began unloading. The men climbed into the Higgins boats and approached the beach at reduced speed to lessen the noise. The first four boats, two each from Baker and Charlie companies, reached the shore in twenty minutes and quickly set up a perimeter defense.

The initial landing party stumbled over what looked to be discarded marching packs, which were lined up neatly in rows on the beach above the high-tide line. Each pack had a life preserver and a field bedding roll attached. The latter was filled with rations, toilet articles and personal items. There was no sign of their owners. When Edson arrived with the second wave he had to break up several scavenging groups that were looking for souvenirs among the packs. He ordered the men to get off the beach and into the palm trees. It was obvious that a Japanese landing party had come ashore earlier that same night. The question was, where were they?

Also discovered near the beach were a couple of abandoned 37mm antitank guns. Had they been manned they could have blown the Raider landing boats out of the water. It was another stroke of good fortune for this star-crossed unit.

Edson was clearly worried, however. Should the enemy strike before Able Company was ashore they might not have the firepower to fend them off. For the next forty minutes, the Raiders were very vulnerable.

It was at this juncture that a convoy of ships appeared off Taivu Point heading west. None of the Raiders knew whether they were enemy or friendly.

"We considered ourselves doomed,"[2] said Captain Antonelli, who watched the ships pass while waiting to debark from one of the "Yippies" anchored offshore. Ashore, the Japanese, who had fled deep into the jungle, obviously felt the ships were American and part of a large invasion force.

It was a confusing situation for both sides. The ships were American but not part of an invasion force. The convoy consisted of a couple of transports (*Fuller* and *Bellatrix*) and several escorts and was headed toward the Marine perimeter. Edson had no idea these ships would be in his area and neither did the Japanese, who fled into the jungle believing they were being attacked by a much larger force.

Edson left Dog Company behind to secure the landing area and got his forces lined up and headed west along the shore road. He took time to get off a message to division headquarters that said: "Came in back door. Overran two field pieces. Enemy withdrawing to Tasimboko, strength unknown. Keep bombers in air."

The Cactus Air Force spent most of the day supporting the Raiders. Four Army P-400s, each loaded with 300-pound bombs and six .30-caliber machine guns, carried out the day's first mission at 0635. After flying back to base to rearm, they returned at about 0830 with three Marine dive bombers for another strike at Tasimboko. A heavy rain grounded the planes until just after noon when a third sortie left Henderson Field as support for the Raiders. Three hours later, a fourth flight of three P-400s took to the air to strafe enemy positions in support of Edson.

Communications with division was a complex maneuver, one that took much practice and teamwork. The Raiders had a single TBX radio with them on the raid. It weighed 120 pounds and broke into three parts, roughly weighing forty pounds apiece. Cpl. Fred Serral headed the radio team and carried the transmitter-receiver, Pfc. David Tabor carried the accessory package and Pfc. Herschel "Bull" Sterling was in charge of the twenty-four-foot antenna and hand-cranked generator. Because they were beyond range of division headquarters, all messages, coming and going, had to be relayed through another TBX aboard the *Manley,* which was being manned by Sgt. James "Horsecollar" Smith.

Every time the command group moved, the TBX had to be broken down into three parts and carried to a new destination, where it would be reassembled, a process they would perform thirty-seven times on the raid. Later, to save time, Private First Class Sterling wound up dragging the antenna through the jungle to keep from erecting and dismantling it.

If Edson wanted to talk with Griffith, he sent his runner, Corp. Walter Burak.

"I remember lugging this heavy load of TBX equipment and hearing the sounds of artillery flying really low overhead," Serral said. "It was so loud that the sound of it alone would force you to the ground. I remember looking up once to see Walter running really fast through the brush, zig-zagging back and forth like he was running with a football. I was amazed and perhaps startled and also concerned for his safety. Then this loud burst of artillery came close overhead and knocked us all back to the ground. I looked up and saw Walter get up unhurt and continue running through the brush as if nothing had happened. It was amazing that none of us were killed."[3]

In the meantime, the *McKean* and the *Manley* hurried back to Kukum landing to pick up the rest of the raiding party. On the way, they lobbed a few dozen shells into Tasimboko as a parting gesture. Also opening up on the village was a squadron of P-400 fighters, the first of four sorties during the day. The added firepower also served to convince General Kawaguchi's rear echelon that a major invasion was underway.

Around 0900, Edson sent another message to Vandegrift. It said: "Have 3,000 Japs bottled up Tasimboko. Propose they surrender or be annihilated. Request landing party support."

Vandegrift and Colonel Thomas looked at each other in horror. Each was thinking of Colonel Goettge's twenty-five-man patrol back on August 12, one that was ambushed by superior Japanese forces and all but wiped out.

"Negative," Vandegrift radioed Edson. "Can't spare troops. Return to base."

Edson ignored the order, later claiming a communications failure. He would also ignore two more orders to reembark his battalion and return to Kukum. He was determined to push on and finish the job. Unsure of the enemy's size or intentions, he would proceed cautiously, however.

He ordered Baker Company to advance along the coastal trail and sent Able Company on a long swing southwest through the jungle to envelop the village from the south. Charlie Company would guard the beach until the rest of the raiding party arrived with the second APD lift. Lieutenant Colonel Griffith, with three native scouts, would accompany Able Company to keep a close watch on young Captain Antonelli while Edson would go with Baker Company to ensure it maintained a proper level of aggressiveness and speed.

Captain Sweeney's 1st Platoon took the point. After sloshing through an unmapped swamp and crossing a waist-deep stream, Sweeney's lead squad came upon a partially cleared area where they captured an abandoned 75mm field piece, along with several boxes of ammunition stacked to the side. Nearby, one of Sweeney's squads discovered another 75mm gun, this one with a crew. Three enemy soldiers ran to the gun, depressed its muzzle and fired off a round at the advancing Raiders, who immediately hit the deck.

Two more rounds burst among the palms, showering shrapnel on the Raiders below before two of the gunners were silenced by a rifleman and the third fled into the jungle. Tregaskis wrote that he was so close to the enemy gun that he could feel the blast of hot air each time the gun fired.

The Raiders had one man killed and two seriously wounded from shrapnel before the gun was silenced. One of the wounded, Corp. Maurice Pion, would surely have died had it not been for the quick and efficient work of two Navy corpsmen, according to Sweeney.

"Using a penknife as a scalpel they amputated his shattered left arm at the shoulder, pinned the skin around the stump and applied a field dressing," Sweeney said. Pion was sent to the rear where a doctor redressed the arm and offered his congratulations to the two corpsmen for the professional job they did. Both received decorations, with one of them, Pharmacists Mate 2nd Class Karl B. Coleman, earning the Navy Cross for his lifesaving action.

At about this time it began to rain hard. But the advance continued, with Able Company pressing deeper into the jungle and Baker Company inching its way down the coastal trail, each headed for Tasimboko. Able Company was cut off from the rest of the Raiders for over two hours, hacking its way through thick foliage and crossing deep, swift streams before the scouts finally found the back door trail to Tasimboko.

Sweeney's point squad had reached the outskirts of the village where it was held up by one well-placed machine gun nest and pinned down for more than an hour. Sweeney sent part of a squad inland to flank the gun while he went the other way to try and draw the enemy's fire with some well-placed insults in Japanese he had learned in New Caledonia from the battalion's language officer, "Tiger" Erskine.

Using what he had learned from Erskine, Sweeney yelled out "Ba-Ka, Ba-Ka," several times. Each time, he drew fire from the enemy machine gun as the flanking squad drew closer.

"I believe it means 'son of a turtle,'" Sweeney said of the Japanese taunt many years later. "I've used the phrase since on other Japanese but they don't quite get it."[4]

It worked at Tasimboko, however. While Sweeney occupied the gunner's attention, three of his men maneuvered through the jungle to outflank the enemy position and killed the three Japanese manning the gun.

Edson got on the radio again at around 1045 asking for air and naval bombardment of Tasimboko and a landing west of the village to cut off any Japanese attempting to flee the scene. The reply came back negative on both accounts. It was simply raining too hard and visibility was near zero.

Edson began to have a feeling that all had been too easy so far. He was concerned that his men were walking into a trap and that they might become cut off from their landing area. He got back on the radio again, telling division that he was facing an estimated "1,000 well-armed, well-equipped troops," adding that "hostile pressure increasing, request instructions."

Division told Edson to withdraw and reembark aboard the APDs. It was the second such order he had received and the second time he ignored it.

Suddenly, things began to brighten for the Raiders. It stopped raining. Their four-ship convoy had returned with Easy Company and the Parachutists at 1130 and began unloading them 2,000 yards east of Tasimboko, where they provided rear and flank protection.

Able Company, which had been hacking its way through the jungle on the left flank, finally reached the rear of Tasimboko and swept through the village from the south. Baker Company scouts quickly followed and the village was overrun at about 1230. A few Japanese soldiers attempted to defend their positions but they were quickly dispatched. Others fled into the jungle to the west.

There was some good-natured kidding between the two companies, even the suggestion that Able Company may have gotten itself disoriented during its long inland trek.

"Griffith would never admit that the column became lost in jungle ('only temporarily' he would say)," Alexander wrote, adding that it was Sergeant Smith who tried to set the record straight. "We knew where WE were—the rest of the battalion was lost."[5]

The spoils of victory were enormous and were to have a decisive impact a few days later on a future battle, one that saved Henderson Field and the 1st Marine Division from being overrun.

In all, twenty-seven Japanese were killed during the raid with the loss of two Raiders killed and six wounded. Tasimboko was as decisive a victory as anyone would have imagined

The Raiders, who hadn't eaten all day, gorged themselves on captured Japanese food and beverage stocks. They also began stuffing their pockets with cans of sliced beef in soy sauce, tins of crabmeat and fancy British cigarettes. Besides food, they discovered huge stores of ammunition, medicines and other supplies. They were all neatly packed in boxes and stacked ten feet high.

Ordered to destroy what they couldn't carry back on the ships, the Raiders slashed open more than 100 sacks of rice and then either urinated or poured gasoline on them. Other foodstuffs, clothing and sundries were taken to huts and then set afire. Rifles were smashed and ammunition of all kinds dumped into the nearby sea. They either blew up captured artillery pieces or rolled them to the sea where they were dragged by a Higgins boat into deep water and sunk. Also destroyed were ten collapsible boats, complete with outboard motors, and a radio generator.

Among the stuff carted back to the waiting ships were a radio transmitter, boxes of medical supplies and intelligence documents, which included maps, notebooks and personal papers. Tregaskis helped gather up the latter in a large captured blanket and carried it aboard the APDs.

The information proved to be of immeasurable assistance in helping Vandegrift and his staff prepare for the coming storm.

Kawaguchi later wrote in his memoirs that the Tasimboko raid, which resulted in the destruction of his food and medical supplies, was a crippling blow to his campaign to retake the airfield. He admitted that he couldn't afford to send reinforcements to Tasimboko because it would have upset his timetable for attacking the airfield.

Lieutenant Colonel Twining had an interesting take on why Kawaguchi stood by almost within view of the raid on Tasimboko and failed to intercede. Twining opined that the code of Japanese military honor precluded voluntarily rendering assistance to a neighboring unit. Assistance must be requested.

Another view has it that Edson's attack was ignored as only a diversion that should not have been allowed to disrupt the carefully planned attack schedule aimed at Henderson Field. Because of his "prickly character," Kawaguchi was not easily persuaded to deviate from his primary mission.[6]

Kawaguchi's paralysis of action can also be explained by the fact that he had moved inland with the main body and, because his main radio had been destroyed, could not be reached to secure permission to commit forces to Tasimboko. Either way, his inaction still puzzles historians.

The Tasimboko raid threw Rabaul into a tizzy. The enemy felt the Marines had established a large new front in the area, one that would cut off Kawaguchi's forces and leave him little room to maneuver. Even after Edson's forces left Tasimboko, the Japanese would continue to bomb the area, killing its own men, and divert reinforcements to the west, fearing a nonexistent Marine presence in the east.

"More than any man, 'Red Mike' Edson would have enjoyed every aspect of the major flap his foray had generated," Griffith said.[7]

The Tasimboko raid not only spooked the Japanese Army headquarters at Rabaul, it also rang alarm bells at the Imperial Navy headquarters at Truk, which increased its patrolling and nightly bombardments on Guadalcanal.

The Raiders were lucky once again. Their timing proved just right. Had they landed a day earlier, they might have had to deal with Kawaguchi's main body, which had not yet left on its inland trek to the southwest. Such a confrontation could have been fatal for the Raiders.

The Raiders departed Tasimboko just before dusk and no more than an hour before a Japanese naval bombardment of the village. The Japanese even sent aircraft the next day to attack the "new Marine stronghold" at Tasimboko, bombing and strafing many of Kawaguchi's hungry and disorganized rear echelon.

Meanwhile, the unescorted four-ship convoy of the Raiders, loaded to the gunwales with food, medicine, intelligence and souvenirs, crept westward down the coast, keeping one step ahead of the Tokyo Express, which had been sent to destroy them. By 2000, the entire convoy had reached the safety of the perimeter and finished unloading.

At breakfast the next morning, Tregaskis learned that a small group of Japanese destroyers and cruisers had shelled some allied shipping anchored off Tulagi during the night. One of the friendly ships hit and set afire was Captain Theodore's "Yippie," which had just participated in the Tasimboko raid.

"I heard that Capt. Theodore had been wounded through the chest in the course of the engagement," Tregaskis said of his new friend. "But he had beached his little craft, and saved it from sinking, despite his wounds. I am glad to hear that he is expected to live. This is the second time that I have left a ship in the evening and it has been attacked and lost before morning. This fact gives rise to the thought that my luck has been good, so far."[8]

When Edson reported to Vandegrift after the raid, he had a special present for the general. Among the booty discovered by the Raiders was a large trunk that belonged to General Kawaguchi. Inside was a clean, white uniform, complete with epaulets and battle ribbons. It was the uniform he intended to wear to a surrender ceremony when his forces recaptured Guadalcanal.

Edson handed the uniform to Vandegrift, who smiled weakly and then cast it aside without comment.

At breakfast the next day, Vandegrift had a present for Edson. It was a radio message from the theater commander, Admiral Ghormley. It read: "To Edson and his doughty warriors . . . Well done."

14

Storm Warnings

It was obvious from Edson's report and a quick reading of all the intelligence documents captured at Tasimboko that the Japanese were planning a large-scale attack on the Marine perimeter in a matter of days. The big question was where they would strike. On this, there was a difference of opinion.

Edson was convinced the attack would come from the south along an open ridge. Colonel Thomas, his deputy, Lieutenant Colonel Twining, and artillery commander, Col. Pedro del Valle, all agreed that the ridge "represented a natural funnel from the south" for an attack. General Vandegrift wasn't so sure. He felt there was a good chance the attack would come from the east along the same path Colonel Ichiki had taken the previous month. Vandegrift didn't have enough troops to sufficiently defend both perimeters.

As more and more intelligence information on Japanese movements from Clemens' scouts filtered in on September 9, Edson became certain that the attack would come from the south along an open 1,000-yard-long grassy ridge, barely a mile south of the airfield. The ridge, as seen from the air, resembled a giant crocodile that had crawled away from the airfield heading south into the jungle. The southern end of the ridge had a knoll rising to 100 feet above sea level that marked the crocodile's head and a second knoll closer to the field rose to an elevation of 120 feet, marking the high point of the animal's spine. A dirt path ran down the entire length of the spine with little spurs, or legs, branching off both sides into deep, dark jungle.

Just that day, Vandegrift, against the animated advice of his staff, had moved into his new division command post on the ridge to the south of the airfield. He said he had grown sick and tired of jumping in and out of bomb shelters and hoped the new setting would give him some peace. The new CP was also a lot more comfortable than the old one, which had acquired the nickname of "impact center."

Adjacent to Vandegrift's quarters was an operations tent that also served as air raid bunker. A third structure nearby served as the general's mess tent.

Vandegrift was proud of his cook, Sgt. "Butch" Morgan, and would often sing his praises to visiting dignitaries, lauding him as much for his ingenuity as for his culinary skills. The much-tattooed Morgan, a colorful figure known throughout the division, took over a Japanese blacksmith shop on the second day on the island and was boiling beans on the forge while wearing a smithy's apron.

With very little to work with, Morgan "lived a life of quiet despair," according to Lieutenant Colonel Twining. "He did manage to console himself by occasionally serving a dish utterly incongruous with our otherwise frugal menu. This was a millionaire's salad, a by-product of our daily bombardment. Whenever a palm tree was toppled in our vicinity, Butch would race to the scene, cut out the large crown buds, and serve hearts of palm, which I understand costs real money down in Florida."[1]

Morgan's pièce de résistance came on a visit by Admiral Halsey in early November. After a meal of steak and apple pie and listening to Vandegrift gush about his chef, Halsey said he'd like to meet the "world's greatest cook." Taken to the galley, Halsey pumped Morgan's hand and told him that it was "the finest meal" he'd ever had.

An embarrassed Morgan, shuffling his feet and pulling on his walrus-like mustache, replied: "Aw shit, Admiral, you don't have to say that."[2]

Also moving into the new CP area on the ridge were the correspondents, who had grown in number to five with the recent arrival of Till Durdin of the *New York Times*, Tom Yarbrough of the Associated Press and Bill Kent of the *Chicago Times*.

Vandegrift's staff had all agreed that moving his command post to the ridge was much too dangerous and could prove disastrous should the enemy attack where Edson and Thomas said they would.

Vandegrift was not to be dissuaded, however. When Twining made a last-ditch attempt to convince the general it was a bad move, Vandegrift snapped at him. "I may not always be right," Vandegrift said, going eyeball-to-eyeball with Twining, "but I'm always the general." And that was that.[3]

Edson and Thomas didn't give up easily, however. The two, who had become such staunch allies in looking out for the best interests of their general, had arrived at a solution that would temporarily please both sides. If Vandegrift was so determined to move into harm's way, why not relocate the Raiders to the ridge as a security force?

The general agreed.

Meanwhile, Kawaguchi's forces were still clawing their way through the humid, putrid jungle under excruciating conditions. Using faulty compasses and outdated maps, each of his four battalions took a separate route to their jumping-off points. On the afternoon of September 10, three of the units ran into each other in utter confusion, creating a "jungle traffic jam." Kawaguchi, deprived of native scouts because of prior treatment toward them by sadists like the infamous Ishimoto, lost contact with his fourth battalion (III/124) and didn't hear from them until the morning of September 12.

After a brief rest, the Japanese general led two of his units (I/124 and II/4) to the southwest while the third (Kuma Battalion) headed off on its own toward Alligator Creek and the eastern boundary of the Marine perimeter.

Rain-soaked and covered with sweat, the men grew tired and hungry the first day. It only got worse after that. Everyone had underestimated the difficulties of moving through the dense jungle. There were few trails and none wide enough to transport heavy equipment. Hand carts broke down, forcing the men to carry mortars and ammunition on their backs. Artillery weapons were abandoned.

Each step was made difficult by the thick vines and heavy mud. The men stumbled over the gnarled roots and slipped going up and down steep ravines. Swamps and stagnant streams slowed their pace. Thick mud grabbed at their boots, forcing them to yank hard to get free. River crossings took hours. And, there was always the danger of discovery by an enemy airplane or patrol. They were soon way behind schedule.

To the west, where Colonel Oka was to deliver a diversionary attack on the night of the 12th, Kawaguchi was informed that Oka was still assembling his forces. Oka told the general that he would have only two companies, not two battalions, ready for an attack on the night of September 12 and asked for a delay of one more day to get the rest of his forces assembled. Kawaguchi decided to stick with the schedule and not postpone the assault.

• • •

Edson returned to the Raider bivouac area late on the night of September 9 and immediately called a meeting of his staff and company commanders. On his way back from division headquarters he debated in his mind whether to tell all that he knew or even what he was feeling. He decided to keep what he knew to himself for the time being.

Looking as calm as ever and without giving away any of the intelligence information he already had, he told his staff that the unit, to include the remnants of the 1st Parachute Battalion, would be moving to a "rest area" the next day to a ridge south of the airfield. The move would be made first thing in the morning.

"Too much bombing and shelling here close to the beach," Edson said. "We're moving to a quiet spot, a rest area."[4]

"And," he added as the men rose to their feet, "bring all the barbed wire you can find."

The "rest area" comment raised more than a few eyebrows in the audience. Edson had never gone anywhere that was "restful." What has the "glory hound" volunteered us for this time? many of them wondered.

"We'll all know more tomorrow," Edson said before dismissing his staff.

After breakfast of captured rice, the two units, Raiders and Parachutists, about 840 men in all, picked up their gear and marched south across the airfield toward the ridge. Around noon, they heard the clang of a dinner bell signaling the imminent arrival of a flight of Japanese aircraft overhead.

Most of the men had reached their new positions well before dark and looked forward to grabbing a good night's sleep.

"It was a peaceful place and not far from the Lunga River," Sgt. Frank Guidone of Able Company remembered. "Hot chow was served the first evening and we settled in for a relatively quiet night. It didn't last long."[5]

Edson hardly slept at all. He stayed up almost the entire night deciding how to deploy his men and how to maximize the use of his scant barbed wire, called "cruel black lace" by those who tried to breach it. He also selected dozens of artillery targets and picked out several possible patrol objectives for the next day.

He would be a very hands-on commander in the coming days.

The men were awakened at dawn on September 11 and told to dig in.

Many of the Raiders, particularly those assigned to listening posts deep in the jungle, had spent a nervous night reacting to strange noises. Although they tried to maintain fire discipline, scattered gunfire could be heard throughout the night as jumpy sentries shot first and challenged later. For most of them, it was their first experience spending the night in a hostile jungle environment since the operation began.

Between the periodic firing and a naval bombardment around midnight, none of the Raiders really got a good night's sleep.

With daylight came the real work of getting the Raiders ready for what everyone now knew would be a major Japanese assault.

"It was evident from some of the things that we saw going on, [like] artillery forward observers from the 11th Marines looking for observation post locations and plotting likely target areas, staff officers from division headquarters checking out the situation and observation planes circling over the jungle and ridge lines [that] enemy activity was suspected," Sergeant Guidone said. "On top of this were our own officers and NCOs constantly pushing us in the laying of barbed wire, digging foxholes, building machine gun emplacements and cutting fire lanes."[6]

Digging in was easier said than done. There were few shovels or entrenching tools. Many men used bayonets. The ground was soft dirt for ten or twelve inches and then the men struck rock-hard coral. It took hours of backbreaking work just to carve out a foot-deep depression in the ground.

"Rest area, my ass," more than one Raider, dripping in sweat, griped at his platoon sergeant. Some of the men blamed Edson for their predicament, claiming that he lobbied his friends at division headquarters for assignments that would win him another promotion and more medals.

Just before noon, the men looked up and saw twenty-four U.S. Navy Wildcat fighter planes flying into Henderson Field to supplement the "Cactus Air Force," which had dwindled to eleven planes in the past few days. The replacement aircraft had been "beached" at Espiritu Santo since the loss of the *Saratoga* two weeks earlier. Admiral Ghormley had been given authorization to use these "homeless planes" as he saw fit but apparently was under the impression that specially trained carrier pilots should only fly off flattops, even though they were desperately needed on Guadalcanal. Wiser heads finally prevailed on September 11 and a whole squadron was flown to Henderson Field.

Sporadic gunfire could be heard in the jungle to the front. Scuttlebutt swept through the Marines that the firing was coming from patrols that had spotted the Japanese headed their way. The firing got closer as the day went on.

Edson was all over the ridge, personally putting his units into place, picking out machine gun locations to take advantage of the terrain, identifying dead spots for the mortar crews, inspecting the barbed-wire emplacements and even going on one short patrol. The latter almost got him shot.

"What the hell is he doing out there?" one sentry said, lowering his rifle, as Edson and his faithful companion, Corporal Burak, emerged from the jungle right in front of his position.

Edson had placed his men as far forward on the ridge as he could, with listening posts in the jungle on all sides.

The Paratroopers, who had been whittled down to about 215 men, a little more than half their original force, were deployed to the left of the path along the ridge with B Company (about ninety-five men) on the front line and C Company (about 120 men) in echelon to the rear where they helped guard the left flank.

The Raiders' front stretched some 900 yards westward to the Lunga River. Baker Company (a little over 100 men, including a machine gun platoon) was positioned on the nose of the ridge, tying in with B Company of the Chutes on its left and a long, narrow lagoon of water on its right. The lagoon itself was some sixty feet wide by 150 feet long. Charlie Company of the Raiders (about 130 men, including a machine gun platoon) manned an area on the right flank from the lagoon to the east bank of the Lunga River and was backed up by Able Company (some 150 men), which also included a machine gun platoon from E Company (Weapons).

The remnants of Dog Company, which had been cannibalized to beef up the other units, and Easy Company, minus the machine gun platoons that were attached to the line companies, formed the reserve on the main ridge

(Hill 120) around the battalion command post, which was just 500 yards to the rear of the front lines.

Edson had struck a balance between putting his strongest forces on the front lines and husbanding the rest as a reserve to counterattack expected penetrations and flanking moves by the enemy. Considering the terrain and the fact that his entire force was a little more than 800 men, it was the very best he could do.

"The thin ranks of Edson's mongrel battalion and the denseness of the jungle surrounding the ridge precluded anything like a continuous line," Frank wrote. "A series of strongpoints with fields of fire for mutual support behind a single-strand barbed-wire fence occupied the jungle frontage."[7]

Some of the terrain was deceiving because patches of jungle crept nearly to the top of the ridge in certain spots. Should the enemy attack out of these spots, they would be too close to the ridge to give the Raiders time to react and counter the move. Listening posts in these thickly forested areas were needed to give the Raiders advanced warning or they could be quickly overrun.

Edson's command post was a shallow trench just to the rear of the highest point of the ridge. It had no overhead cover, wire or sandbags. A few telephone lines ran out to his front-line units and another snaked its way back to division headquarters, less than 1,000 yards to the rear. The CP and ridge area was crowded with runners, forward observers, medical personnel and members of Edson's staff, including his executive officer, Colonel Griffith, his operations officer, Major Brown, and his chief of intelligence, Sergeant Pettus.

In the meantime, both Colonel Thomas and Lieutenant Colonel Twining had been trying to get Vandegrift to move his reserve unit, the 2nd Battalion, 5th Marines, closer to the ridge where they could be quickly plugged in should the Japanese break through the Raider line. Vandegrift, still not completely sold on a full-scale attack from the south, finally relented and moved 2/5 to a new position between the ridge and the airfield where they could be committed in any direction as needed. He also approved reorienting some of the 105 howitzers toward the ridge where they could begin to register likely targets of opportunity.

Edson seemed to be everywhere on September 11, barely stopping to have something to eat. Accompanied by his runner, Corporal Burak, Edson personally inspected the entire front, pointing out expected Japanese assembly areas and routes of possible attack to his artillery forward observers. Later in the day, he, Lieutenant Colonel Griffith and Corporal Burak went on a small patrol well forward of the C Company strongpoint to see for himself what the enemy was up to. He heard the distant sound of voices and the chopping of trees and vines in the jungle. He inspected the single-strand barbed wire that had been strung from tree to tree. These defenses, he realized, would only slow the enemy down. They weren't strong enough to stop him.

He even plotted fallback positions and withdrawal routes for his men should they have to shorten their defensive positions.

Boxes of ammunition, particularly grenades, were brought forward to be of easy access to the men. Edson made sure that everyone knew where the first-aid station was. No detail was too small for him.

Everyone on the ridge could see Col. Pedro del Valle and his forward observers from the 11th Marines carefully surveying the front lines and plotting fire missions. It made the men dig harder and deeper.

Edson kept patrols, accompanied by native guides, in the jungle throughout the day to try and gauge exactly where the Japanese would most likely strike. He knew for certain they would, either that night or the next.

One such reconnaissance patrol was led by Able Company platoon sergeant Joe Buntin early on the morning of the 11th. One of the members of the twenty-five-man patrol was Sgt. Frank Guidone, who only got to go along because he lost a coin toss with another sergeant, Harold Floeter.

"[Buntin] told us that our mission was to obtain information as to the enemy's location and strength and that after we made contact and he could determine Jap strength we would disengage and withdraw," Guidone said.

"We moved out in column on a trail leading to the Charlie Company front line position, passing through its still-under-construction barbed wire protection and on into the unknown—to us—jungle with the Lunga River on our right flank. Buntin, with two point men ahead, was leading the patrol, which now had strung out nearly 100 yards on the faint trail being followed.

"Our forward progress was slow and cautious," Guidone said. "Shortly before noon the point halted when the sound of Jap voices was heard along with noises from the chopping of underbrush.

"As Buntin and his scouts were sizing up the situation they were taken under fire and a lively firefight quickly developed. I led my group forward quickly and then cleared the trail to await developments. The rifle and BAR firing tapered off but no word came back from those engaged in the firefight. We remained very alert. I got behind a large banyan tree along with my BAR man, Sylvester Niedbolski.

"Suddenly, in the distance we heard the drone of aircraft at high altitude. Here come the Jap bombers with their noontime raid. Henderson Field will get pasted again," Guidone thought.

It was a flight of twenty-seven bombers and fifteen Zeros but instead of attacking the airfield, they began dropping their loads on the ridge to the south.

"The enemy formation now appeared to be almost overhead from our location," Guidone recalled. "That's when the WHAM, WHAM of the first bombs could be heard directly ahead of us. As the bombs continued exploding they walked right up to our location and continued on toward our battalion positions on the ridge. One exploded near Niedbolski and me. The concussion picked up both of us and slammed us down and covered us with debris. I looked over at Ski and he was flat as a pancake, as was I. He had a rosary in one hand and was well along into his prayers. Luckily, no one in the patrol was injured. What was good about this raid was that the Japanese ahead of us also got bombed and broke off the firefight."

Guidone and the patrol quickly hustled back to their bivouac area and hardly recognized the place.

"Our tents and lean-tos were scattered and personal gear was strewn throughout the jungle," Guidone said. "The one personal loss that I suffered was 40 dollars in cash that I had left behind in my khaki trousers, which were destroyed."[8]

That wasn't the worst of it, however. Sitting against a banyan tree with his rifle between his legs was Sergeant Floeter, the man who had won the coin toss with Guidone. He had been killed in the bombing raid. He was one of four Raiders killed in the surprise bombing attack, which had clearly been aimed at the ridge and not the airfield. Fourteen more were wounded and had to be evacuated.

Any lingering doubts about the ridge being a "rest area" were answered in a most forceful way.

The night of the 11th was another sleepless one for Edson, who was filled with doubts about the upcoming battle. He didn't like the terrain he had to cover for an attack he knew was coming. The jungle crept up the sides of the ridge and left the Raiders without any maneuvering room. He had no choice but to accept the conditions at hand. He had to position men in the jungle if only to slow down a Japanese assault. Such a deployment, of course, left the Raiders vulnerable to be outflanked and overrun.

He also didn't like being on the defensive. It went against all the training his men had endured the past six months. It was also against his nature.

He had deployed his men the best he could but the terrain wouldn't allow him to protect his flanks. For that, he needed more men. If he concentrated his men on the ridge, he could easily be flanked by enemy troops moving uncontested through the jungle. If he spread his forces out more, extending them into the jungle, they could be destroyed piecemeal. He would have to be flexible.

Early on the morning of the 12th, Edson was surprised and elated to see a familiar face limping down the path toward his CP. It was Maj. Ken Bailey, still wearing his trademark tennis shoes. Looking a little pale, Bailey had suffered a leg wound on Tulagi and been hospitalized in New Caledonia for the past month. Apparently he and his weapons platoon leader, Lt. Astle Ryder, who was also wounded on Tulagi, had gone AWOL from the hospital and hitchhiked their way back to Guadalcanal to rejoin their unit.

The two also brought along many sacks of mail, which had been collecting dust in the rear for some six weeks. It was the first mail call since the Raiders arrived in the Solomons. It provided a big boost to morale.

Pfc. Henry "Popeye" Poppell recorded in his diary that he received 100 letters.

"Our first mail in three months!" he wrote. "My most prized possession . . . was a toothbrush. I had gone five and a half weeks without brushing my teeth . . . within five minutes I had an offer of $50 for my brush, but no sale!"

Many of the men who were to die in the coming battle had been given at least one final connection with home and family. The letters had provided the Raiders with a new zest to fight on. They would need it.

Edson was worried about the leadership situation of his battalion on the eve of what could become a life-and-death struggle to hold the ridge. His intelligence officer, Capt. Henry Adams, and Able Company commander Lew Walt were still in the division hospital with malaria (as were ninety other Raiders). Baker Company commander Lloyd Nickerson was hospitalized on the 12th with severe stomach cramps and his exec, Capt. Louis Monville, would be sent to the rear with heatstroke the next day. Young John Sweeney, who had come ashore on Tulagi as a demolition's platoon leader in Easy Company, would become the third commander of Baker Company in three days on the 13th. He was the only officer left in the company. And, rising to the occasion, he would earn a Navy Cross for his bravery.

Other platoon commanders hospitalized with malaria included lieutenants Tom Mullahey and Ed Dupras of Able Company and Capt. Rex Crockett and Gunny Cecil Clark of Baker Company. In addition, Charlie Company lost Capt. Clay Boyd to a freak accident when, after becoming tangled in some vines, he accidentally shot himself in the foot.

Rather than return Bailey to his old post as CO of Charlie Company, Edson decided to keep him close by to help in coordinating the defense of the ridge. He felt he needed Bailey more than his company did. Bailey became Edson's second set of legs and would become the unit's "roving linebacker" in the coming battle, racing here and there to plug holes and lift the morale of the men when they most needed it.

As a team, they would prove unbeatable.

Later in the afternoon of the 12th admirals Richmond Turner and John S. McCain flew in from Espiritu Santo for a visit with Vandegrift and Geiger. Shortly after they shook hands at the airfield, the air-raid siren went off, sending everyone to the nearest bomb shelter.

After the all-clear, Vandegrift escorted his guests to his new command post near the ridge. Turner, who was unusually quiet, reached into his breast pocket and handed Vandegrift a folded piece of paper without saying a word. As the general read the typewritten note, the color drained from his normally ruddy Dutch face. He appeared to wince as he read the words.[9]

He quietly passed the note to Colonel Thomas, who read it with the same reaction. Thomas folded the note and put it in his shirt pocket.

The note was from Admiral Ghormley stating his estimate of the situation in the area, which forecasted a major Japanese effort to retake Guadalcanal within ten days.

"This was bad enough but I read next of Ghormley's situation—his shortage of ships and airplanes, his lack of supply," Vandegrift later wrote. "Compared to the size and strength of the enemy this meant, according to the staff paper, that the Navy no longer could support the Guadalcanal operation."[10]

Ghormley, it appeared, had simply thrown up his hands, concluding there was nothing he could do.

Turner and Vandegrift were not so quick to give up, however. Turner proposed to use all his influence to convince Ghormley to release the 7th Marines from Samoa and bring them to Guadalcanal as soon as he could to give Vandegrift "a fighting chance."

"Vandegrift, I'm not inclined to take so pessimistic a view of the situation as Ghormley does," Turner said. "He does not believe I can get the 7th Marine Regiment here, but I believe I have a scheme that will fool the Japs."[11]

Turner, who still fancied himself as an infantry tactician, then offered a bizarre plan to break up the 7th into smaller units and position them along the north coast to interdict and destroy Japanese landings wherever they might occur.

Vandegrift and Thomas looked at each other with raised eyebrows as if to say, "Here we go again."

Thomas later wrote in his memoirs that Ghormley also passed along to Vandegrift "a personal note that described the Guadalcanal situation in dire terms and suggested that Vandegrift might have to surrender."[12]

Surrendering was not an option to Vandegrift. After sleeping on the news for a night, he called in Thomas to give him his decision.

"Jerry, we're going to defend this airfield until we no longer can," he wrote in his memoirs. "If that happens, we'll take what's left to the hills and fight guerrilla warfare. I want you to go see Bill Twining, swear him to secrecy and have him draw up a plan."

The plan was to be kept strictly top secret to avoid creating any panic or talk of defeatism among the troops.

Twining, in his own memoirs, said he did prepare a plan of withdrawal but not into the jungle. His plan, which was classified top secret and kept locked in a safe, called for a withdrawal eastward along the coast, which would give the Marines a chance to be evacuated.

Shortly after nightfall, the Japanese launched an attack on Raider positions less than two miles from where Turner and Vandegrift were meeting at the Division Command Post. The two men had raced to the same bomb shelter to escape a naval shelling. It was a new experience for Turner, who at first thought it was friendly fire. A half hour later, after several near misses, Turner had acquired a new appreciation for what Vandegrift's forces were facing on a daily basis, one that was far more descriptive than any message or radiogram. By the time he flew out early on the morning of the 13th, having endured a harrowing night of bone-rattling enemy air and naval fire, he was determined to see to it that Vandegrift got the 7th Marines as soon as possible.

Twining later wrote that Turner was seen crawling on his hands and knees toward the foxholes dug that afternoon. "I have it on good authority that as the admiral headed for his hole, along with the rest of us, he was still clutching a half bottle of Dewars. He seemed to enjoy the situation immensely."[13]

"In the morning I showed Turner the results of the night attack including the pitiful and bloody annex of our field hospital, struck by a large Japanese shell," Vandegrift wrote. "I think he was impressed.

"At dawn his party left for Noumea. At the airfield his parting words to Vandegrift were, 'When I bring the 7th Regiment I'll land them wherever you want.'"[14]

Vandegrift confided with his old friend and air commander, Brigadier General Geiger, about Ghormley's doomsday estimate of the situation. He told Geiger he had no intention of surrendering and would take to the jungle to fight on, if he had to.

"If the time comes when we no longer can hold the perimeter I expect you to fly out your planes," Vandegrift told Geiger.

"Archer, if we can't use the planes back in the hills we'll fly them out, but whatever happens I'm staying here with you," Geiger said.[15]

Turner, meanwhile, flew directly to a meeting with Ghormley at Noumea. The 7th Marines had been moved from Samoa to Espiritu Santo on September 2 where they were waiting for further assignment, either to combat or to New Zealand. Apparently, Ghormley had been reluctant to commit the regiment because they were his only Marine reserve. Turner must have made a good pitch to his boss because Ghormley gave the order to release the 7th for duty on Guadalcanal the very next day. The Regiment, complete with two battalions of artillery and 147 vehicles, sailed from Espiritu Santo aboard five transports and two supply ships at dawn on the 14th.

Help was finally on the way.

15

The Ridge, Round One

Edson called a get-together with his staff and company
commanders just after the noontime bombing of the 12th
to let everyone know what was at stake. They must hold
the ridge, he told them, or the airfield would be lost, and
perhaps the whole island. He seemed to be speaking directly at his two front-line company commanders, Capt.
Robert Thomas of Charlie Company and Capt. Louis
Monville of Baker Company.

Should they fail, Edson warned, pausing briefly for
effect: "It'll be us, not the Japs, roaming the jungles and
eating raw coconuts."[1]

Charlie Company had about 800 yards of jungle to
cover on the right flank, from the lagoon to the east bank
of the Lunga River. Captain Thomas put all three of his
platoons on line but the jungle was so dense he could
only deploy single strands of wire. Fields of fire had to be
cleared for the three machine gun squads. Some of them
were so broad the Japanese would mistake them for
native trails and be on top of them before they could fire.

One of the fallback routes was through a swampy area
by the lagoon over a slippery fallen log. It was a tough
chore to negotiate the log in the daytime. At night it was
sure to become a bottleneck.

"As the long afternoon was drawing to a close it
became apparent to even the dim-witted that we were in

for big trouble," said Pfc. Joe Rushton of Charlie Company's second platoon. "If our positions became untenable we were then to withdraw back across the log, or that not being possible to fight our way out as best we could . . . We were expendable."[2]

Rushton, who would undergo a hellish night for survival, had a prophetic meeting with one of his platoon mates, Pvt. Paul Ratcliffe, that shook him. Ratcliffe had a wan, far-away look in his eyes as they chatted, one Rushton and others would see more of in the coming days. It was almost as if Ratcliffe had a premonition of his impending death. Eerily, no one ever saw him again.

Backing up the thinly spread Raiders of Charlie Company was a thirty-man machine gun platoon of Easy Company, which spread out along the Lunga River on the right flank. Further to the rear was Able Company, dug in and prepared to assist Charlie Company and eliminate any infiltrators.

Griffith, Bailey and Edson made last-minute rounds of the front-line positions. Edson had made preliminary plans to go on the offensive the next morning if the Japanese attack didn't come this night. He wanted to beat the Japanese to the punch, throw them off-balance and dissipate their forces before they could launch an attack. In the meantime, the Raiders had done all they could to get ready. What happened next was out of their hands.

At precisely 2130, a green flare dropped from the sky and slowly fell to earth over the ridge. It was the signal for a bombardment by a Japanese cruiser and three destroyers that had moved into position off the coast. Most of the shells fell to the east in an empty jungle. Five shells struck in the area of Edson's command post, however, but only one exploded, causing little damage. The

Raider luck still held. The cruiser then turned its powerful searchlight on the ridge, turning night into day.

The searchlight undoubtedly helped the Japanese infantrymen orient themselves on their target and the noisy bombardment served to pin the very alert Raiders in their holes and helped mask the approach of the assault troops.

Kawaguchi's troops never did get themselves organized. One battalion (I/24) reached its assembly area just as it got dark and the other two (III/124 and II/4) didn't reach their jumping-off points until an hour before midnight.

"When the three battalions, numbering 2,506 men, went forward they lost their sense of direction, almost entirely missed the ridge, and instead drifted into the low, waterlogged swath of jungle between the ridge and the Lunga," wrote historian Richard Frank. "Units became lost; lost units became scattered; scattered units became intermingled. Control slipped away from Kawaguchi and his battalion commanders and it became a struggle of captains, lieutenants, sergeants and privates against a few Marines and a mass of jungle."[3]

One battalion (II/4) never made it into action and a second (I/124) wound up west of the Lunga and too far away to assist in the attack. As a result, only one battalion made the assault on the Raider position and it was more a series of uncoordinated surges than any massed frontal charge.

The Japanese had only reached their jumping-off points after dark and never had time to reconnoiter the area. Tired, hungry and weakened by their seven-day march through the jungle, they were being asked to assemble in the dark and blindly attack an objective they had never seen before. Confusion reigned but their courage never wavered.

On the Japanese left flank near the Lunga River, elements of I/124 and III/124 became entangled and order wasn't restored until just before daylight.

236 GEORGE W. SMITH

"On the Japanese right front," according to Frank, "[elements of] the III/124 advanced until it encountered the Marine line about 0100 by Japanese watches. Presumably this unit made the penetration between the Raider companies (B and C), but it could not exploit the situation because of the jungle and intense American artillery fire, which killed two company commanders. The movements of the reserve unit, II/4, cannot be reconstructed."[4]

Kawaguchi himself wound up on the west side of the Lunga and in no position to direct the attack. He revealed his frustration many years later in a memoir, writing that "because of the devilish jungle, the brigade was scattered all over and completely beyond control. In my whole life I have never felt so helpless."[5]

Meanwhile, the Japanese diversionary attacks scheduled east and west of the Marine perimeter were comical affairs. The Kuma Battalion thrashed about in the jungle, never getting close enough to assault the Marines along Alligator Creek and Colonel Oka's motley crew in the west arrived at their jumping-off point too late to conduct much of an offensive.

Back on the ridge, those Japanese troops who eventually got themselves organized, probably a total force of about 700 men, led by a sword-wielding Maj. Yukichi Kokusho, came straight at Charlie Company with everything they had. Slapping their rifle butts and chanting "U.S. Marines be dead tomorrow," they crashed into the strands of barbed wire erected in front of Charlie Company, creating a traffic jam for those behind them.

Edson called in artillery fire and the enemy scattered to find safety. It brought the Japanese attack to a halt, but only briefly.

Jumping over the bodies of their comrades, the Japanese moved around the wire and charged up fire lanes cut by the Raiders earlier in the day. Charlie Company machine guns mowed them down but they kept coming. Artillery and mortar fire, grenades and individual rifle fire took their toll as the enemy closed in on the Raider foxholes, finding gaps and racing through them. A withdrawal was ordered and Charlie Company slowly moved back, dragging with them all the wounded they could find.

On their left flank, the Japanese waded through the Lunga River rather than approach through the dense jungle. Within an hour, the machine gun platoon attached to Charlie Company became surrounded. Many began falling back to higher ground. Others who were hit, like Pfc. Charles Everett, crawled into the jungle to hide. Everett, badly wounded, hung on throughout the night before he was finally rescued the next day.

Meanwhile, Capt. John Salmon, a platoon leader in C Company, led a group of his men to the rear across the lagoon to Captain Sweeney's position on the lower ridge.

"[Salmon] was visibly shaken, in bad shape, and deeply concerned about several of his men who had been cut off during the withdrawal," said Sweeney, who had a ringside seat for all the action going on to his right flank.

Corp. Bob Gray of B Company's 3rd Platoon also watched most of the action from the lower part of the ridge.

"When the attack began it was hard to know who was killing whom," Gray later wrote. "Who were the enemy and who were friends? Who was winning, who was losing? All we knew was C Company was overpowered. The screams in the jungle only told us of men dying or about to die."[6]

B Company maintained excellent fire discipline this night, never revealing their positions on the right flank of the enemy attack.

• • •

Private First Class Rushton led some members of his platoon in C Company on a withdrawal across the log bridge over the lagoon but the Japanese had it flanked. He told his men to hit the ground where they lay in sheer terror, listening to sounds of the enemy finishing off Raiders with their bayonets, swords and machetes.

Suddenly, a Japanese soldier stepped on Rushton's leg. He thought he heard the sound of a sword being pulled from its scabbard. Rushton jumped up only to be knocked down by an enemy machine gun. Pissed off, Rushton rose again and emptied his BAR on a crowd of Japanese soldiers. "Eighteen frigging rounds," he said later.

Just as feared, the log bridge had become a bottleneck. "People were crawling in all directions, mainly away from the log crossing," Rushton said. "It wasn't long before they were overrun by the swarming attackers of the main charge. It was horrible and frightening hearing our small group of overrun Raiders screaming as the bastards bayoneted and hacked them with their Samurai swords."[7]

According to several sources, the Japanese captured one or two Raiders and tortured them to death with their knives and swords.

Within an hour of the initial frontal assault, the enemy seemed to pause to either reorganize or wait for reinforcements. Some historians believe that had there been any reinforcements they might have gone all the way to the top of the ridge and broken through to the airfield. Instead, the Japanese milled around in confusion, bumping into scattered Raider units, who were equally confused and desperate to escape the carnage taking place.

Private First Class Rushton spent the night trying to crawl his way to safety. Though seriously wounded, Rushton dragged Pfc. Ken Ritter, who was in shock from a wound to his back, with one hand while trying to keep his BAR out of the mud with the other. He could hear Japanese voices all around him.

When they reached the northern end of the lagoon, they were spotted by three Japanese soldiers. One of them bayoneted Ritter in the leg. Rushton shot the assailant but then his mud-covered BAR jammed. Jumping to his feet, an enraged Rushton butt-stroked the second Japanese soldier in the face with the nonfunctioning BAR. The third enemy soldier fled into the jungle in a panic.

Rushton continued dragging Ritter to the rear but just before dawn, he died. Rushton left Ritter's body under a fern and somehow found the energy to keep crawling up the hill to safety.

Charlie Company had taken the Japanese assault right on the chin. Many were either killed, wounded, surrounded or in full retreat. Yet, the Japanese failed to capitalize on the situation.

Higher on the ridge, Edson, Bailey and several NCOs were running around trying to stop a panic, directing the stragglers who crawled out of the jungle into new fighting positions and bolstering their morale. How they distinguished friend from foe in the darkness was a tricky situation. Everything was done by voice and physical contact. In the hours before dawn, a steady trickle of Raiders carrying or dragging wounded comrades slowly, and painfully, made their way up the ridge.

Charlie Company had been creamed but they were far from beaten.

Also making an early-morning withdrawal was the thirty-man machine gun unit from Easy Company, which had provided right flank cover for Charlie Company on the

Lunga River. Soon after dark, Japanese troops could be heard advancing in the river, heading their way.

"We heard them splashing across the river," Cpl. Robert Youngdeer said. "They weren't very quiet. We could hear them jabbering away. They weren't attacking; they just were coming down the fire lane trying to find us. Soon they were all around our position. I could hear the bolts being pulled back on their weapons. Next they sprayed the bushes near us. We didn't fire because we knew if we did, we'd give away our position and they'd overwhelm us. So we threw grenades. There isn't the kind of fear you might think. There wasn't any panic or anything.

"They came back through us again. Like I said, they weren't very quiet. They were making a lot of noise, talking, yelling to one another, and I heard someone beat up on the left. I can still hear the screams. He was begging for mercy. They [the Japanese] were beating him. Later on I found it was one of my friends, Ken Ritter. I'd seen him the day we went into our position. He had dysentery and was in bad shape, laying along the trail. As I went by, he looked up and smiled real weak-like. He didn't have anything to say. I heard from people later on that they bayoneted him."[8]

Pfc. John Mielke also remembered hearing a lot of noises that night. Shapes began to form directly in front of one of their machine guns, manned by Pfc. Warren Morse.

"Morse was always a real eager beaver and he had cleared his fire lane so well the Japanese thought they had found a trail to follow, and they did so right up to the muzzle of his gun," Mielke wrote. "[Morse] fired incessantly [and] there were cries of pain from the Japanese. The rest of us could only sit there silently, not knowing what to expect from our front."

"There was some sporadic rifle firing by our troops. We

had no way of knowing what their situation was and we occasionally heard one of our riflemen cry out in pain as though being tortured. All through the night we expected the Japanese to probe further into our position but they failed to do so."[9]

Shortly before daylight, Mielke's unit could hear Japanese voices to their rear. He realized they had been bypassed and now were surrounded. They pulled their guns into a tighter circle and began a search for some of their missing men. Sgt. "Pappy" Holdren and Corporal Youngdeer crawled through the brush listening for voices. They quickly found Pfc. Charles Everett, who had become separated from his squad early in the night after being shot and had hidden in some deep brush.

"[Everett] was shot through the legs and could not walk," Youngdeer said later. Mielke and others rushed out to help drag him to safety. The Japanese saw them coming and opened fire, killing one man and injuring another. Youngdeer was shot in the face and fell hard to the ground. Mielke maneuvered behind a fallen tree and wiped out an enemy machine gun emplacement, which earned him a Navy Cross.

Youngdeer blacked out for a few seconds after he was hit. The bullet had struck him under the left nostril and exited under his right ear.

"In a moment I was able to see," Youngdeer said, "but I was breathing through a hole in my neck. My teeth were shattered and my tongue creased so that I couldn't speak distinctly."

Ordered to withdraw, Platoon Sgt. Lawrence Harrison gathered up the survivors and led them through enemy lines to the rear by way of the river. Sergeant Holdren managed to get the badly wounded Youngdeer and Charlie Everett out safely. Harrison and Holdren would each be awarded the Navy Cross for their skill and bravery this night.

In a quiet moment, young Mielke asked Sergeant Holdren, who had served in World War I at Belleau Wood and the Argonne Forest, if his earlier experiences were worse than Guadalcanal.

"No," replied "Pappy" Holdren. "This is the worst situation I've ever been in."[10]

16

Buckling Up

Soon after daybreak, Edson called a conference of his staff officers and company commanders.

"They were testing, just testing," he told the men. "They'll be back." He looked up and smiled weakly. "But maybe not as many of them. Or maybe more.

"I want all positions improved, all wire lines paralleled, a hot meal for the men. Today: dig, wire up tight, get some sleep. We'll all need it."[1]

An earlier-than-usual air raid took place soon after sunrise. It was a reconnaissance mission by the Japanese to determine if their forces had captured the airfield. The signal for success was to be two lighted torches sixty meters apart on the airfield. One quick pass over the field revealed no torches and the planes hurried back to Rabaul with the news that the Americans still held the airstrip.

Later in the day when the Japanese bombers and Zeros returned for their usual noontime air attacks, they avoided the airfield and the ridge to keep from hitting their own men. Instead, they dropped their bombs and strafed what they thought was an American stronghold at Tasimboko.

"Their targets, frenzied members of Kawaguchi's signal and supply detachments, were slaughtered as they attempted to spread 'meat-ball' banners on the sand near the water's edge," Sam Griffith wrote. "These perforated, bloodied flags were later brought in by native scouts."[2]

Edson wanted Vandegrift to commit the division reserve (2nd Battalion, 5th Marines) to the ridge but the general, erring on the side of caution, still wasn't ready to do that just yet. He was still wary that the enemy could attack in force from the east or west. His only reserve force might be needed elsewhere.

In the meantime, Edson wasn't going to sit still and wait for the enemy to come to him. He ordered a probe of his own to keep the Japanese off-balance and to find out the latter's strength and disposition. He sent his intelligence chief, Sgt. Pete Pettus out on a five-man patrol to the south, ordered the Parachutists to patrol southeast in their sector and got Able Company ready for a larger reconnaissance in force to try and regain some of the ground lost the previous night and eliminate the bulge in the line.

Pettus, with "Horsecollar" Smith as his radioman, trudged down the southwestern slope of the ridge, crossed the infamous log bridge over the lagoon in single file and came upon several fighting holes abandoned by Charlie Company the night before. Moments later, they came under fire from a couple of machine guns that sounded familiar.

Pettus at first thought his patrol had run into some Raiders who had been bypassed during the night. He yelled out seeking recognition, only to be answered by heavy fire. He later learned that the firing was by the Japanese who had captured several .30-caliber machine guns from the Raiders during the night.

Pettus gave the signal to withdraw. Everyone saw it except Smith, who suddenly found himself all alone in enemy territory. He could hear movement to his front that sounded like troops moving through the brush. He calmly fixed his bayonet and lowered his rifle, awaiting a rush. Just then he heard some firing to his rear as Pettus and another Raider came to his rescue. The three of them turned around and, with an anxious Smith galloping to the head of the column, raced as fast as they could back up the trail, bullets buzzing all around them like annoyed yellow jackets.

Bursting from the jungle upon the open ridge, Pettus' patrol surprised the forward elements of Able Company, who were getting ready for their recon mission. Pettus briefed company commander Captain Antonelli on enemy strength and then retired to the rear. Antonelli passed the word back to his men about the captured machine guns and told them to proceed slowly, watching for ambushes and any stragglers from the previous night.

Shortly after entering the jungle, Able Company came upon a group of eleven Raiders slowly making their way up the ridge. It was the remnants of Platoon Sergeant Harrison's machine gun unit that had become surrounded near the Lunga River the night before. Among the walking wounded was Corporal Youngdeer, whose face was a bloody mess.

Antonelli assigned a squad to help get the wounded back to the aid station and then resumed the patrol. The Japanese, alerted by Pettus' earlier patrol, were waiting, many of them occupying fighting holes dug by Raiders the day before.

"We formed a skirmish line with two platoons on line and a platoon in support," Sgt. Frank Guidone said, providing the following narrative. "As we moved slowly into the jungle, loud, shrill Japanese voices broke the stillness. The line froze. The voices continued—the Japanese officers or NCOs were placing their men into position to halt our attack.

"I was on line with my squad and we were trying to stay on line with the squads on our flanks but the thickness of the jungle made this difficult. We were moving forward slowly—we only had about thirty feet of visibility ahead of us. It was difficult to maintain silence. We were constantly brushing aside long stems and branches and the thorny ones would cause one to curse aloud.

"The Japanese were now quiet. This was a bad omen because it meant they were all in position and awaiting our attack. Finally, it came. The Japanese fire was heavy, mostly Nambu machine guns, but since we all fell to the prone position and crawled for cover their initial fire was ineffectual. We returned fire with our Springfields and BARs. There were no targets—we were only firing in the direction of the Japanese positions. We could actually see the jungle foliage just above our position being moved by the Japanese bullets. You could not move to any upright position—you would be cut down quickly.

"I remember off to my left someone tossed a grenade toward the Japanese positions. Suddenly we saw a tail of smoke heading toward us. It was our grenade coming back. We rolled around for cover and fortunately when it exploded no one was hurt. Now there was sporadic shooting, some more Japanese commands. We were waiting for a decision. We did not have the force to move through the Japanese. Fortunately, Capt. Antonelli was readying the mortars for action but he was not certain of the target area. Apparently he decided to move all hands back to the riverbed and then he would have a chance to shoot the mortars freely. As the order came to start pulling back I sent most of my squad back and kept a couple of men with me as a rear guard.

"It was during this time that I heard a voice from our front and it sounded as though someone was saying 'Marine.' I heard the voice again. This time it was clear. It had to be someone from Charlie Company who was there the previous night. Of course we were highly suspicious because of the many tricks the Japanese were noted for and how some of them spoke English very well. There was also intermittent fire from the Japanese positions so this required us to be in the prone position.

"I decided to move ahead a few yards to try and see where this person might be. It seemed he was not too far away. We crawled ahead toward the Japanese position. At this time, Captain Antonelli had his mortars ready to fire until one of the noncoms told him I was still up there with some of my squad. Antonelli then detailed Staff Sgt. 'Red' Hills to go into the bush and bring me out or at least find out what was holding me up.

"Finally we could see a body on the ground lying still. He was dressed in Marine garb and from all appearances was one of us. We were now close enough to talk to him. He was from Charlie Company and had been there all night and he was wounded. The Japanese had walked all around him during the night but did not see him. He said he was wounded in both legs from machine gun bullets. He had removed his web belt and used it to wrap around both legs to immobilize them and help to cut down the bleeding. This Marine was not small and we had to drag him out of there with everyone being in a prone position as the Japanese were still firing in our direction. We also knew that we were in a most vulnerable position if the Japanese came charging toward us. Three of us in a prone position dragging a limp body with us while he groaned and moaned was no easy task, this coupled with intermittent gunfire from the Japanese who knew something was going on toward their front. Finally we reached a small knoll and had some protection and more help.

"We never learned the name of the Charlie Company Marine but as he was being evacuated he looked in our direction and nodded his appreciation. That was worth more than his name to us."[3]

It was Pfc. Charlie Everett, the man Corporal Youngdeer had tried to rescue the previous night before he was shot in the face.

Both Everett and Youngdeer would recover.

Based on information he received from Pettus and Antonelli, Edson knew the Raiders were facing a large, well-armed Japanese force. He knew he couldn't recapture the lost territory on his right flank, so he decided to pull back all his lines and establish new fighting positions on the ridge closer to his command post. He also called division and asked for more men.

Division sent up Lieutenant Colonel Twining to take a look for himself. Twining was shocked at what he saw. He "found the men glassy-eyed, mumbling their words and displaying the mechanical high-stepping gait that betrayed utter exhaustion."[4]

When he returned to division headquarters a few hours before dark, Twining recommended that the division reserve force, Lt. Col. Bill Whaling's 2nd Battalion, 5th Marines, be moved at once to reinforce Edson, but once again Gen. Vandegrift demurred. As a compromise, Vandegrift agreed to a partial deployment, moving two companies of the reserve into position near the ridge where they could be quickly rushed to Edson's aid should a breakthrough occur. By the time the units got moving, however, it was already dark.

Twining, who would retire in 1959 as a four-star general, pulled no punches over this needless delay in his memoirs by criticizing the division command for not fully appreciating Edson's situation on the ridge.

Specifically, Twining said that division headquarters disregarded "the clear indications that Kawaguchi's attack would be a major thrust fully capable of reaching Henderson Field: and most important of all, not listening more attentively to Edson's views and estimates of the threat confronting him.

"[Edson's] awareness of the gravity of the situation was obviously far greater than our own. Quite apparently, Edson felt that we had written him off and that he was very much on his own."[5]

In fairness to Vandegrift, however, he really didn't have the manpower to establish an airtight perimeter defense. Many areas termed "likely avenues of approach" were defended by lightly manned outposts. Gaps existed everywhere. In truth, his emergency reserve had to be kept available to plug gaps in dozens of places.

"The dense jungle," Vandegrift wrote, "represented a terrific obstacle to be overcome only by weeks of labor at a time when it was all too obvious that only days remained open to us . . . A penetration was almost a certainty."

He wouldn't know where until it happened.

Edson didn't fret over this denial of reinforcements. Instead, he got busy placing the men he did have where they were needed most. He sent Able Company, which was virtually untouched the previous night, to the right flank in the low ground along the Lunga. Charlie Company, which had suffered nearly 50 percent attrition the night before, was moved back on the ridge as a reserve.

He pulled the Parachute battalion and Baker Company of the Raiders back some 500 yards, extending the latter's right flank farther west into the jungle. To help fill the gap between Baker and Able companies, he brought up the 115-man Dog Company of the 1st Engineer Battalion, which had been providing security for the division CP, and made them front-line riflemen. The company commander, Capt. Bill Stiles, was given orders "not to move or fall back under any conditions."[6]

All these moves were made to shorten the perimeter and give the Raiders less ground to defend and more open ground between themselves and the attackers, providing killing zones for the machine guns and artillery. Lieutenant Colonel Griffith supervised the emplacement of Able Company and Major Bailey personally guided the engineers into position between Baker and Able companies as well as the positioning of the reserve troops surrounding the command post. Despite a blazing sun that sapped the energies of his exhausted men, all the moves were completed by 1700.

The password for the night would be "Lola's Thigh." Most of the men smiled at the image the password brought to mind. All agreed it had a nice ring to it.[7]

Edson decided to make one more check of the front line. He was particularly concerned about Baker Company's position on the nose of the ridge, which he felt would be in the eye of the coming storm.

As the three platoons of B Company began their withdrawal from Hill 100 to new positions nearer Hill 120, Captain Sweeney of the 1st platoon was met on the trail by Captain Monville. Monville had assumed command of the company only the day before when Major Nickerson was evacuated with malaria.

"[Monville] was babbling incoherently and his face was flushed," Sweeney said.

It was then that Edson came over and told Sweeney that Monville was about to be evacuated with heatstroke and that he, Sweeney, was the new company commander "as of now."

"I had no officers—they were all gone," Sweeney later wrote. "But the NCOs were all strong. At the time I was too tired to realize the situation I was handed."[8]

Earlier that day, Gunny Sgt. Cecil Clark, leader of the 3rd platoon, was evacuated with malaria and the 2nd platoon leader, Capt. Rex Crockett, had been sent to the hospital the day before with malaria.

Sweeney and his company first sergeant, Brice Maddox, attended a brief meeting with Edson and Major Brown, the operations chief, to learn the details of the company mission and disposition for the coming night. It had been another brutally hot day and the men, used to much cooler bivouacs closer to the sea, were sweating profusely. They were in need of a rest, not another night of what promised to be more hand-to-hand combat.

It was now about 1630.

Edson saw the look in the men's eyes. He knew what they were thinking. He approached Sweeney and in that calm demeanor of his, coolly presented the defensive plan of action.

Owing to the late hour, Major Brown would guide the 2nd platoon, now led by Gunny Clint Haines, to a position on the right flank that tied in with Able Company. The 1st platoon, now under Plt. Sgt. Robert Aneilski, would be positioned forward on a piece of high ground overlooking the swampy area near the lagoon. The third platoon would dig in on the ridge itself, tying in with Baker Company of the Chutes to its left. Sweeney would learn later that the 3rd platoon leader, Gunny Clark, had also been sent to the hospital.

The total company strength was just over 100 Marines, according to Sweeney.

Sweeney had a bad feeling about the 1st platoon's position. Maybe it was because it was his old platoon. It was a hasty defense in an entirely new jungle setting, one without any protective wire or telephone communication and nightfall only a few minutes away. Each man on the line had sufficient ammunition for his rifle or BAR but only one or two hand grenades apiece.

Also bothering Sweeney was the fact that all three platoons were on line, which meant there was no reserve.

Sweeney returned to where the understrength 3rd platoon (three squads of about eight men each) was digging in on the forward slope of the prominent spur off the main ridge. The platoon was augmented by a machine gun squad, bringing the total force to about thirty men. The command post was only a few yards to the rear on the spur's reverse slope. First Sergeant Maddox reported that battalion had promised that a telephone line would be pushed forward soon. The telephone connection was never made.

The company command group was made up of First Sergeant Maddox, Corp. John Gann, a communication specialist, and a young private messenger who had recently joined the company as a replacement. Sweeney didn't even know his name. Without a telephone, the only communications with battalion would be done by runner or by walkie-talkie.

Sweeney closed ranks on his left flank with Marine Gunny Manning, platoon leader from Baker Company of the Parachutists. The identical unit designation of the side-by-side platoons would cause plenty of confusion later in the night when both units withdrew to fall-back positions at the same time.

After leaving Sweeney, Edson conducted a personal reconnaissance of much of his extensive front—some 1,000 yards from the open ridge to the Lunga River. Whether he and Burak went as far as the Lunga is doubtful but he did go forward of the Dog Company engineers and Baker Company strongpoints.

Corp. Joseph J. Sweeda of the latter unit was busily digging in when he and his men were startled by movement in the jungle underbrush to their front. Quickly discarding their entrenching tools for weapons, they waited to see who or what would emerge from the jungle in front of them. As Sweeda later described it, "Of all people, it was Colonel Edson and Burak returning from a reconnaissance to the south."

Stopping only long enough to look over the position and tell Gunny Haines to hold, Edson hurried on to the 1st platoon for a brief stop and then returned to the Baker Company command post on the ridge for a last look.

Edson, his face a stony gray, stood next to Sweeney, peering through his field glasses at the long axis of the ridge to the south and the adjoining jungle. If he saw anything his face didn't reveal it. Nor did he say a word as he adjusted his glasses.

The responsibility must have been overwhelming. His understrength force of Raiders and Chutes were being asked to hold off a much superior force or lose the island to the enemy. He would have artillery help but that was it. He had no reserve and neither of his flanks had any direct physical or visible contact with other friendly units.

After no more than a minute, Edson placed his field glasses in their case and prepared to go. He stopped and then slowly turned toward Sweeney. "John, this is it," he said softly but firmly. "We are the only ones between the Japs and the airfield. You must hold this position."[9]

With that, he turned and departed with Burak. It was nearly 1800.

Kawaguchi was anxious to make up for the disappointing showing the night before when more than half his force, himself included, never got involved in the attack. This time he would make sure that all three of his battalions, perhaps as many as 2,000 men, would participate. There would be no reserve.

On the west, Major Kokusho's 1st Battalion, 124th Infantry (I/124), which had been whittled down somewhat during the previous night's action, gathered for an attack through the lagoon area; Major Tamura of the 2nd Battalion, 4th Infantry (II/4), which spent the previous night hopelessly lost in the jungle, moved his rifle companies to a jumping-off position in the jungle at the southern nose of the ridge in front of where Sweeney's platoon had been earlier; and the 3rd Battalion, 124th Infantry (III/124) swung to the right to get in position to sweep around the left flank of the Parachutists.

By late afternoon, the command group of the latter unit, including its leader, Lieutenant Colonel Watanabe, had yet to arrive. Apparently, Watanabe, who had been injured on the long march inland from Tasimboko, became disoriented in the jungle and never did show up to take charge. The unit, effectively leaderless, would engage in disjointed and piecemeal attacks this night, much to Kawaguchi's dismay.

17

The Ridge, Round Two

Captain William J. McKennan was commanding officer of Able Company of the badly depleted 1st Parachute Battalion. His outfit, which consisted of less than fifty men, was in defensive reserve around Edson's command post this night. He was told to be ready to move out and plug any holes that might develop to the front.

"The men had had practically no sleep for the past 48 hours, so we decided to let them turn in, maintaining a sufficient number on guard to bring them out if we were suddenly called for," McKennan said. "At dusk, or around 6:30 in the evening, there were evidences of a renewal of the conflict. I could hear considerable artillery fire, but I was not particularly worried about it at the time because the shells were hitting far over the ridge. I dropped into a doze ... I awoke to find a runner from battalion headquarters telling me I was wanted at the CP. I made my way through the dense jungle in the pitched darkness to headquarters and was advised there that the situation up front was threatening and that our company was called for at the ridge.

"Most of us realized this was to be the big night. We took all the ammunition that could be packed in, plus case upon case of hand grenades, for which we were later to be very thankful."

McKennan, as ordered, deployed his company around

the nose of Hill 120 just to the right of the road running
along the ridge, tying in with some Raider units on the
right flank. Before they could find the unit to their left,
the enemy struck.

"The sky and jungle were blazing with fireworks and a
hellish bedlam of howls," McKennan wrote. "Firecrackers, a cheap imitation of machine-gun fire, exploded in
front of us . . . and from the jungle below this umbrella of
fire and noise came the rhythmic, bloody chant, learned
by rote and shrilled to the accompaniment of the slapping
of gun butts: 'U.S. Marines be dead tomorrow. U.S.
Marines be dead tomorrow.' "[1]

Forward of McKennan's position and closer to the taunts
and curses of the Japanese, the Raiders of Baker Company gave as good as they took.

"Eat shit," was a simple, yet effective response to the
Japanese taunts.

Major Kokusho, sword in hand, ordered his lead units
of 2/4 to attack. Screaming "Banzai" and "Death to Roosevelt," the enemy came forward, crashing through thick
jungle and running in a crouch through the open areas.
They hit Gunnery Sergeant Haines' 2nd platoon of Baker
Company head-on.

"The jungle seemed to come alive in front of us,"
Corp. Joe Sweeda said. "We could hear the shouts of the
Japs and their movements in the brush. Suddenly, they
threw grenades into our position on the right flank. We
exchanged rifle and machine gun fire and threw all of our
hand grenades into the jungle. We could hear screams
and moaning, so we got some of them."[2]

The first wave was beaten back but the enemy mortar
and machine gun fire never stopped. Then, a fresh assault
came forward. This one bounced off the entrenched 2nd

platoon and swept the flanks. Sweeda gathered his squad and joined another led by Corp. Al Camlin as they both moved to the rear, all the way to the ridge.

As Sweeda's squad was repositioned into foxholes atop the ridge, many of the wounded were taken back to the aid station. One of them, Pvt. Robert Schneider, was covered with his own blood from an enemy grenade. He looked much worse than he was, however. While being patched up at the aid station, Schneider could hear Marines on the ridge yelling for more ammo.

Covered with bandages, Schneider took it upon himself to organize a group of wounded to help him hunt up the needed ammunition and get it to the men on the ridge. He would spend the rest of the night racing back and forth atop the ridge to resupply his fellow Marines. His "indomitable fighting spirit and fearless devotion to duty" earned him a Navy Cross.

Shortly after the assault on the 2nd platoon, Sgt. Bob Aneilski's 1st platoon was struck and, after a wild firefight, was cut off and overrun when hit from the front and flanks. The deadly firefight quickly became a melee between individuals. The squad leaders and the platoon sergeant lost control in the eerie darkness. Flashes of gunfire and grenade explosions lit up the night. There was screaming, both in English and in Japanese, as the enemy moved through the position. The Raiders began crawling to the rear, dragging as many wounded comrades as they could find with them.

The Japanese infiltrators would crawl forward as far as they could and then jump up and rush the Raider defenses when they were almost on top of them. As soon as a weak spot was identified, more enemy soldiers would rush to the breach and push forward. The Raiders opened fire and called in preregistered artillery fire before pulling back to the ridge. Those who delayed got cut off, surrounded and were left to their own devices.

Quickly, it was every man for himself. Camouflaged Japanese soldiers crashed through the bush firing their light Nambu machine guns and throwing grenades on the run. Terrified Raiders could see enemy bayonets glistening in the flickering light. Suddenly, one of the Japanese soldiers collided with Corp. Gene Eleston, who quickly dispatched him with his knife.

While the 1st and 2nd platoons of Baker Company were reeling from the brunt of Major Kokuska's assault, the 3rd platoon on the ridge only had to deal with probes and sporadic rifle fire from individuals. Captain Sweeney, whose command post was directly behind the 3rd platoon, was kept busy reorienting those who were falling back while 1st Sergeant Maddox was on the phone coordinating artillery fire missions on the now deserted positions to the front. The enemy was also probing positions on the left flank being manned by the Parachutists.

Sweeney prowled the ridge warning his men to conserve ammunition and be careful who they were shooting at. "Don't shoot at noises or shadows," he reminded them time and again. Sweeney had no orders to fall back from his position.

"My group was now around sixty or so people," Sweeney said. "We had some people who disappeared, and that's something that I think needs to be said. We had stragglers. The 1st Parachute Battalion had stragglers—not stragglers in the sense they were lagging behind but a few men that were leading a charge to the rear."[3]

The initial action was much lighter on the extreme right flank along the Lunga River where Able Company was dug in. It was also lighter in the area of Dog Company of the engineers, who were dug in just to the east of Able Company. They received more of a glancing blow. The "eye of the storm," as Edson had predicted, crashed up against Baker Company around the nose of the ridge.

One of the reasons the main attack was confined to Baker Company's front was because Marine artillery was playing havoc with the other two Japanese battalions trying to form up in their assembly areas. One report claimed that the Japanese formations "scattered like a school of frightened fish" when the 105s came screaming in on top of them. The bombardment also prevented General Kawaguchi from directly coordinating the enemy attack.

The barrages also helped a few isolated Raiders escape to safety, though very nearly at the cost of their own lives. Corp. Jim Mallamas and Sgt. John "Squeaky" Morrell, cut off and left on their own in no-man's-land, found themselves in the middle of a Marine artillery barrage and thought they were goners.

One of the shells landed nearly on top of them, lifting both into the air and throwing them to the ground. Bleeding from the nose and ears and reeling from the explosion, the two men somehow found the energy to start crawling to the north out of the killing zone. Morrell made it to the Raider lines while Mallamas somehow made it to the Engineers' front line.

Another fortunate Raider this night was Pfc. James Hall, who, after being knocked to the ground by an artillery shell, played dead while a Japanese soldier stripped him of his rifle and cartridge belt.

The 1st and 2nd platoons of Baker Company, the "speed bumps" of Edson's defensive plans, had done their job, though at heavy cost. They had blunted the first Japanese attack and channeled them into prepared killing zones for the artillery. They also identified the enemy's route of attack, which helped Edson realign his much smaller force to achieve maximum results.

To Captain McKennan, perched on the highest hill around, it looked as if the Japs were moving forward in three thrusts.

"One had filtered through the jungle on our left, a second had been launched frontally against the hill to the south and the third was coming from the southwest," McKennan said. "The latter, for some inexplicable reason, was momentarily held up just around the corner of the hill, but so close we could hear the Japs blabbering while they organized for an assault. They were perhaps 75 yards away.

"In the uproar the commanders of the companies on the advanced slopes were ordered to withdraw from their exposed positions to a point where the battalion could be consolidated and a stronger defense set up."[4]

The units to the front that McKennan was talking about were Baker Company of the Raiders and Baker and Charlie companies of the Chutes. No such orders to withdraw were given at this time, however. While Captain Sweeney's Baker Company of the Raiders held fast, the two parachute companies, led by battalion executive officer Maj. Charles Miller, began an unauthorized move to the rear, which would later draw Edson's wrath and cause him to relieve Miller.

Sweeney's position now "stuck out like the prow of a ship into a sea of maddened Japs."[5]

At about 2100, "Washing Machine Charlie" appeared over the perimeter and a few moments later dropped a flare over the airfield. This signaled the start of a bombardment by seven destroyers cruising off Lunga Point. Their shells were aimed at Henderson Field.

Near the end of this thirty-minute shelling, the ground attackers fired what appeared to be a mortar round from the edge of the jungle to Baker Company's front, Sweeney remembered. The round, trailing sparks, hit on the forward slope of Hill 120 in front of Edson's CP and burned brightly for several minutes. The shell, probably a magnesium flare, caused the dry kunai grass to catch fire. The blaze gave off an acrid odor and a heavy cloud of smoke, which started cries of "gas" and "gas attack."

At first the shouts were attributed to the Japanese, who were obviously trying to create some confusion and panic. Others who were there were convinced that the shouts came from nearby Marines, both Raiders and Paratroopers. Whatever, the incident did cause a few individuals to begin an unauthorized withdrawal. These moves were quickly dealt with, averting any headlong flight to the rear.[6]

The smoke attack, Sweeney believes, served a dual purpose for the assault units of Major Tamura's 2nd Battalion, 4th Infantry and the 1st Battalion, 124th Infantry, which lost its leader, Major Kokusho, on the night's first attack. He believes it was a signal to renew the attack and a "marker" to identify the objective as well as to assist the Japanese assault units in the jungle flat to regain their direction of attack.

By this time, Sweeney's first two platoons were reduced to a few isolated squads desperately trying to reach the safety of the ridge. One of the lucky ones was Pfc. Ed Shepard of the 1st Platoon, who, despite bullet wounds to the chest and both arms, made it back to the battalion aid station. His best buddy, Pfc. Frank "Russ" Whittlesey, wasn't so fortunate.

"Russ and I were attached to each other like no other

people could ever be," Shepard wrote. "We lived together several months before seeing action and shared everything from small bits of food to each other's personal affairs and feelings. Being scouts we were alone together a great deal and learned to depend upon each other. I knew his past life like a book, the food he liked best and even his favorite music and songs. We went through several battles together, never leaving each other's side."[7]

Their friendship reached its apex on the night of September 13 as Shepard described in his letter.

"We had just returned from the raid of [Tasimboko] and set up positions on a bare ridge (later called 'Bloody Ridge'). At dusk we were ordered to advance several hundred yards into the jungle and dig in at the edge of a lagoon which the Japs were expected to cross to reach Henderson Field. All was quiet until about 9 o'clock except for the movement of small animals in the lagoon and surrounding jungle, a half moon hung on the [Canal] and then we could hear the Japs cautiously advancing. They reached the far edge of the lagoon. The word was passed to hold our fire until they started crossing.

"Then all hell broke loose, the jungle was lit up like a stage, battle cries broke out from both sides above the screams of dying and wounded men. We were outnumbered five to one and were soon hand to hand. After about thirty minutes, I was hit and dropped to the ground. Russ stood over me and fought like a madman. I asked him to leave me and he only said, 'Go to hell Shep!'

"Things began to quiet down and reorganization began. Russ worked over me about an hour trying to stop the blood flow, tearing his shirt into strips for bandages. His rifle had been shot from his hands and mine had fallen into the lagoon and all we had were knives. With Russ's assistance I could walk a bit. My right lung being punctured made it difficult to breathe, the bullet had penetrated both my arms which made them useless. We found ourselves behind the Jap lines and we had to go through to get to our own outfit.

"Moving along a narrow trail, we ran into a Jap patrol, and Russ, instead of getting away, chose to die fighting to save my life. He dropped me to the ground and stood with a knife in hand and the three Japs charged him with bayonets. With the cool art of a true Marine he used certain tricks (we had often practiced together) to kill the first two, and the third one stabbed him in the back with a bayonet. He fell and the Japs ran. He put a finishing touch on the two Japs and lay down beside me.

"He was hit in the stomach several times, of which I was not aware. He said, 'Well Shep, I guess this is where we came in' and smiled, and began to try to hum his favorite tune 'I'm getting tired so I can sleep.' Then he just went to sleep. I put my hand on his heart and started crawling toward the Jap lines. By some miracle of God, I reached the hill and a corpsman gave me a shot and I went to sleep."[8]

Before passing out, Shepard remembered seeing Major Bailey calmly walking along the ridge directing and encouraging the withdrawing Marines as if it was a training exercise.

Pvt. Irving Reynolds, another member of B Company, also had a close call that night. Scattered by the initial Japanese attack, Reynolds fell head over heels down a steep slope into the jungle, breaking the strap on his BAR and plugging it with dirt. Joining up with other Raiders, Reynolds and his group soon found themselves intermingled with some Japanese soldiers.

"It was so dark you could only make out forms but you could smell them," Reynolds said. "We were so close we bumped into each other. To this day I believe they knew we were there but they were either scared too or disorganized and didn't start anything."

Both sides then went on their way without firing a shot.

Most of the stragglers made their way back to the top of the ridge where they were positioned in a horseshoe around Edson's command post. They would be needed later in the night to help repel three banzai attacks on the crest of Hill 120.

After the initial thrusts by the enemy, the attack seemed to stall. Kawaguchi's forces became confused and disoriented. They paused to take cover from the relentless artillery barrages and lost any momentum they might have had. Kawaguchi later wrote that his force became "scattered all over and completely beyond control."

Some historians believe this momentary confusion, as well as the stepped-up artillery fire, allowed many of those Raiders in the 1st and 2nd platoons of Baker Company who were overrun to escape annihilation and make it back to the ridge.

Meanwhile, Sweeney's third platoon of about thirty men was still holding out on the nose of the lower ridge with an open right flank and part of a Parachute company to his left.

As the incendiary shell burned itself out, Sweeney's men could hear the distinct sounds of troop movements along the ridge line to their front. The Japanese were equally vocal on the jungle flat to the right where it appeared they were getting ready to attack Edson's command post on Hill 120.

It is at about this time that Edson called Sweeney on the radio for an update.

"What's your situation?" Edson asked.

Before Sweeney could reply, another voice broke in and replied in precise English: "My situation is excellent, sir."

Sergeant Maddox, who had been monitoring the radio nearby, cursed and slammed his helmet to the ground.

"The bastards have one of our radios," Maddox said in disbelief.

"While the Japanese might have located our frequency on one of their own radios," Sweeney said, "it is more likely that they were using one of our own 'walkie-talkie' sets discovered after they seized C Company's position the previous night."[9]

Sweeney quickly broke in to "cancel that last transmission." He then gave Edson a brief status report, adding that he needed more men and concluding with a comment to bring the artillery barrages in closer to the front lines.

In no more than five minutes, 105mm rounds were falling to Sweeney's front. The artillery forward observer at Edson's CP, Corp. Thomas Watson, did such a fine job that he was spot-promoted to 2nd lieutenant the next day on Edson's recommendation.

Watson brought the fire to within 150 yards of Sweeney's front line.

"That's right on. Now walk it back and forth on the ridge and into the jungle on each side," Sergeant Maddox told Watson.

It stopped the Japanese in their tracks—at least temporarily.

Sweeney took advantage of the brief lull to check on his men, who now numbered less than thirty effectives, chiefly from the 3rd platoon. He and a couple of NCOs moved along the line encouraging each man to fire only when they saw definite targets.

Many of the men were understandably frightened. Some left their foxholes and started to the rear. They were quickly stopped and forced back into their holes.

Sweeney called for his runner to give him a message to deliver to Edson. At first, he couldn't find him. Then he spotted him hunched over and looking very much like a shell-shocked victim.

"The lad appeared without his rifle and when I asked where it was, he stared off into the darkness," Sweeney said.

"I don't know," the young private finally answered. "I . . . I lost it."

Sweeney grabbed him by the arm and looked into his eyes.

"His arm, his entire body was frozen stiff with fear. He was out of it," Sweeney said. "He was scared shitless. As a runner, as a Marine, as a fighter, he was worthless."[10]

While Sweeney was inspecting his line, Corp. John Gann, who had been posted on the extreme right flank to observe enemy activity, crawled back to report that the enemy appeared to be massing for an attack in his area.

"This development posed the threat of the position being cut off should the enemy move around the open flank and up the ravine which separated the spur from Hill 120," Sweeney said.

Sweeney had orders to hold and he was determined to do just that.

At about 2230, two red flares rose up from enemy positions and drifted down the ridge toward Hill 120. These signaled another series of attacks against the defenders around Hill 120 and the Parachutists on Sweeney's left flank. The latter was preceded by a heavy barrage of mortar fire that caused the Chutes to fall back—or charge to the rear—to new positions nearer Hill 120.

That left Sweeney's 3rd platoon all alone on the nose of the ridge.

Edson recognized Sweeney's predicament immediately. Shunning a radio transmission that could be intercepted, Edson told his runner, Burak, to go forward and shout a message in the clear to Sweeney. Burak, running in a crouch, raced down the ridge and through some jungle to within a few yards of Sweeney's position where he cupped his hands to his mouth and bellowed, "John Wolf. This is Burak. Do you hear me?"

Sweeney heard. He recognized both his code name and Burak's voice and quickly answered, "Yes. Affirmative."

Burak then delivered the message that "Red Mike says it's OK to withdraw."

Sweeney conferred with 1st Sergeant Maddox and told him to contact the artillery forward observer, Corporal Watson, at battalion to arrange a covering barrage to their front. He then sent Maddox to the rear to assemble the men as they moved back along the path.

Sweeney moved along the line to inform his squad leaders of the imminent move, then gave the order to withdraw, one squad at a time. As they were leaving, the enemy raked the position with rifle and machine gun fire as the Raiders lobbed a few farewell grenades.

"Miraculously, no one was hit," Sweeney said.

The men started down through the waist-high kunai grass in the ravine to the road east of Hill 120 when they heard and felt the promised artillery barrage rolling across the spine of the ridge and into the adjoining jungle not more than 100 yards forward of their abandoned position.

Sweeney, who would earn a Navy Cross for his leadership, believes that the artillery barrage coincided with a two-company attack by the enemy on the hill they had just occupied.

"They were pressuring both the 3rd platoon position

and the Paratroopers about the time Edson ordered the withdrawal," Sweeney said. "The [enemy] 5th company apparently was shattered by Marine defensive fires, especially the accurate and deadly artillery barrages crafted by Maddox and Watson."[11]

Maddox met Sweeney on the road where he was trying to corral the Raiders, who had withdrawn. They had become commingled with Baker Company of the paratroopers, who had also pulled back.

"NCOs of both units were shouting as they desperately tried to bring order out of a near-chaotic situation," Sweeney said. "Shouts of 'B Company, Parachutes, assemble here,' and 'B Company, Raiders, assemble here' pierced the darkness as artillery shells whistled overhead."

Sweeney said that more than words were needed to keep the men from panicking and fleeing all the way to the beach. He and his NCOs moved among the milling throng and soon assembled "about twenty-five of the thirty odd Raiders who earlier were defending the ridge spur."

Edson and Bailey also moved among the men doing their best to halt a potential stampede to the rear. Edson challenged the men with sarcasm, telling them that "the only difference between you and the Japs is they've got guts." The six-foot-three Bailey, a former football star at the University of Illinois, used a more physical approach, waving his pistol in the air and threatening to shoot any man who left his post.

Pfc. Dave Taber distinctly remembered Bailey getting in his face.

"[Bailey] said something like this: All you fellows have buddies and friends that have been wounded and killed, and it will all be in vain if we lose the airfield. Now let's get out, hold the line, and save the airfield. If we lose the airfield, we're going to lose the island. That was the gist of it. It was quite dramatic and got everybody moving. I thought to myself it was almost like something out of a movie."[12]

By midnight, Company B had made it safely to the knoll. "From then on," Edson would later say, "we had them licked."[13]

As the Raiders were counting noses, both Edson and Bailey ran up to Sweeney to offer their assistance.

"Red Mike began speaking just as the battalion communicators at the Command Post, about fifty yards up the road, kicked off their gasoline-powered generator," Sweeney said. "The start-up had a distinctive sound— 'pop-pop-pop' like a machine gun, although not as sharp. With the first sound Bailey, standing between Edson and me, grabbed both of us around the shoulders and dived headlong into a roadside ditch, covering Edson with his body.

"For Crissakes, it's only a generator," Sweeney said, a bit disrespectfully.[14]

Edson, after dusting himself off, smiled weakly and Bailey looked a little embarrassed. Sweeney thought to himself that he was about to catch a little hell for his impertinent remark but it never happened.

Edson ordered Sweeney to "take what you have and form a blocking position across the road in case the Paratroopers get pushed back." Bolstered by a few stragglers, Sweeney's fractured company, which consisted of about two dozen Marines, stayed in their new position until daylight, fighting off several attempts by the enemy to take the hill.

Edson had also managed to round up a squad of communicators from his headquarters and dispatched them to Sweeney as reinforcements. When Sweeney first saw the detail, led by Sgt. James "Horsecollar" Smith, he thought it was a company of men.

"Deploy your company over here," Sweeney said, pointing at a gap between his men and the Parachutists.

"We're not a company, just seven men," Smith answered.

"Oh, shit," Sweeney replied before ordering Smith to place his makeshift squad adjacent to the Paratroopers on the very apex of the position. Six of the communicators, including Sergeant Smith, would become casualties this night.[15]

Edson then met with Capt. Henry Torgerson, the newly elevated commander of the 1st Parachute Battalion (Edson had relieved Maj. Charles Miller, later calling him a "dud"), and ordered him to counterattack on the left flank to try and regain some of their former position, as well as tie in with Sweeney's force on the ridge.

Edson hustled back to his CP and phoned division headquarters to give them an update. He spoke with Lieutenant Colonel Twining and told him that the Raiders had now withdrawn to their "final defensive position." He also warned Twining that he should shore up the Division CP defenses or the Japanese could "come through you like shit through a tin horn."[16]

Concerned by what Edson had said, Twining departed the Division CP around 0200 to check on the readiness of the reserve force (2/5) and then went forward to see for himself what Edson was dealing with. When he got there the ridge was under a heavy mortar attack.

"Edson was up there roaring like a lion getting his men ready to throw back what proved to be the final 'banzai' charge of the night," Twining later wrote. "Where he found such strength and energy I will never know. Thirteen hours before, I had thought him close to collapse but he seemed to grow stronger as the night moved on."[17]

The Paratroopers, meanwhile, counterattacked as ordered and managed to gain some ground. More importantly, however, they blunted any further infiltration of Japanese troops on the left flank, an action that Edson later praised as "a decisive factor in our ultimate victory."

18

Situation Critical

Edson made a quick assessment of his position and it did not look good. The Japanese had driven a huge wedge into his right flank, bypassing Able Company and Dog Company of the engineers, and were now poised to make a push to overrun Hill 120.

Edson had about 300 men dug in, in a horseshoe around Hill 120. It was the last defensive position before Henderson Field. The two Baker companies manned the left flank and center positions while the rest of his battalion—Charlie, Dog and Easy companies, all supplemented by stragglers—were dug in on the right flank of the hill. All were way understrength. The situation was critical.

At about 0230, the enemy launched a full-scale mortar attack on the knoll and the Raiders answered with their own mortars. A red flare signaled the ground attack and on the Japanese came, moving rapidly up the hill in a crouch, chanting slogans and firing their weapons. The Raiders met the charge with a shower of machine gun fire and grenades, rolling the latter down the hill as fast as they could pull the pins.

One of the enemy mortar rounds severed Edson's communications line with division headquarters, leaving him completely on his own.

One Raider wrote later that he saw Edson and Bailey

standing together shouting toward division headquarters "Bill Whaling! Bill Whaling!" at the top of their lungs, repeating the cry two or three times. They were literally calling for reinforcements. Whaling was the commanding officer of the 2nd Battalion, 5th Marines, the division's only reserve unit, which had been brought up near the ridge earlier in the night.

When the communication line was severed, Edson sent Corporal Burak back to division to report the line failure and to tell the artillery coordinator to continue the previously requested firing missions. Burak then took it upon himself to run a new reel of commo wire back to Edson's CP, running through a hail of fire for some 300 yards.[1]

When Edson got back on the line to division, around 0300, Colonel Thomas asked him how he was doing.

"I've been hit hard and I need more men," Edson said, trying to keep as calm as he could.[2]

General Vandegrift came on the line and asked Edson, "Can you hold?" Edson said he could but he needed more ammo and more men.

Thomas put in a call to Colonel Whaling and told him to get his battalion on the move to Edson's location immediately. Whaling sent his men forward one company at a time but because of the darkness and unfamiliarity with the terrain, the first company didn't reach the ridge until just before daylight.

Meanwhile, the Japanese were plastering the ridge with mortar fire as a prelude to yet another all-out banzai charge. Calls of "ammo, ammo" swept the ridge. Now and again, the men could also hear the soft moan of "corpsman, corpsman." To those who already hadn't done so, the order was given to fix bayonets.

It was now about 0330.

• • •

"From the beginning of the fight until dawn, there were never more than a few minutes of surcease," Captain McKennan later wrote. "The attack was almost constant, like a rain that subsides for a moment and then pours the harder. In most of these assaults the Japs never reached our lines. I believe now that they had no definite plan other than the general order to attack, attack and attack. When one wave was mowed down—and I mean mowed down—another followed it into death. There was never a moment when there were not Japs in front of us.

"Some of the Jap rushes were now carrying them into our positions and there was ugly hand-to-hand fighting. But not one of our men, to my knowledge, met death that night by a Jap bayonet. We were thankful for our grenades. We used them constantly and with deadly effect. We took them out of their cases by the hundreds, pulled the pins and rolled them downhill into the noise below. They wrought havoc and a shrill chorus of shrieking rose."[3]

Edson and Bailey had foreseen the ammunition shortage and the latter had organized a resupply mission to the rear with Sgts. James Childs, Pete Pettus and Corporal Burak. While the mortar barrage was still underway, the Raiders could hear a small truck chugging its way down the path toward their lines. It was loaded to the hilt with boxes of grenades and belted .30-caliber machine gun ammunition, which was provided by the 1st Marines.

Bailey, Burak and others grabbed the boxes off the truck and struggled from foxhole to foxhole, crawling on hands and knees, dragging and carrying the heavy crates of ammunition. Then they would return to the truck for more, dodging enemy fire both ways. When the truck was emptied, it took away a half dozen seriously wounded to the division hospital.

Bailey, who would earn the Congressional Medal of Honor for his bravery, would be shot twice this night. The first bullet just grazed his cheek and the second punctured his helmet, glanced off his head and exited out the back of the helmet, leaving him with a huge headache and a bloody face.

When he wasn't delivering ammo, Bailey was limping along the line in full view of the enemy, exhorting his men to hang tough and maintain their positions. Occasionally he would grab a man who had thoughts of heading to the rear and physically shove him back into his foxhole.

"Do you want to live forever?" he was heard to yell, quoting a line used by Marine Sgt. Maj. Dan Daly at Belleau Wood during World War I.[4]

The Japanese literally beat their brains out against a wall of steel from artillery, mortar, machine guns, rifles and grenades. They became disoriented and sought refuge in foxholes already manned by Raiders. Those who strayed into a Raider foxhole were knifed and thrown back out like so much refuse.

Some made it all the way to the crest of the ridge where they were thrown back in hand-to-hand combat. They came on again and again, never having quite the push they needed to roll over the top. It was close but not close enough.

By 0400, the enemy had hit the wall and had neither the will nor the manpower to continue the assault. The Raiders smelled victory. Egged on by Edson and Bailey, the Raiders stood their ground and threw back a final assault.

Edson, too, roamed the battlefield, standing defiantly

with his hands on his hips and yelling at his men to stand fast. Bullets whizzed over his head, some piercing his clothing.

"Go back where you came from," he was heard to yell at some of his men who had left their foxholes. "The only thing they've got that you haven't is guts."[5]

When he spotted a potential breach of the line, he sent his "linebacker," Bailey, over to plug it up. The line bent but never broke. Some of the men certainly thought about leaving their holes but men such as Edson and Bailey wouldn't let them. The horseshoe became tighter as the night progressed. And, as the enemy's will waned, that of the Raiders grew stronger.

The athletic Burak, who was Edson's only secure means of communication for much of the night, was as heroic as his boss. He roamed the entire length of the ridge many times, delivering messages and ammunition without regard for his own safety, earning him the Navy Cross. Other heroes who were awarded Navy Crosses on Hill 120 for their actions during the early morning of September 14 included Pfc. William Barnes of Easy Company, a mortarman-turned-infantryman, and Pfc. Herman F. Arnold, a radio-operator-turned-infantryman, and three members of Charlie Company, Sgt. Dan Hudspeth, Pfc. Jimmy Corzine and Platoon Sgt. Stanley Kops.

Hudspeth personally stopped an attempted breakthrough atop the ridge in hand-to-hand combat, Corzine led a bayonet charge that routed an enemy force and Kops gathered up some stragglers and led them in a charge that seized their positions. All but Barnes lost his life in these desperate hours just before dawn.

Three members of Edson's command group, Maj. Robert Brown (operations), Capt. William Stevenson (communications) and Sgt. Francis Pettus (intelligence), were also awarded the Navy Cross for extraordinary actions above and beyond the call of duty.

Also performing heroically this night were the two Navy doctors, Edward McLarney and Robert Skinner, and their brave group of corpsmen. The doctors, who treated more than 200 wounded during the thirty-six-hour battle, operated by flashlight in a small tent not thirty feet from Edson's command post. Each doctor would receive a Navy Cross as would eight corpsmen. One of the latter, Karl Coleman, had also earned a Navy Cross on the Tasimboko raid for some lifesaving surgery in the field.

Another corpsman, Robert L. Smith, survived the wild action on the ridge during the night only to suffer a cruel fate a couple of hours after dawn. Resting with a buddy and enjoying a well-deserved cigarette, Smith spotted a wounded Raider lying near the crest of the ridge and rushed out to perform his duty. While he hovered over the stricken Raider, providing assistance, a Japanese sniper took his life.

Shortly after 0400, Edson got on the line with General Vandegrift at division headquarters one last time.

"I'm committing my last reserves, General," Edson said. "Have you got anything left to replace it?"

"I'm afraid it's negative, Mike," Vandegrift answered. "They've got us tied down on the Matanikau and at Alligator."

"Well, I'm sending in the 2nd Battalion [of the 5th Marines]. Is that okay with you, sir?"

"Go ahead, Mike. Sorry I can do no more for you. Daylight'll be here soon," Vandegrift said.

There was plenty of anxiety at division headquarters, as well, as Dick Tregaskis related in his award-winning book.

"The whispered word went 'round that the Japs were landing parachute troops (later proved false)," he wrote. "More reinforcements came through our position on the ridge, while the Japs were firing. If the Japs drove down the ridge in force, and broke through Col. Edson's lines, they would be able to take the CP. If they had already cut in behind our position, as we suspected they had, they would box us in, and perhaps capture the general and his staff.

"But the general remained calm. He sat on the ground beside the operations tent. 'Well,' he said cheerfully, 'it's only a few more hours till dawn. Then we'll see where we stand . . .' He was amused at my efforts to take notes in the dark."[6]

The enemy mortar barrage at 0430 turned out to be a last hurrah. The Japanese infantry tried to mount a serious attack but they were spent. The Raiders had held Hill 120 and the American artillery, almost 2,000 shells, had broken up the enemy force into little pieces. But, many of them didn't retreat.

How close did the Japanese come to succeeding? In a word, very.

"The attack of one more battalion would probably have brought Kawaguchi a breakthrough," wrote historian Richard Frank, "and that battalion was available. Kawaguchi learned that the two assault battalions had lost nearly half their strength, but he became enraged upon discovering that the III/124 had hardly entered the action."[7]

That battalion belonged to Lieutenant Colonel Watanabe, who spent the night wandering around in the jungle, dazed and confused. He also had badly swollen feet and had difficulty walking. Without their leader, the battalion never got into position to reinforce the main body and help provide the final push over the ridge.

"This powerful battalion, the one I had counted on most, was completely mismanaged," Kawaguchi later wrote in his memoirs. "When I heard of this I could not help shedding tears of disappointment, anger and regret."[8]

Edson managed to hang on without the help of his Able Company, which was bypassed by the Japanese and left stranded on the far right flank without any means of communication. Nearly full strength, Able Company could only bear witness to a night of wild fighting, wondering when they would be attacked as well.

"It was a long night waiting for the Japs to attack our front," Sergeant Guidone remembered. "The noises of the various weapons to our left, flares, screams all combined to increase our awareness to the inky black to our front. I could not tell you what was happening two or three foxholes to my right or left. My world was to my front where the smallest noise could be the Japs assembling for an attack.

"It is amazing what you think you are seeing to the front at night. Outlines of the brush take on the shape of a figure and if you stare long enough it will move. We heard the Japanese voices which appeared to sound closer to us than we thought. What went through my mind during those moments I am certain were the same for my buddies. Is this the ending of my life? Eighteen years—ending up in a dark jungle as a corpse."[9]

As the main attack fizzled, small groups of Japanese carried on independently, penetrating deep behind Raider lines around daylight. They held out until they were hunted down and eliminated one by one. Surrendering was not an option for them.

One enemy squad-sized unit intercepted George Company of 2/5 moving up to reinforce Edson and inflicted thirty casualties on the Marines. Easy Company of the same unit had fourteen casualties, including five dead, moving to the ridge just before dawn. The Japanese would not give up or go down easily.

The division command post also came under fire just before dawn, according to Tregaskis and Lieutenant Merillat, who were both on the scene.

"Snipers were moving in on us. They had filtered along the flanks of the ridge, and taken up positions all around our CP," Tregaskis wrote. "Now they began to fire. It was easy to distinguish the sound of their rifles. There were light machine guns, too, of the same caliber. Ricocheting bullets skidded amongst the trees. We plastered ourselves flat on the ground."[10]

Merillat headed for the message center to find refuge and immediately hit the deck.

"Tracers started coming into the CP," he wrote. "Firing seemed to come from all sides [a common impression, I am told, on such occasions]. We could make out the distinctive ping of a Jap .25-caliber rifle close by. At least one seemed to be right on the spur where the CP stood, firing at random. Now and then bullets kicked up the dirt nearby. I could have sworn the Jap was right in front of the general's house. I slipped further down into the ravine to the north and crawled under a log that stuck up at an angle from the ground. I watched the time closely, praying for dawn.

"Then, as it began to grow light, it became clear that my refuge was in full view of snipers on the west side of the ravine. Others nearby had already begun to find better cover. I dashed up the slope into the [intelligence] tent and hit the deck. Two others closely followed. Just as they got inside a bullet clanged against a steel plate propped near the entrance. Ducking around behind the [intelligence] tent I saw Colonel Buckley, also looking for cover, and asked him where everyone was. He said I could hop into one of the [intelligence] shelters, which I did with alacrity, to find I shared it with Martin Clemens (who didn't recognize me in the dark and was inclined to dispute my right of entry), a wounded Raider, two British missionaries, and a couple of [intelligence] Marines. By now it was about 0500. I stayed until the sky was bright."[11]

By then, Vandegrift's command post had acquired a most apt nickname. The men began calling it "sniper's roost."

Fearing another banzai attack at dawn and itching to take the fight to the Japanese, Edson requested and received approval for an air strike on enemy positions at first light. He sent Bailey and Field Sgt. Maj. Jim Childs to Henderson Field to arrange the mission.

The two Marines would have to fight their way to the airfield, however.

"The major had to stop at division headquarters to inform Gen. Vandegrift of the situation first," Childs said. "As we approached, a sniper in a tree overhead, within a hundred feet of the headquarters let go a round at us. I let loose about half a clip from my Reising gun and out he tumbled. When we got to division, Major Bailey told the general that snipers were in the trees along the ridge, especially on the east side."

Vandegrift didn't need to be told. A few minutes earlier, he nearly fell victim to a Japanese machine gun, according to Tregaskis.

"As the first light of dawn came, the general was sitting on the side of the ridge, talking to some of his aides," he later wrote. "A Jap machine gun opened up, and they high-tailed it for the top of the ridge, with me right behind. We were heading for a tent, where we would at least have psychological shelter. Just as we reached the tent, a bullet clanged against a steel plate only two or three feet from us."[12]

Bailey and Childs continued on toward the airfield where they met with Army pilot John A. Thompson. Lieutenant Thompson told them they only had a few P-400s in commission and he only had enough fuel for three of them. Bailey, he remembered, "was holding a helmet with a bullet hole through it and blood was on his head and face . . . [Bailey] drew a crude map of the area showing Marine positions and the area below where the Japanese were amassing for their attack."

"It was getting light and time was critical," said Thompson, who led a group of three P-400s on the mission. The P-400, distinguished by its shark-toothed nose, lacked superchargers and oxygen equipment for high-altitude combat but it was an excellent strafing plane. Each was equipped with three .30-caliber machine guns on each wing.

"As I came in just over the treetops I saw the Marines on the ridge [Hill 120] and below in a clearing were hundreds of enemy troops huddled together. They were caught completely by surprise," Thompson said. "I tilted the nose down and depressed the gun switch. Six machine guns poured bullets into the troops. I pulled up and the next plane did the same thing."[13]

All three planes were hit by ground fire during their runs but each one made a dead-stick landing back to Henderson Field.

Vandegrift was so pleased with Thompson's skill and enthusiasm he nominated him for a Navy Cross.

• • •

Dawn came to the ridge but the killing was far from over. Most of the Japanese survivors drifted back into the jungle, withdrawing as ordered, but many others remained on the battlefield where they were determined to cause as much damage as possible. Many of the wounded waited in ambush to take a curious Marine with him before he died.

Corp. Joe Sweeda was fighting off the urge to catch a couple of winks shortly after dawn when he heard the familiar "thunk" of an enemy mortar discharge. Looking up he saw the projectile "headed right for me," he said. Sweeda rolled over several times trying to get away but was wounded by some fragments. He then crawled on all fours to the rear looking for a corpsman.

"Tregaskis, in his book, told about seeing a Marine crawling like a dog with only three serviceable legs toward the aid station. He may have been referring to me," Sweeda said.

Just a few minutes later, a small truck made its way from the airfield to the ridge to help evacuate some of the badly wounded to the field hospital. Sweeda was lifted into the truck bed along with several other wounded and three stretcher cases. Other wounded draped themselves on the fenders. Major Brown, the operations officer, sat in the passenger seat holding the bloody stump of his right hand, which had been shattered by a Japanese grenade. He had tried to throw the grenade back at the enemy but it went off in his hand.

The truck was overloaded as it began its bumpy ride to the rear. The makeshift ambulance hadn't gotten more than fifty feet when a Japanese machine gunner opened up on the vehicle. The driver was hit and the truck came to a stop, providing a stationary target. Before the enemy gunner was silenced, he had killed three helpless Raiders.

One of them was Major Brown. Corporal Sweeda survived, however.

The hero of the event, according to Tregaskis, was a young private named Lewis E. Johnson, who was in the rear of the truck with a leg wound.

"Johnson painfully crawled from the rear of the vehicle, dragged himself to the cab, got into the driver's seat and tried to start the motor," Tregaskis wrote. "When it would not start, he put the car in gear, and, using the starter for traction, pulled the truck a distance of about 300 yards over the crest of the ridge. Then he got the engine going and drove to the hospital. By that time, he was feeling so refreshed that he drove the truck back to the front and got another load of wounded."[14]

A platoon-sized group of Japanese had slipped past the division command post through the jungle to the east and reached the southwest end of the new Fighter One airfield, some 2,000 yards east of Henderson Field. They briefly overran a company of engineers and captured two machine guns. But the defenders, which included clerks and headquarters personnel, rallied and took back the position as the Japanese fought to the last man.

Just after dawn, a sword-wielding officer and two other Japanese soldiers with fixed bayonets, shouting "banzai," suddenly burst out of the jungle near Vandegrift's command post. Vandegrift, who was about thirty feet away, was unarmed when the intruders appeared. He stared in disbelief as the enemy officer threw his sword at a Marine guard, killing him. Two of the Japanese, including the officer, were knocked to the ground and shot by Sgt. Maj. Sheffield Banta and the third fled unharmed into the jungle.

Perhaps the most tragic scene of all, however, was witnessed by Captain Sweeney.

"I saw two men from the Parachute battalion walking to the rear, laughing and juggling a Japanese mortar round between them. Then one of them dropped it. It killed both of them instantly," Sweeney said.[15]

The battlefield below the ridge was strewn with the bodies of dead Japanese soldiers, some very still and others writhing in the midst of grass fires started by explosions. The scene left an unforgettable image in the mind of Edson's executive officer, Lt. Col. Sam Griffith.

"[Kawaguchi] left behind him a bloodstained ridge littered with corpses," Griffith wrote. "In the grotesque attitudes of those who meet sudden and violent death lay the twisted bodies of more than 500 men who had died gloriously for the Emperor. With heads lolling and mouths agape, the inscrutable dead stared with glazed and sightless eyes at the morning sun."[16]

At first light, the area around Hill 120 was littered with ammo boxes, empty shell casings and the tangled and twisted bodies from both sides. It was strangely quiet except for an occasional shot or the low boom on a booby-trapped body. The Raiders could also hear a strange moaning from the battlefield below. It sounded like "okasan, okasan." Later, they learned that the word "okasan" meant mother in Japanese.

Correspondents Robert Miller and Tregaskis walked out along the ridge to see the carnage for themselves.

"At the crest of the knoll we looked down the steep south slope where the ridge descended into a low saddle," Tregaskis wrote. "On this steep slope there were about 200 Jap bodies, many of them torn and shattered by grenades or artillery bursts, some ripped, a Marine told us, by the strafing planes which we had seen this morning. It was up this slope that the Japs had sent their heaviest assaults many times during the night, and each time they tried they had been repulsed.

"Beyond the saddle of the ridge rose another knoll, and there we could see more bodies and the pockmarks of shelling. The whole top of this knoll had been burned off and wisps of smoke still rose from the smoldering grass."[17]

"Credit on the American side for defeating Kawaguchi must be shared," according to Richard Frank. "The Cactus Air Force contributed importantly in keeping one infantry battalion (III/4) completely out of the battle and slaughtering or dispersing nearly half of another (II/124). These men represented one-quarter of Kawaguchi's potential strength. The American fliers also forced an exhausting and time-consuming jungle march on Kawaguchi's assault units and harried the Japanese in retreat. The gunners of the 11th Marines likewise played a critical role. The 1,992 rounds of artillery fire on the night of September 13–14 by the 105mm howitzers of the 5th Battalion, 11th Marines inflicted between two-thirds and three-quarters of all of Kawaguchi's losses on the ridge and protected the withdrawal of the defenders at a desperate moment."[18]

A "detailed" Japanese report, according to Frank, reveals that of Kawaguchi's total strength of 6,217 men, 708 were killed or missing and another 506 wounded. On the American side, "one contemporary report" lists 111 Marines killed or missing and 283 wounded. The number of Raiders killed or missing varies from 34 to 37. Raider historian Oscar Peatross reported the latter figure and listed the names of all 37, even breaking them down by company (Able 3, Baker 3, Charlie 19, Dog 1, Easy 8 and HQ 3).[19]

Certainly, hundreds more Japanese died on the long withdrawal march to the west. Thanks to the Tasimboko raid, the Japanese had no supplies of food or medicine and suffered horribly on their forced retreat. Also because of the Tasimboko raid, Kawaguchi decided to withdraw toward the west through uncut jungle rather than head back the way he came, believing that a second front had been established by the Marines to the east.

The Parachute battalion was finished as a fighting force. Of the 377 men who landed on Gavutu-Tanimbogo on August 7, 212 had either been killed or wounded, a little over 55 percent. (Capt. Torgerson had eighty-six able-bodied men under his command when he left the ridge.) The Raiders had absorbed almost 25 percent casualties from its available personnel of some 750 men. At least 100 Raiders missed the battle because of illness or injury.

Looking back on the climactic battle of the ridge, one realizes how close it came to being a Japanese victory. Edson's forces on the ridge during the early morning hours of September 14 were no more than 300 men while the Japanese had about 1,500 troops to throw at the defenders.

Most of the credit for the victory has to go to Edson and his combined Raider-Parachute battalion. He persevered in his belief that the attack would come from the south despite doubts stubbornly proffered by Vandegrift, who was disinclined to act promptly on the available intelligence. Special recognition should also be given to Colonel Thomas and Colonel Twining, who both believed Edson's estimation of the situation all along.

In summary, it is more than reasonable to assume that without the Raiders and Chutes defending the ridge, Henderson Field would have been lost. Second, without the curtain of artillery fire provided by Colonel del Valle's

11th Marines, the airfield would have been lost. And, third, had Kawaguchi been able to delay his attack one day to conduct a proper reconnaissance of the area, the ridge would likely have been overrun.

Vandegrift later said that the battle of the ridge was the only time during the entire Guadalcanal campaign that he had doubts over the outcome.

Had they prevailed, would the Japanese have had enough troops to hold the airfield until reinforcements arrived? The answer here is probably yes. That's how close the outcome at Guadalcanal was. Had Guadalcanal fallen, it certainly would not have changed the outcome of World War II but it assuredly would have prolonged its course.

"It had been a close call," Merillat later wrote. "We can only speculate about what would have happened if several hundred soldiers of Nippon had overrun the airfield. Their primary targets were the planes and artillery. They would have overrun the division CP, putting the Marine nerve center out of action at a crucial time. Japanese ships and naval air force units were poised to surge in quickly if the field were captured. Marines outnumbered the attackers by three or four to one, but were spread throughout the perimeter. Presumably they would have had a reasonable chance to retake the field, depending on how quickly the Japanese had run in reinforcements by air and sea, unopposed this time by Cactus planes."[20]

By midmorning, what would later be called "Edson's Ridge" was officially turned over to the 2nd Battalion, 5th Marines. The Raiders, looking like walking ghosts, shuffled slowly to the rear and most were given the rest of the day off. Many of them spent the day sleeping.

A weary Edson shuffled off the ridge looking very much

relieved. He stopped to chat with an equally weary Raider, Pvt. Ernie Gyenese, who was sitting on the ground enjoying a smoke.

"Son, could you spare a cigarette?" Edson asked.

"Yes sir," Gyenese answered, "but I got these at Tasimboko and they don't taste too good."

"Beggars can't be choosers," Edson replied before striking a match.

Edson took a couple of drags and looked out over the battlefield. Softly, he muttered to himself: "Now I know that I have a really great outfit."[21]

A few minutes later, a relieved Vandegrift smiled broadly when Edson and Bailey arrived at his command post, pumping each man's hand in gratitude for a job well done. Colonel Thomas joined in on the celebration, calling the Raiders "the best gang of cutthroats you could find anywhere in the world."

Vandegrift, wearing a pith helmet because his steel pot gave him a "devil of a headache," couldn't help noticing the rips in Edson's uniform at the waist and collar, obviously caused by enemy gunfire. The general was at a loss for words.

He then glanced over at Bailey and kidded him about the holes in his helmet and his bloody face.

"Better draw another [helmet] from supply, Ken," the general said with a big grin.

Vandegrift looked around his command post and admitted to the two Raiders that maybe moving his CP to the ridge hadn't been such a good idea after all. He had already issued orders to move his CP back to its original position northwest of the airfield.

This time it was Edson's turn to smile.

19

A Brief Lull

Early that afternoon, scuttlebutt swept the area that the Raiders would be leaving the island on the next transport for a long rest. The rumor was given life when it was announced that the 1st Parachute Battalion had been given orders to prepare to do just that.

"If they leave, doesn't it mean we have to go, too?" one Raider asked his platoon sergeant. "It makes sense, doesn't it?"

Morale was at a low point. Many men were beginning to feel sorry for themselves despite the adulation of the entire division for their gallant stand on the ridge. Some believed they should be rewarded with a rest, maybe even sent back to the United States.

Edson sensed the mood. As he had done two weeks earlier when the battalion crossed over to Guadalcanal from Tulagi, Edson spoke directly to the men, telling them what he knew about the situation. It was a business-like talk. He told them they were not being relieved, at least just yet, and reminded them that it would be a long war. Like his earlier speech, the words had an empty ring.

Some of the men were openly resentful, blaming their misery on Edson. They began calling him "Mad Merritt the Morgue Master." There was some griping, but then again, there was always griping.

Scuttlebutt swept the Raiders that Edson was leaving the Raiders to take over as regimental commander of the 5th Marines. For once, the Marine grapevine was accurate.

"We cussed him for trying to get us all killed. I was glad to see him go," Pvt. Irv Reynolds said, "yet we knew we were losing a great leader."[1]

The Raiders rested on the 14th and 15th before resuming a light schedule of patrolling. Most of the men took advantage of the down time (no Japanese air raids reached Guadalcanal between September 14 and September 26) by taking baths in the Lunga River or in the sea. They received mail, wrote letters and listened for news on the radio. It was nice to know that the folks back home had not forgotten them.

They also got used to some hot meals again, although the diet was heavy on rice and coffee and light on meat and potatoes. Standing at the chow lines were medical personnel making sure the men took their Atabrine pills. No pill, no food.

Malaria had become nearly epidemic within the division, from almost 900 cases that required hospitalization in August to nearly double that figure in September.

Meanwhile, the immediate job of cleaning up the battlefield fell to the 2nd Battalion, 5th Marines. The grim task of searching the dead for intelligence and burying the already decaying Japanese bodies was a job for strong stomachs and stout hearts—but it had to be done. Japanese prisoners were again pressed into duty to help the Division Graves Registration section in burying their former comrades.

The Army air strikes early on the morning of September 14 was the final hammer that convinced Kawaguchi that the battle was over. The strafing runs had been deadly, ending any hope Kawaguchi may have had to gather enough men to make another attack the next night.

He issued the order to withdraw back into the jungle—but that didn't mean everybody got the word. The Marines remained on the alert for snipers and enemy pockets of resistance. They were especially wary of Japanese soldiers feigning death on the battlefield and then ambushing an unsuspecting Marine looking for intelligence or souvenirs.

Not all those given a chance to surrender declined, according to Tregaskis, who interviewed a dozen or more Raiders immediately after the battle of the ridge.

"[I] heard some interesting stories about the Japs; how, for instance, they often ask to be killed when they are captured, but seem relieved when we do not oblige," Tregaskis wrote. "Then they feel they have complied with their part of the death-before-dishonor formula, and make no further attempt to deprive themselves of life.

"Several of the Jap prisoners captured on the ridge, it seems, said 'knife' when they were captured, and made hara-kiri motions in the region of the belly. But when no knife was forthcoming, they seemed relieved, and after that made no attempt to kill themselves."[2]

The prison camp on the island had grown to over 400 and the occupants provided instant reminders of what kind of enemy the Marines were up against.

"Looking at the prisoners, who squatted inside a barbed-wire rectangle like animals on exhibit, brought mixed feelings," Tregaskis wrote. "One could not but feel at least a trace of sympathy for the group of labor troops, a meek-looking, puny lot, most of them well under five feet in height and physically constructed like children. After all, most of them had been conscripted into service, and had always been unarmed.

"But the military prisoners, Japanese naval troops, were different. They were a surly-looking, glowering group, and by no means puny. They were cooped up in a little barbed-wire pen of their own, since they had refused to mix with the laborers. We stared at them and they stared back at us. There was no doubt as to what either we or they would have liked to do at that moment—if we had not remembered our code of civilization or if they had not been unarmed."[3]

The majority of the enemy troops honored their Bushido Code and departed the world in a messy fashion. A bulldozer appeared on the scene and a large trench was dug to bury the bodies of the Japanese. American dead were transported to the division cemetery on the north side of the airfield by the beach.

To make sure the Japanese had left the area, Vandegrift ordered patrols out to probe and push the enemy deeper into the jungle.

Two companies of the 1st Marines were sent on a combat patrol south of the ridge on the first day and ran into an ambush. One platoon was almost wiped out and the two companies suffered a staggering twenty-four killed.

Meanwhile, Captain Sweeney had been replaced by Capt. Ed Wheeler as CO of B Company. Wheeler, who had come over from Able Company, had been a classmate of Sweeney's and was commissioned on the same day. His service number was slightly lower, however, so he had seniority. "It was a big disappointment," Sweeney said about losing command of the company.[4]

Sweeney led a patrol beyond the area of the ridge he had defended just a few days before and discovered the body of one of his men, Pfc. Frank "Russ" Whittlesey. Young Whittlesey was overrun by the Japanese on the night of September 13 after helping one of his wounded comrades, Pfc. Ed Shepard, to safety.

Sweeney's men buried Whittlesey where he fell and took one of his ID tags to give to the medical people with information on where he had been buried. The story didn't end there, however. In 1989, a local farmer discovered some bones and a dog tag bearing the name of Frank R. Whittlesey. A series of tests conducted by the Army's Central Identification Laboratory confirmed the identity of the remains and they were returned to the United States for reburial next to his parents in Pittsfield, Mass.

Thomas and Edson were urging Vandegrift to press ahead and chase down the remnants of Kawaguchi's weakened force but the general eased off a bit waiting for the arrival of the 7th Marines, which he knew were on the way. Besides, reports of enemy activity to the east and west caused him to husband his forces for what could be another Japanese attack.

Kawaguchi's main assault on the ridge was supposed to be supported by simultaneous attacks from the east by the Kuma Battalion and the west by forces led by Colonel Oka. The force to the east got tangled up in barbed wire and came to a halt well short of the Marine lines while Oka's forces in the west were late getting into position and, except for one company which made a half-hearted attack, became bogged down in the jungle.

Though neither force played a significant role in the battle of the ridge, Vandegrift still considered them dangerous. He knew he would have to deal with them again in the future.

News of Kawaguchi's failure was greeted by the Imperial Army and Navy with "shock and incredulity" and a new resolve "to meet the total American commitment in kind by tossing in every plane and literally bringing its big guns to bear on the Marine perimeter," according to historian Richard B. Frank.[5]

The key to the next all-out effort to regain Guadalcanal would be the troops from the 38th Infantry (Sendai) Division, the conquerors of Hong Kong, Sumatra and Timor. This unit, which was in training for a planned attack of Ceylon, would be funneled to Guadalcanal aboard barges and destroyers on nightly runs over the next few weeks.

Kawaguchi's withdrawal from the "ridge" would prove to be a nightmare, a six-mile journey through some of the worst terrain on the island. Of the 1,500 or so men pulled from the battle, fully half of them were either wounded or desperately ill. There were an estimated 160 stretcher cases, many of them needing at least four men to carry them. There was no food or medicine. These vital stores had been destroyed by the Raiders back on September 8 at Tasimboko.

Kawaguchi was faced with a desperate decision. He had to decide whether to retreat the way he came to the east toward Taivu Point or break through the jungle and head west along the west bank of the Matanikau River. The Tasimboko Raid paid another dividend here as he was almost compelled to choose the latter course believing that the Americans had set up a major base to the east.

It was a horror show from beginning to end. After pulling back from the ridge out of artillery range and resting a day, Kawaguchi's desperate troops began their withdrawal on the night of the 15th. The healthiest of the bunch were sent ahead to scout a trail that had been previously cut by another unit. Others served as stretcher bearers. They made less than a mile that first day. The sobbing of the wounded and the horrible smell of their gangrenous wounds kept the others from sleeping that first night and every night thereafter.

As the days wore on, the starving men were reduced to eating tree roots and bark. They drank river water and developed terrible cramps. Packs, helmets and crew-served weapons were discarded as they trudged along in their misery but the men hung onto their rifles. Soon, these were tossed aside. As the ill and wounded died, they were left on the side of the trail. The men did not have the strength to dig graves. Finally, the vanguard reached Japanese lines.

"Colonel Oka blanched at the sight of them. He had never seen such human wrecks," Robert Leckie wrote. "They did nothing but beg rice from his own hungry troops or wander among them with lit fire cords in their mouths pleading for a few crumbs of tobacco. . . . Some of these survivors who had been with Colonel Ichiki had horrible tales to tell of the Marines. They said they were foul-mouthed beasts, the refuse of jails and asylums. They cut off Japanese soldiers' arms and legs and ran over their bodies with steamrollers."

The Japanese command felt it would be unwise to allow their men to mingle with these "scarecrows and catch that most deadly of military diseases; defeatism. So the survivors of Bloody Ridge were sent farther west" to look for food and shelter.[6]

The lull after the battle gave General Vandegrift time to do some personnel housecleaning. He had been authorized by Marine Headquarters to weed his command of an excess of colonels, who were now needed stateside to help train a rapidly expanding Marine Corps. Vandegrift sent his chief of staff, Col. Capers James, to Australia, and the commander of the 5th Marines, Col. Leroy Hunt, home to the States. He quickly elevated the division's operations officer, Col. Gerald Thomas, to take James's place and Lt. Col. Merrill Twining moved up to take Thomas' place.

Vandegrift then named Edson as the new commander of the 5th Marines with Lieutenant Colonel Griffith taking over the 1st Raiders. Edson took Maj. Lew Walt with him as his operations chief and later as a battalion commander. He also kept Capt. Hank Adams from intelligence and his runner, Corporal Burak. He wanted to take Major Bailey, too, but Griffith put up such a stink that the order was canceled even before it was issued.

Edson's elevation to command of the 5th Marines was a case of "ironic justice," according to Herb Merillat. "When Edson had been appointed to lead the 1st Raiders early in 1942 he (as well as the 7th Marines) had skimmed off the cream of officers and noncoms in the 5th Marines to fill his own ranks. If the regiment had not measured up thus far on Guadalcanal, it was due in part to the 1st Raiders' raid on its best men."[7]

A number of senior lieutenant colonels, some of them battalion commanders, were also sent home to make way for younger, more aggressive men. Some of the reassignments were nothing more than clearing away dead wood as the challenges of combat had exposed inadequate performances of a number of key officers. All of the changes went into effect on September 21.

Just after dawn on September 18 the reinforced 7th Marines—the first major reinforcements of the campaign—finally arrived off Lunga Point and began to come ashore. In the eyes of many of the silent, unshaven men who watched these fresh troops disembark, the U.S. Navy finally stood vindicated.

Vandegrifts's 1st Marine Division was finally whole.

The reinforcement didn't come without a price, however, as Japanese submarines sank the carrier *Wasp* and badly damaged the battleship *North Carolina* three days earlier while they were providing distant escort duty for the Marine convoy. The sinking of the *Wasp* left the ancient *Hornet,* which had served as the platform for Jimmy Doolittle's stirring Tokyo bombing run back in mid-April, as the only remaining U.S. carrier in the South Pacific.

Vandegrift and his staff stood near the pier at Kukum, almost cheering, as 4,157 Marines in fresh new uniforms and helmets stepped onto the soil of Guadalcanal. The reinforcements included the 1st Battalion, 11th Marines and Company C, 1st Tank Battalion. Support units included an engineer company, a service company and a medical company. Also unloaded were 4,323 drums of aviation gas, 137 vehicles, 1,000 tons of rations, much-needed ammunition and barbed wire and some engineering equipment. The ammunition included 10,000 rounds of 37mm canister and 10,000 hand grenades, which were ordered nearly a month earlier.

Admiral Turner had delivered this much-needed convoy with great skill, timing the landing for dawn and then getting away before it got dark, a procedure he had used often during the campaign.

The convoy, according to Lieutenant Colonel Griffith, had also brought in some "post-exchange supplies," which were put to use in ways they were never designed for.

"In breakfast lines several days later each Marine was issued three 'Trojans' gratis," Griffith wrote. "If not too tightly knotted, these proved most effective for preserving such perishable items as cigarettes, matches, candy, and letters from sweethearts in the States."[8]

The 7th endured some good-natured ribbing by the battle-hardened Marines ashore. One of the targets was Lt. Col. Lewis B. "Chesty" Puller, the legendary commander of the 1st Battalion. Puller, forty-four, had already won Navy Crosses in Haiti and Nicaragua and would earn three more before his career was over. He was also that very rare bird of war, a man who actually loved combat and who was beloved by his men.

"Well, Puller, you finally found the war," Lieutenant Colonel Twining kidded his long-time friend. "Did you get lost on the way? Where have you been?" he asked with a smile on his face.

Puller, ever ready to live up to his colorful reputation, asked Twining where all the Japs were. Told they were in the hills beyond the perimeter, Puller is reported to have said: "Well, let's go get 'em." Edson, who was also part of the greeting party, turned to his executive officer, Sam Griffith, and said: "The Raiders will have some competition now."[9]

Some of the Raiders, standing nearby in ragged-looking uniforms, watched the 7th Marines come ashore with mixed emotions.

"I think we might have been glad to see them and yet sorry for what they had to look forward to—which we knew only too well," Sergeant Guidone said.[10]

By 1800, the troop ships began taking aboard the remnants of the 1st Parachute Battalion and some 162 wounded personnel from the division hospital. The convoy got underway for New Caledonia as darkness fell.

"Speaking for myself, the Chutes leaving the island was good news for us," Guidone said. "We knew that we would probably be the next in line. We were mostly glad for them and we held them in high esteem—especially after their fight at Gavutu-Tanambogo and the Ridge."[11]

The 7th Marines, meanwhile, were exhausted after unloading transports all day. Nightfall had come quickly and there had been no time to dig foxholes. Many of the new men plopped themselves on the ground and covered themselves with their ponchos. Around midnight, a Japanese plane circled overhead and dropped a brilliant green flare, turning the night into day. Then came a bombardment from the sea. The earth shook and palm trees toppled to the ground and the men frantically began scratching out some cover in the dirt with their bare hands.

At dawn, the 7th Marines reported three dead and two wounded on their first night on Guadalcanal.

Meanwhile, Vandegrift's toehold on Guadalcanal had grown into a foothold.

20

New Blood

The arrival of the 7th Marines finally gave General Vandegrift the option of offensive action, particularly to the west along the Matanikau River where intelligence information indicated the Japanese were beginning to stockpile troops and equipment for a major push toward the airfield.

Vandegrift realized he was in no position to gamble but he could be a little more aggressive with his patrolling to keep the enemy off-balance and under constant strain. His moves, however, had to be calculated to tweak the Japanese any way he could without risking heavy casualties.

Division headquarters came up with a two-battalion patrol to get Puller's feet wet on the island with a minimum of risk. At dawn on the 20th, Puller's 1st Battalion, 7th Marines, 900-men strong, patrolled south along the west bank of the Lunga River while Edson led what was left of his Raider battalion (now down to no more than 200 effectives) for the last time south along the eastern bank.

The Raiders, by then, had attained an almost legendary status within the 1st Division. Men stopped and stared in awe as the ragged remnants of the unit trudged by en route to yet another tough assignment. They had not only come to be known as Vandegrift's "fire brigade" but were often referred to by the general himself as his "do or die men." Admiration for their courage and fortitude was just about universal and resulted in a special commendation from Vandegrift.

As they readied themselves for another patrol on the evening of September 19, the division's public relations officer and historian, Lieutenant Merillat, took out his notebook and wrote: "These Raiders are really rugged. Less than a week after taking 50 percent casualties [actually 30 percent] on the Ridge they are back on the job—at the colonel's own request. I saw them marching across the airfield last evening, on their way to take up positions to the west. I felt my throat tighten as they filed past, but saw no gloom in those faces. What an outfit."[1]

The patrol went looking for any stragglers from Kawaguchi's failed attack a week earlier. Other than a few snipers and some abandoned bodies and equipment left alongside some trails, there were no signs of any fresh buildup of forces. The most dangerous aspect of the patrol occurred at dusk when they were greeted by some friendly fire from the green troops of the 7th Regiment, who were now defending the "Ridge" sector.

Even though the 7th had been in training for many months in Samoa, there was a big difference between simulating warlike conditions and actually experiencing them. Their first night standing guard on the ridge was a scary experience for all of them.

"There were 10 of us in my platoon," one of the newcomers said, "and we all tied strings around our fingers and then connected it one to the other, so we could keep alert. We agreed if we saw one fellow starting to doze, we'd yank the string and wake him up. But everytime one of us moved or relaxed his muscles, the string would usually pull and the rest of us would get scared that it was a signal that the Japs were on top of us. So we gave up the string."

They had been given orders not to shoot unless the Japanese opened fire so as not to give their positions away.

"It seems inevitable that troops never before under fire will shoot all night at nothing," Lieutenant Merillat wrote, quickly adding the caveat that "it's easy to talk, of course, when you are not in the firing line yourself."[2]

The days also took some getting used to.

"Nights were bad but the days weren't much better," said one of the rookies. "The jungle fried us alive and the humidity was like a Turkish bath. The rains came fast and sudden, soaking us and then making us crawl around in deep mud. Then there were the jungle insects—malarial mosquitoes kept buzzing around and bugs and scorpions crawled inside our clothes and down our backs. We had land crabs as big as turtles. I used to wear my shoes day and night because I was afraid the crabs would snip my toes off. I never took my clothes off except to wash myself in the rain."

On September 21, Edson turned the Raiders over to Lieutenant Colonel Griffith and took on the job of commander of the 5th Marines. There were no speeches, no change-of-command ceremony or emotional farewells. He simply published a Battalion Order expressing his pleasure and honor at having been the commander of such a great outfit and had it posted on a bulletin board.

Edson then quickly turned all his energies five miles west of the Lunga around the lower region of the Matanikau River, where he would direct two bloody engagements in the next three weeks that had decidedly mixed results.

The Marines had tested this area a month earlier in a retaliatory raid following the massacre of Lieutenant

Colonel Goettge's intelligence patrol but it was more of a hit-and-run operation and accomplished very little. This time, the Marines would go with greater force and with the mission of breaking up an increasingly threatening concentration of enemy troops between the Matanikau and Point Cruz further to the west. The enemy had begun moving long-range artillery into the area with the capability of reaching the airfield.

Vandegrift thought the area was manned only by scattered units and the remnants of Kawaguchi's beaten forces when, in fact, there were some 2,000 or so fresh troops in the area, and more on the way. The general wanted to break up the enemy forces before they could cross the river to menace the airfield with their artillery. He also wanted to deny the enemy the east bank of the Matanikau itself.

Puller's 1/7, a force of 900-plus men, was chosen to lead this "exploratory" mission while the 1st Raider Battalion was given the ambitious assignment of establishing a patrol base at the village of Kokumbona—four miles beyond the Matanikau and deep in enemy territory.

Puller moved south on September 23, hacking his way toward the northwest slope of Mount Austen. By nightfall, his men were exhausted and Puller was out of breath—from swearing at them. On the next day, Puller's point surprised a group of sixteen enemy relaxing and cooking rice and quickly dispatched them. Later in the day, 1/7 ran into heavy resistance and suffered thirteen dead and twenty-three wounded in a protracted firefight. Puller called for help so he could evacuate his dead and wounded.

The 2nd Battalion, 5th Marines was sent forward the next day. Puller sent two of his companies (A and B) back with the casualties and pushed on westward with 2/5 and the remainder of his battalion, which was basically one company. After digging in the night of the 25th, Puller continued his mission, moving north along the east bank of the Matanikau River. All attempts to cross the river were blocked and violently resisted. His column was under constant mortar fire from the opposite bank practically all the way.

"By this time the Japanese had over 4,000 fighting men on the line of the Matanikau and in reserve behind it," Colonel Griffith wrote. "Some of them were hungry and others ill. But reinforcements had arrived and fresh troops were on the way."[3]

Division headquarters ordered the Raiders to join Puller at the mouth of the Matanikau and Edson came forward to assume command of the combined force. Puller would be his second in command. Right from the outset, the operation dissolved into a complicated series of blundering actions, one Colonel Twining called "the only thoroughly unsuccessful operation of the entire Guadalcanal campaign."[4]

A quick change of plans called for the Raiders, along with Puller's Charlie Company, to move up the east bank of the Matanikau, cross the river at the so-called "one-log" bridge and attack Matanikau village from the south. In effect, Griffith's understrength unit was being asked to do what Puller had been unable to do a few days earlier.

The plan also called for the 2nd Battalion, 5th Marines to cross the mouth of the river along the sandspit and attack from the north. While this was going on, three companies of Puller's 1/7 (A, B and D, under the command of the executive officer, Maj. Otho Rogers) were to proceed by Higgins boats, along with the destroyer *Monssen*, from Lunga Point to a beach well beyond the Matanikau near Point Cruz and attack the enemy from the rear. Air and artillery covering fire was hastily arranged to support all areas of the three-pronged attack.

The Raiders moved out at first light on September 27 and the Japanese were waiting on both sides of the "one-log" bridge. Moving up to the point to assess the situation, Major Bailey, now the battalion executive officer, was shot and killed by machine gun fire. Bailey's loss sent shock waves through the Raiders. The very embodiment of an indestructible Marine officer, Bailey was standing with 2nd Lt. Richard Sullivan and his squad leaders of the point platoon when an enemy machine gun suddenly erupted.

"Everyone hit the deck except Bailey, who had dropped to his right knee and was holding his head in his hands," Sullivan had told Raider historian Oscar Peatross. "The machine gun continued to fire and Sullivan yelled at him to get down and when he didn't move, grabbed him by the ankle and pulled. As Bailey fell he rolled over, and Sullivan could see that he was dead, shot squarely between the eyes. No one else in the group had been touched."[5]

Sgt. James Smith helped carry Bailey's body back to the rear but he was already dead.

"I remember when we pulled Bailey into the aid station in a poncho," Smith said. "A couple of guys [were] sitting on logs and doctors [were] treating them. There was a kid by the name of Dobson who had been shot right in the groin. His face was absolutely dead white, you couldn't believe it. He just sat there and held his stomach. Everybody knew he was going to die, and he knew he was going to die. Not a murmur out of him; talk about stoicism. He died shortly after that. He just slid off the log and was dead."[6]

Bailey's widow, Elizabeth, would receive the Medal of

Honor he earned for the battle of the ridge the following March from President Roosevelt at the White House.

No more than an hour after Bailey was killed, Colonel Griffith, who had assumed command of the Raiders only six days earlier, was shot through the shoulder as offensive action came to a halt.

A few hours later, Griffith turned his command over to Maj. Ira "Jake" Irwin, a sandy-haired reservist from Boston. Irwin, who had been the battalion's supply officer, was the senior man remaining in the Raiders.

Downstream from the Raiders, the 2nd Battalion, 5th Marines was stopped cold by the well-entrenched enemy in repeated attempts to force a crossing near the mouth of the river.

Both these actions took place during a Japanese air attack, the first one in two weeks, that apparently caused division headquarters to lose radio contact with its front-line units. HQ thought the Raiders had crossed the Matanikau and were fighting their way north down the west bank. Believing that, division ordered 2/5 to renew its attempt to cross the river and then gave the final go-ahead for the three companies of 1/7 to implement its amphibious landing behind enemy lines.

Major Rogers was barely ashore when his 500-man unit was attacked by a superior force and nearly cut off from the sea.

"Unfortunately, the landing was made immediately in front of a Japanese battalion bivouac area," Griffith said. "The alerted Japanese pulled out and allowed the Marines to penetrate about 400 yards. Then they fell upon them from three sides."[7]

Rogers was killed by a mortar round and Capt. Charles W. Kelly took command. The toll mounted alarmingly as the Japanese moved to cut the Marines off from the beach. The situation was critical. Lacking a working radio, a few Marines used their white T-shirts to spell out the word "Help" to a pilot circling overhead.

Edson could sense that things were going wrong. He decided to call off the attack on the sandbar by the 5th Marines before a bad situation got worse. Puller, who was temporarily assigned as Edson's executive officer for the operation, objected strongly to the halt, claiming that it was needed to take some of the pressure off his trapped battalion to the west. His claims that his men were being abandoned went unheeded so Puller raced back to Kukum where he boarded the destroyer *Monssen* and, with 10 Higgins boats following behind like a parade of ducklings, he headed for the landing site of his beleaguered men.

Through his field glasses, Puller could see his men on a distant hilltop. Using blinkers and semaphore flags, Puller had messages sent to return to the beach.

"Engaged. Cannot return," came the reply.

"Fight your way. Only hope," Puller ordered. He then instructed the ship's captain to blast a trail through the coconut grove and had the Higgins boats stand by. Puller went to the beach himself to help direct the rescue. Slowly, the men, carrying the dead and wounded, fought their way down to the beach and established a defensive perimeter waiting for the landing craft to arrive.

The first Higgins boat reached the beach at about 1630 and was immediately taken under fire by Japanese machine guns and mortars. Signalman Douglas Munro of the U.S. Coast Guard, who led the landing craft to the shore, died while placing himself between the attacking Japanese and the embarking Marines. Munro was posthumously awarded the Medal of Honor for his bravery.

With several Army planes providing covering fire,

most of the beleaguered Marines made it back to the ship. Casualties were high. One report gave a figure of twenty-four dead and twenty-three wounded but the real numbers may have been twice that total.

Whatever the figure, the operation was a fiasco. One historian called the dramatic seaborne rescue "a kind of tropical Dunkirk."

The media-friendly Puller, who risked his life by directing the operation from the beach, later summed up the desperate operation in one sentence when he told a correspondent: "We're just damned lucky we didn't get the royal shit kicked out of us."

As the day ended and the Marines totaled their casualties (some sixty-seven dead and 125 wounded, most to Puller's battalion), General Vandegrift could only shake his head in dismay. There was little to show for this sacrifice save the realization that the enemy buildup in the area was indeed real. The operation only served to bloody Puller's battalion and further dissipate the Raiders. The Raiders suffered only one killed and a dozen wounded but they had lost some irreplaceable leaders in Bailey and Griffith.

Vandegrift would later criticize the operation for "drifting aimlessly into action." His new operations officer, Merrill Twining, shouldered much of the blame, writing that "what began as a sound and sensible reconnaissance operation ended as an improvised, complex, jury-rigged attack for which we had no plan and had made no preparations. I am the first to offer my own mea culpa. I should never have gone along with Edson's and Puller's idea of recommitting the 1st Battalion, 7th Marines in an improvised, off-the-cuff landing near Point Cruz . . . My conditional acquiescence may well have swayed General Vandegrift's judgment when he gave final approval. In this operation we were lucky. We let ourselves drift aimlessly into action."[8]

The operation also revealed the problems of utilizing the lightly armed Raiders in a static jungle environment. As skilled and resourceful as they were, such tactics only defeated their very purpose as a swift shock unit.

The Marines had been guilty of the same tactical blunders that had plagued the Japanese early in the campaign. They relied on intelligence that badly underestimated both the terrain and the enemy and then they fed in troops piecemeal instead of concentrating on a single point of attack.

Historian Richard B. Frank was equally harsh in his assessment, writing that "the Marines found that the operation had an improvised, purposeless flavor. It had been initiated without meaningful intelligence on the enemy situation or the terrain, and the attack was characterized by the commitment of battalions along unreconnoitered axes, beyond mutual support range, and without coordination of movements or of air or artillery support."[9]

Just a few weeks earlier, Colonel Thomas had voiced concerns that Marine troops could lose their value as a striking force by staying too long on a particular objective. He told a colleague that Washington had better make up their minds whether they want to use Marines as garrison troops or attacking units.

"Offensive troops should never lie behind barbed wire," he said. "They get dugout minded. I saw it happen in the last war."[10]

Much to Vandegrift's credit, the busy Marine general never ducked the newspaper reporters who were growing in number on the island. On the contrary, he went out of his way to be courteous and helpful to the media, even when the news wasn't very good.

New York Times military affairs correspondent Hanson Baldwin, a man very much respected by members of all the services, flew into Guadalcanal on September 19 shortly after the battle of the ridge for a first-hand analysis of the situation, which resulted in a series of articles that earned him a Pulitzer Prize.

Baldwin, who had graduated from the U.S. Naval Academy in 1924 before changing careers, told Vandegrift that the American people had little idea what was going on at Guadalcanal. Many believed the Marines occupied the entire island rather than just a beleaguered perimeter. The plain-speaking correspondent also said he had heard talk in Washington that indicated the politicians were about ready to give up on Guadalcanal

Baldwin also told the general what he saw at New Caledonia on his way to Guadalcanal. There was a "spirit of defeatism" at Admiral Ghormley's headquarters, he said, adding that he saw upwards of sixty ships lying at anchor in the harbor of Noumea because of confusion and a squabble over overtime pay to unload them.

This was the first Vandegrift had heard of this. He didn't know what to say. After letting this sink in, Baldwin looked him in the eye and asked him point-blank: "Are you going to hold this beachhead? Are you going to stay here?"

"Hell yes," Vandegrift answered. "Why not?"[11]

Ghormley wasn't the only one who had believed the Guadalcanal operation to be doomed. General MacArthur and Admiral Fletcher were also skeptics and so was Maj. Gen. Millard F. Harmon, the senior Army officer under Ghormley, who told General Marshall back in Washington that there was "considerable room for doubt" whether the Marines could hold on to Guadalcanal.

Even Admiral Nimitz would express some skepticism,

telling reporters on October 15 in Hawaii that "it now appears that we are unable to control the sea in the Guadalcanal area. Thus our supply of the positions will only be done at great expense to us. The situation," he said, "is not hopeless, but it is certainly critical."

There were other doubters as well, including the award-winning author William Manchester, then a young intelligence sergeant with the 5th Marines.

"At a time when a dozen high-altitude fighter planes would have saved Marine lives, [Gen.] Hap Arnold, the chief of the Air Force, refused to send any on the grounds that they would be sacrificed in vain," Manchester wrote. "Delos Emmons, who was Arnold's air general in the South Pacific, reported categorically that the island could not be held.

"Ghormley, all but writing the campaign off, refused to strengthen the landing there, to the point of ignoring an order from King to do so. Even Vandegrift later said he himself would have listed 'a hundred reasons why this operation should fail.' Vandegrift's plight may be measured by his surprise and gratitude when [Gen.] Alexander Patch, commanding the Army's Americal Division in New Caledonia, withdrew twenty thousand pairs of shoes from his quartermaster's shelves and sent them to the Canal so Marines would no longer have to fight barefoot.

"It took a presidential order and a scrappy admiral—William Halsey, who replaced Ghormley—before the troops began to receive real support from their rear echelon."[12]

Baldwin's reports, which were printed by the *New York Times* during the last week of October, were factual and insightful. They gave the American people their first clear picture of the struggle going on in the Solomons and carefully explained what it would take to achieve victory.

"Japanese domination of most of the Western Pacific and much of Eastern Asia has not yet been seriously challenged in almost a year of war," Baldwin began. "But the U.S., aided by a clear-cut qualitative air of superiority, has assumed the offensive. And if we can hold our Solomons foothold, we shall have taken the first small step in a campaign that may someday lead to the gates of Tokyo."

Baldwin pulled no punches in identifying where blame should be assessed for early failures, particularly the sea disaster at Savo Island.

"Perhaps our greatest problem, as it is the problem of any peace-loving nation flung suddenly into war against a nation of professional militarists, is leadership," he wrote. "Errors of judgment or professional mistakes on the part of some, but by no means all, of our naval leaders—errors that stem in large measure from overcaution and the defensive complex—have resulted in costly and unnecessary losses. . . . Some of our commanders have been overimpressed with the effectiveness of air power upon surface ships and this has resulted in an overcaution."

Baldwin recognized that the worst was probably over for the Marines on the ground.

"The situation on Guadalcanal was for a time almost touch-and-go," he wrote, "but the Marines remained cheerful and hard-working . . . though the enemy had succeeded by mid-September in building up his forces on the island . . . The first crises came—but it will not be the last, if we repeat the same mistakes—in the intensive Japanese attacks of September 12, 13 and 14, which were finally beaten back after a hard struggle."

The most important factor in this Pacific war, according to Baldwin, was who controlled the seas.

"The greatest stakes in the Solomons are not the Marines and Army troops on Guadalcanal—not even the planes based on Henderson Field or the New Hebrides, New Guinea and Australia but the fleets of Japan and the United States," he said. "The outcome of the battle of the Solomons, and indeed the battle of the Pacific, depends primarily upon ships—ships to supply the land forces and the planes, ships to protect and convoy the supply ships, task forces to help secure domination of the seas."

Baldwin also talked with many of the foot Marines during his stay.

"Say," one of the Leathernecks asked Baldwin before he left, "is it really true they are singing that song in the States?"

"What song?" asked Baldwin.

"Oh, you know—the one about Guadalcanal.

"Say a prayer for my pal

"On Guadalcanal . . ."

Vandegrift, an exceedingly affable man, seemed to enjoy his interaction with all the correspondents who covered the Guadalcanal campaign but he appeared to have had a special relationship with the six-foot-seven-inch Tregaskis. Harvard educated, Tregaskis was an original member of the "Guadalcanal Press Club" (along with Robert Miller), which landed on the island the first day.

An excellent conversationalist, the twenty-five-year-old Tregaskis and the much-older general had an obvious mutual respect for each other. Vandegrift appreciated the fortitude and common sense of the young reporter, particularly his decision to gather up valuable intelligence on the Tasimboko raid. The two chatted often, on and off the record, and shared many light moments together.

The modest and soft-spoken Vandegrift was practically unknown back in the States. He was almost never mentioned in news dispatches, perhaps because he never held a formal press conference in all the time he was on Guadalcanal. In fact, Vandegrift had remained so much in the background during his entire career that few people outside the Marine Corps had ever heard of him before Guadalcanal.

It was not until he was awarded the Congressional Medal of Honor in Washington by President Roosevelt in February of 1943 that his grandfatherly face became familiar to the American public. Some people found it difficult to believe that such a kindly-looking man could really have led and won the bloody fight for Guadalcanal.

When Tregaskis came to Vandegrift's tent in the last days of September to ask permission to leave the island, the general smiled at his friend and, in that humble and courteous way of his, said: "They're putting in a shower for me in a few days. And when such luxuries come, the correspondent should go."[13]

A day after the Matanikau debacle, Vandegrift received a letter from his immediate boss, Admiral Turner, saying that he had been meeting with Lt. Col. Evans F. Carlson, the commander of the 2nd Marine Raider Battalion, which had just arrived at Espiritu Santo, about future operations.

Vandegrift was furious that Turner was once again meddling with Marine ground troops and proposing future actions without consulting him. Turner, who often considered himself a ground tactician, had irritated Vandegrift early in the campaign by initially withholding three battalions of the 2nd Marines for another operation he was planning at Ndeni in the Santa Cruz Islands 350 miles to the east. He also had offered a harebrained scheme to break up the 7th Marines and utilize them at several outposts on the north shore of Guadalcanal instead of landing them intact within the Marine perimeter.

When Turner was forced to pull his transports from Guadalcanal on August 9, more than half of the men from the 2nd Marines were ashore, which effectively killed any immediate campaign at Ndeni. The other half of the regiment, about 1,400 men, were still aboard ship where they were being used as stevedores when the convoy sailed.

Turner then attempted to form these men into a "provisional Raider battalion" under his control. He went so far as to write his boss, Admiral Ghormley, to recommend the overhaul of all Marine regiments so that each one would carry a Raider battalion for special missions. Again, he had not consulted Vandegrift, who was able to work behind the scenes in getting Admiral Nimitz to scuttle Turner's plans.

"Vandegrift's constant problem in dealing with his nominal superior in the chain of command was to keep the sailor in his nautical place," Colonel Griffith wrote. "Every now and then Richmond Kelly Turner behaved like a frustrated general."[14]

Vandegrift, using his customary tact, answered Turner's letter by saying that he had had his eye on the 2nd Raider Battalion and its commander, Carlson, since their well-publicized raid on Makin Atoll in mid-August. He felt they would be ideal replacements for the 1st Raiders, which were badly undermanned after nearly two months of action.

"I regret that Major Bailey of the Raiders was killed and that Lieutenant Colonel Griffith, the present commander of the Raiders, was wounded in the shoulder," Vandegrift wrote. "I believe that with the losses sustained in both officers and men of this battalion, and the strenuous work that they have done, that they should be returned to Noumea or some other place for rebuilding. If this is done, I urgently recommend that the Second

Raider Battalion be sent in to replace them as we will need all the strength we can get for this next push which I feel sure will be a major one."[15]

Turner had already made his own plans for the 2nd Raiders. Two companies would be shipped to the eastern end of Guadalcanal near Aola Bay in early November as security for the possible construction of an airfield, another Turner project. When the area was quickly declared unsuitable for an airfield, the Raiders' mission was changed. Joined by the rest of his battalion and a dozen native scouts, including Jacob Vouza, Carlson's Raiders embarked on a highly successful month-long reconnaissance in force behind enemy lines that greatly relieved pressure on the Marine perimeter at Lunga Point.

The 2nd Raiders would earn a unit commendation for their "long patrol" and Carlson received his third Navy Cross and a great deal of publicity. The following year, the outfit was immortalized in the hit movie *Gung Ho* for their exploits on the Makin Raid. The 2nd Raiders were quickly dubbed "Hollywood" Marines by their contemporaries.

The Raiders had become quite popular with the high Navy brass by September. Orders had already been cut to form a third battalion in Samoa and a fourth, under Lt. Col. Jimmy Roosevelt, which would be trained in San Diego. President Roosevelt, himself, had been personally involved in the planning of the Makin Raid in which his son earned a Navy Cross as the unit's executive officer.

Nimitz, whose staff had planned the Makin Raid, was equally sold on the value of Raider units. In early September, Nimitz radioed Admiral King about the prospects for additional Raider units, stating the "present battalions have proved their effectiveness," and concluding that "more of these special type organizations are desirable for employment."

King sought an opinion from the Marine Commandant, General Holcomb, who, like the rest of the upper
Marine brass, was dead set against it. Holcomb stated
that he objected to additional Raider units on three
grounds. First, he needed every man simply to field three
full Marine divisions. Second, he believed that "hand-
picked" units deprived other organizations of natural
leaders. Third—and most important—he did not believe
hit-and-run raids to be "sufficiently profitable to justify
the organization of special units."

Holcomb didn't push his objections, however. Acknowl-
edging that Nimitz was closer to the field than he was in
Washington, Holcomb consented to the formation of two
more Raider units.

Later, Admiral King went so far as to order Admiral
Ghormley to form a Raider regiment that could be
assigned to General MacArthur, who had been asking for
an amphibious unit for some time. Ghormley and Vandegrift both expressed their astonishment that those in high
places could consider assigning Marines elsewhere when
the fate of Guadalcanal was still very much in doubt.

Lurking in the background of this controversy surrounding the Raiders was a growing resentment within
the ranks of the regular Marine Corps that these units
were getting too much publicity. The issue would come to
a head with the wave of media attention given to Carlson's Raiders after their highly successful "long patrol"
behind enemy lines on Guadalcanal from November 4 to
December 4.

By early 1943, word within the Marine Corps had
gone back and forth from Washington to the Pacific that
something had to be done about the Raiders. They were
being made too much of. It was getting so that people in

the States thought of the Raiders instead of the Marine Corps. The rank-and-file Marines did not agree that the Raiders deserved to be singled out as exceptional.

The prevailing opinion among senior Marines was that so-called "special" units were superfluous, virtually the same position they took early in 1942 when the Raiders were first formed.

The basic training of all Marine Corps infantry units was essentially the same as that of the Raider battalions; therefore all Marine Corps infantry battalions are potentially Raider units, the argument went.

By 1943 when President Roosevelt's attention was diverted to other operations both in Europe and in the Pacific, pressure to disband the Raider concept became more overt. The Raiders, particularly Carlson's unit, were denied many of the creature comforts given other units that were pulled off the line, things like showers, movies, post exchange privileges and even lumber to improve their bivouac areas.

Remarks were overheard in high places that the Raiders were nothing but arrogant prima donnas and a bunch of publicity hounds. Even the 2nd Battalion's colorful motto of "Gung Ho" came under criticism. If the Marine Corps's own slogan of "Semper Fidelis" was often interpreted to mean "I got mine, how'd you make out?" the Raiders' real motto should be, "Which way's the photographer."

More and more, the Marine brass began to realize that merely keeping an eye on the Raiders was not enough. Many felt they had to be stopped if the Corps hoped to survive after the war as a separate fighting force with all its supporting air and artillery. Some felt the postwar Marine Corps would consist only of a regiment or two of commandos.

The Raiders would eventually be disbanded on February 1, 1944.

On September 30, Admiral Nimitz flew to Guadalcanal aboard a B-17 bomber for a firsthand assessment of the situation. The aircraft took the wrong heading after leaving New Caledonia and only some quick thinking by staff officer Ralph Ofstie, who happened to have a *National Geographic* map with him, avoided a dangerous—and embarrassing—situation. The plane, rerouted by Commander Ofstie, landed in a driving rainstorm on a muddy Henderson Field with just a few gallons of gas to spare.

If first impressions are the ones that count most, Nimitz quickly saw what the Marines were up against on Guadalcanal. The airfield was a wreck. Cannibalized planes were everywhere. The men looked filthy and exhausted. Later in the day, he was given a tour of the now famous "ridge" by General Vandegrift and Colonel Edson and then visited with the sick and wounded at the crowded division field hospital.

Nimitz had heard the "pessimistic" talk about whether Guadalcanal could be held or not and wanted to get Vandegrift's side of the story. The two men met and conducted a very frank discussion.

"You know, Vandegrift, when this war is over we are going to write a new set of Navy regulations," Nimitz said, relaxing over a cool drink. "So just keep it in the back of your mind because I will want to know some of the things you think ought to be changed."

Vandegrift seized the moment.

"I know one right now," a haggard Vandegrift said, looking straight at the Commander-in-Chief of the

Pacific. "Leave out all reference that he who runs his ship aground will face a fate worse than death. Out here too many commanders have been far too leery about risking their ships."[16]

It was a direct slap at the Navy for turning tail back on August 9 and leaving the Marines high and dry.

Nimitz smiled weakly and said nothing. The comment had registered, however. A little more than two weeks later, Nimitz would remove the "pessimistic" Admiral Ghormley and replace him with the more aggressive Adm. William F. "Bull" Halsey as area commander.

After spending the night, Nimitz presided over a hastily assembled medals ceremony at Vandegrift's CP. He awarded sixteen Navy Crosses and eleven Distinguished Flying Crosses. Among those receiving the former from the Commander-in-Chief of the Pacific were General Vandegrift, General Rupertus, Colonel Edson and Lieutenant Colonel Carlson. The latter, who had hitched a ride to Guadalcanal with Nimitz, received his award for the Makin Raid. Still harboring a grudge against Carlson over the treatment of some of his men more than six months earlier, Edson snubbed the lanky Raider commander.

En route to the airfield following the ceremony, Nimitz promised Vandegrift he would support him "to the maximum" of his resources.

He almost didn't make it off the island, however.

Climbing aboard his B-17 bomber, Nimitz, under protest from his staff, decided to ride up front in the nose of the plane to get a bird's-eye view of the takeoff. As everyone on the ground held his breath, the plane bumped its way down the muddy runway but couldn't reach takeoff speed. At the last minute, the pilot shut off power and slammed on the brakes as the aircraft slid sideways, coming to a halt with its nose hanging over the edge of the field not too far from the coconut trees.

The plane taxied back to the other end of the runway, and with Nimitz now sitting in the rear of the aircraft and everyone crossing his fingers, the pilot gunned the engines and finally achieved liftoff.

21

One More Time

As the month of October began, the Raiders were comfortably settled into their bivouac area in a coconut grove near the beach knowing that they were next for evacuation. They had been designated as a division reserve force. Soon, they would be off this godforsaken island.

"Our only concerns were the daily raids by the Japanese bombers and some shelling from the Japanese fleet," Able Company's Sgt. Frank Guidone said. "Fortunately for us, their target was the airfield. Lying on our backs in foxholes you could see the large caliber shells from the naval guns streaking toward Henderson Field."[1]

Many Marines had moved out of their foxholes and built themselves shacks and lean-tos, so that the perimeter took on the appearance of a hobo jungle. They used crates, Japanese rice bags, strips of corrugated iron, palm fronds—anything to keep off the torrential rains and to give the position a semblance of civilization, however primitive. There were even quite a few tree houses.

Sergeant Guidone had a feeling the Raiders weren't done quite yet.

"There were reports that some of the division was in contact with the enemy along the Matanikau River," he said. "Colonel Edson, our former commanding officer, was in charge of the Matanikau River operation.

"Word was spread that Army troops were expected to

arrive as our relief within a few days. The 1st Raider Battalion would be leaving the combat zone. Our morale was at a high level but one Marine's level of morale was especially high. PFC Donald Steinaker had just received a Red Cross communiqué that his wife had given birth to a child. Don was really pumped up. Cigars appeared as did many handshakes and congratulations. He beamed when he was called 'papa' or 'daddy.' Joe Connolly, a member of the A Company mortar platoon, of which Don also belonged, ribbed Don. Joe was giving Don advice on the responsibilities of being a father. Everything was falling in place. Don was proud of his new status and our ship would soon be arriving to take us out of the jungle."[2]

Meanwhile, the division's operations staff was working on another plan to drive the enemy from his positions along the Matanikau River. The new Japanese commander, Lt. Gen. Masao Maruyama, was working on a similar plan, hoping to establish long-range artillery positions to shell Henderson Field to support a decisive ground attack later in the month.

Maruyama had about 20,000 troops on the island with another division waiting in reserve at Rabaul. The Japanese had never been more confident that they would finally prevail. They were so confident of victory, in fact, that part of Maruyama's operations order included specific instructions as to where along the Matanikau River he would hold a ceremony to accept Vandegrift's surrender.

To protect his left flank at the mouth of the Matanikau, Maruyama had ordered an advance force of about 200 men across the river to establish a defensive position about 100 yards inland from the river mouth. By October 6, this force had constructed a formidable semicircular defensive system of twelve interlocking machine gun positions, all connected by trenches. By October 7, nearly a regiment of infantry had been moved into assembly areas for a river crossing.

General Vandegrift had his eye on the same piece of territory. He knew that the enemy had recently landed four 150mm howitzers to the west, which had the capability of reaching the airfield. Additionally, the sandspit at the mouth of the river was the only east-west avenue for trucks, tanks and artillery. It had to be denied to the enemy.

This time, Vandegrift would use five full battalions. Two battalions from the 5th Marines, under the command of Edson, would make a demonstration at the mouth of the river while two battalions of the 7th Marines and a third from the 2nd Marines would cross the river upstream near the "log bridge," swing right and march to the sea, three battalions abreast, rolling up the enemy as they went. The operation would be supported by heavy doses of air and artillery fire.

The remnants of the 1st Raider Battalion were assigned to the division as a reserve force.

Vandegrift's attack was to begin on October 7, the same day that General Maruyama had planned a limited operation across the Matanikau.

Edson was surprised when his advance elements met strong resistance from a well-entrenched enemy on the east side or near bank of the river. Though the Japanese force was small, it was well dug in. The defensive positions, 400 yards wide by 500 yards deep, were sprinkled with a dozen machine guns and backed up by mortars. The redoubt was designed to protect the sandbar crossing, which would later allow the passage of tanks and heavy artillery.

Edson spent half a day pounding the area with air and artillery and still his men could not advance. Half-tracks were moved up to within point-blank range and pumped one 75mm high-explosive shell after another into the fortifications without noticeable success. As night fell, the situation had become a standoff.

Disappointed with the efforts of his two battalions, Edson asked Vandegrift if he could have the Raiders. Vandegrift, knowing the condition of the Raiders, hesitated and then reluctantly gave his permission.

Some of the Raiders were bitter about returning to combat. Earmarked for evacuation on the first available transport—a matter of days—the outfit was a shell of its former self and in no condition for a major action.

The Raiders could muster less than 200 men. Major Bailey was dead and Lieutenant Colonel Griffith had been evacuated with a serious shoulder wound. Capt. Bob Thomas, who had replaced Bailey as Charlie Company commander on Tulagi, was now the battalion executive officer under Major Irwin. Lt. Bud "Black Jack" Salmon had taken over Charlie Company, Capt. Ed Wheeler, who was slightly senior to Capt. John Sweeney, was CO of Baker Company and Capt. Robert Neuffer had just assumed temporary command of Able Company from Capt. Tony Antonelli, who was ill with malaria. Each of those companies was no more than fifty men.

Edson ordered Irwin to immediately send up Able Company, which had been reinforced with a machine gun section and a mortar section. Irwin complied and then put the rest of the battalion on alert status.

Able Company was the largest of the Raider units, with a fighting force of about seventy-five men. None of the officers who had landed with the unit on Tulagi two months previously were still with the company. Though they were disappointed that they were called into action, there was no grumbling as they moved toward the front late on the afternoon of October 7. They appeared determined to make the best of a bad situation.

"We were told that we would be used in some patrolling duties," Guidone said. "We moved toward the Matanikau in column along the beach trail. On the way, Don Steinaker, carrying a base plate and with a cigar in his mouth, acknowledged several remarks about his new title (daddy) with a large grin and a wave of his hand. For a unit about to enter the combat zone the morale was still high. There was some apprehension because the small-arms fire we could hear from the front promised more than patrol action."[3]

Corp. Joe Connolly, one of the old-timers, tried to keep the men loose with a running conversation of waiting transports, ice cream, clean sheets and movies. Just one more mission, he told them, and it would all be theirs. Everyone knew the Raiders were through with combat. They were just going along for the ride on this mission. They were the division reserve. This time some other outfit would do the dirty work. Everyone wanted to believe that.

"As we moved into the river area we were placed into the lines next to a battalion from the 5th Marines," Guidone remembered. "It was raining as we tried to move forward toward the river but with not too much success. Later in the afternoon, we were assigned defensive positions and began digging our foxholes."[4]

The Raiders had passed a battery of pack howitzers that were firing full blast at the enemy and ahead could be heard the crack of sniper fire and the "whomp" of mortars. Still, these noises didn't dampen their spirits. They believed some other outfit would spearhead the attack. At worst, the Raiders would be used only to mop up. Colonel Edson was in command of the 5th Marines, and he knew that the Raiders were in bad shape. If anyone could accomplish his mission without committing the reserve, it was Red Mike.[5]

Able Company reached its bivouac area just before dusk. Weary Raiders began digging in close to the shore road, not far from the 5th's regimental command post. It was raining hard. No one would get much sleep this night.

At daybreak, Major Walt, now Edson's operations officer with the 5th Marines, came up to give his old company a little pep talk.

"Men, I am proud to be with you again," he said. "For six days the Fifth Marines have been trying to push to the river, which is four hundred yards from our front lines. They have failed. I have a hundred of you, and I know what you can do, even if you are riddled with injuries. I don't know the Nips' strength exactly, but, men, you are going to be on that river when the sun sets tonight. Prepare to move out at once."[6]

Able Company left the shore road and passed through the forward units of the 5th Marines. The immediate objective was to help eliminate a pocket of Japanese resistance on the east side of the river and then anchor themselves along the mouth. The Raiders were stopped cold by gunfire from the pocket.

The heavy rain, which grounded all planes at Henderson Field, forced Vandegrift to postpone the entire operation for twenty-four hours. Edson, however, kept the pressure on the Japanese pocket to his front, dumping occasional artillery concentrations and mortar fire on them most of the day.

Conditions were miserable. Even the press were "badly out of sorts," according to Merillat.

"They take it out on each other and everyone else within earshot," he wrote in his diary. "Seeing men die around you, watching the stretchers bring out the wounded, with artillery and mortar fire blasting your ears and machine-gun bullets pinging all about does not promote good spirits and bonhomie."[7]

Though Captain Neuffer was the commander of Able Company, Colonel Edson and Major Walt were also giving orders to his men. Either Edson or Walt ordered Neuffer to move his company north along the river to occupy an L-shaped line that would cover the beach, the mouth of the river and the sandbar crossing. They were to dig in, wire up and prepare for an enemy attack from across the sandspit.

In making the move, the Raiders bypassed the strong, dug-in positions of the enemy, now located to their left rear. It was assumed that a unit of the 5th Marines would take responsibility for guarding the enemy enclave and tie in with Neuffer's left flank. That never happened.

Neuffer was told that the enemy would make a major drive across the sandspit that night with tanks and attempt to push through the Marine lines and on down the shore road to Henderson Field. To stop the tanks, the company was supplied with two 37mm guns.

As the rain continued to fall, Able Company got busy stringing a double-apron of barbed wire along the sandbar. Sgt. Joe Buntin's 3rd Platoon took up positions on the right flank between the shore road and the sea, Gunny Sgt. Cliff McGlocklin's 1st Platoon continued the line westward toward the mouth of the river and the sandbar and Lt. Red Sullivan's 2nd Platoon extended the line upstream for about 200 yards.

The only reserve was Sgt. Woodrow Thompson's small 60mm mortar section, which was armed with carbines and pistols.

There was a feeling of unease among the Raiders as darkness began to fall. Sergeant Guidone remembered running into the normally jovial Connolly shortly before nightfall and seeing a look on his face he hadn't seen before.

"He asked me how I was doing and cautioned me to be careful," Guidone said. "It was one of the few times I had seen a serious Joe Connolly. I never saw him alive again."[8]

Lieutenant Sullivan crawled back to talk with Captain Neuffer about getting some help closing his wide-open left flank. Neuffer gave him Sergeant Thompson's mortar section to use in listening posts. Moments later as he was placing the men in the exposed area of his left flank he saw some white smoke floating over the battlefield. Then he heard some noises.

"We didn't have the day's password, so I challenged, thinking it may be some Marine getting through," Lieutenant Sullivan said. "As I did so, all hell broke loose. Japs broke out of the jungle almost on top of us in solid waves. I screamed to the platoon that we were being hit from the rear. As I turned around and started firing with my Reising gun, Joe Connolly was cut down right at my side with a sword or bush knife before he had a chance to get his pistol out of the holster.

"I started backing up in order to direct my platoon. I emptied two magazines [from my foxhole] and was reaching for a third when I was shot in the left shoulder. Sgt. [Donald] Wolf's foxhole was next to mine, so I dove in on top of him. Wolf and a corporal on his left killed three Japs who were almost on top of me.

"By this time, it was pitch-black and the Japs had completely overrun our lines. They ran into our barbed wire, which surprised them. My men were able to account for quite a few of them who were tangled in the wire, mostly by bayonets and rifle butts. The Nips began to search out our wounded in the dark and when they found them, two or three would gather around with knives or swords and with seeming glee hack our men to pieces."[9]

The Japanese, apparently convinced by the Marine artillery and mortar fire that their position had become untenable and deciding they couldn't take any more, had suddenly burst from their foxholes, turned left and raced headlong for the sandbar, yelling and slashing at anything in their way. The route took them straight through the Raiders' left flank from the rear.

Thick clouds of smoke from bursting smoke bombs obscured the battlefield. Shoulder to shoulder the Japanese of the first rank rushed ahead, firing automatic weapons. Behind this wall of fire, a second rank advanced. As fast as they could pull the pins, the Japanese of this rank heaved grenades. Some of the enemy yelled "gas, gas," in English.[10]

Sergeant Guidone had a vivid memory of that night.

"When the darkness came upon us we heard noises and voices coming from the pocket of Japanese. The noises became louder as did the voices. We were being attacked by the Japanese from the surrounded pocket," Guidone said. "There was yelling and screaming, the chattering of machine guns and rifle fire punctuated with sounds of hand grenades exploding. There were grunts and groans as hand-to-hand fighting in the foxholes took place."[11]

Gunny Sergeant McGlocklin, whose 1st Platoon guarded the mouth of the river, was in a terrible dilemma. Turning around to face the noise of the Japanese rushing toward his position, he now had the barbed-wire emplacements to his back. He could see running forms but who were they, the Japanese or Raiders? He finally gave his men an order to stay in their holes and open fire. It seemed to divert enough attention to allow some of Lieutenant Sullivan's men to escape with their lives.

Pfc. Sammy Mitchell had run out of ammunition. Everyone around him seemed to be dead and he appeared to be alone in a sea of enemy soldiers. He jumped out of his foxhole and ran toward what he believed to be Marine lines, yelling, "Gangway. Gangway, this is Sammy Mitchell coming through. Gangway." Mitchell, unlike a lot of his Raider buddies, made it all the way to the beach without getting a scratch.[12]

After overrunning the mortarmen, most of the enemy headed toward the sandspit at the mouth of the river but some veered off toward Raiders dug in on the beach. Pfc. Andy Anderscavage saw three Japanese bunched together with their bayonets fixed rushing right at him. He pulled the trigger of his BAR and heard the dreaded click of a misfire. He then grabbed the BAR by its muzzle and hurled it broadside into the charging Japanese, knocking two of them down. Anderscavage sidestepped the third soldier, grabbed his rifle and bayoneted him. Then he jumped out of his foxhole and bayoneted the other two with the same enemy rifle.

The Japanese kept running toward the river and the sandbar. Many ran into the barbed wire and as they thrashed about trying to get untangled, they were systematically picked off by Raider riflemen.[13]

Even if the Raiders wanted to withdraw, they couldn't. Their backs were against either the river, the barbed wire or the sea. Along the Matanikau, the 2nd Platoon's line had been prepared to withstand an attack from across the river, not from their own rear. Between the line and the river, the double-apron of barbed wire stretched as a barrier against the expected attack. But now, as so often happens in jungle warfare, the Raiders' rear had become the front. The second platoon was in direct line of the enemy charge that headed toward the sandspit.

Machine gunners worked frantically to reverse the position of their guns as a mass of soldiers, both friend and foe, raced toward their positions. Lieutenant Sullivan, who had been wounded three times this day, couldn't find his foxhole and when he did, it was occupied by an enemy soldier. He finally crawled into one manned by Sergeant Wolf.

All around them was chaos.

"I didn't move in my foxhole that night," Sergeant Guidone said. "I just waited for somebody to jump me. That's the kind of night it was . . . I think about Gettysburg; it was probably nothing like it. But I think about the men lying out in those fields not getting any treatment."[14]

Sullivan and Wolf decided to make a run for it. In the pitched darkness, Wolf ran right into a party of Japanese and the unarmed Sullivan, who had dropped his Reisling when he was shot in the shoulder, could hear him swear as he scuffled with them. Sullivan ran into a sword-wielding officer and delivered a kick that knocked him off-balance, allowing Sullivan to keep on running. He ran into some vines and crawled as far under them as he could to take a breather. A few minutes later, he began a slow crawl back to where he thought was Marine lines. His biggest fear, he said later, was that he might pass out from loss of blood and the Japs would find him the next morning and finish him off with a bayonet.[15]

Meanwhile at the company command post, a frantic Captain Neuffer was inundated with terrified stragglers and wounded. He began building a defensive line with the stragglers and moved the wounded further to the rear, making sure each had a weapon to use should the Japanese break through.

As soon as he could, Neuffer got through to Colonel

Edson and reported that Able Company had been over-run and practically destroyed.

Edson knew, from his experience in jungle fighting at night, that situations usually appear worse than they really are. "Neuffer," he said with that cold, yet calming voice of his, "you will hold your position"—just as he had told young John Sweeney the previous month on the ridge. Edson promised reinforcements and then sent up Major Walt to take charge and give Neuffer a steadying hand.[16]

En route to the front, Walt could hear the fire lessen-ing. But he was concerned that it might be a lull before strong Japanese forces began attacking across the sand-spit. He expected to hear the clatter of enemy tanks at any moment. The Raider lines must be rebuilt quickly if they hoped to withstand an armored assault.

Walt arrived at about 2100. By then, the forty-five minutes of fury was over.

Lieutenant Sullivan finally reached the shore road just before daylight. Shouting that he was "coming in," he raised himself up and staggered into the Marine lines. After reporting in to Colonel Edson, he was ordered to the hospital to have his many wounds treated.

Dawn revealed a gruesome sight. Seven of the nine-man mortar section perished in the hand-to-hand fight-ing, including Sergeant Thompson, Corporal Connolly and the new daddy, Private First Class Steinaker. The Raider luck had failed Able Company miserably this night.

Sergeant Guidone and Plt. Sgt. Cliff McGlocklin went on a short patrol through the battle area at daylight and saw a sight neither of them would ever forget.

"As we started into the jungle we passed through the area where the mortar section had been hit," Guidone said. "I stopped in my tracks. I was shocked at the scene. There were my good friends Joe Connolly, [Dennis] Thomas, [Neldon] French and several others all in their death poses."[17]

Another Raider in shock was Sgt. Tom Pollard, who had only recently left the mortar platoon for a rifle platoon in Able Company.

"They ran right over my old mortar squad," Pollard said in a 2002 interview. "They ran right through what I had just left. They were my best friends."

(Pollard left the Marine Corps after the war and when he tried to return, they wouldn't take him. So, he joined the Army and served with distinction in Korea as a member of the 82nd Airborne Division, earning a Distinguished Service Cross, two Silver Stars and two Purple Hearts. He retired to his native Florida as a lieutenant colonel in 1964.)

A total of eleven members of Able Company earned Navy Crosses this night, nine of them posthumously. The company reported losses of twelve killed and twenty-two wounded, nearly all of them occurring during that forty-five minutes of frenzied mayhem when the Japanese made their mad dash to the rear.

Enemy casualties caused by the Raiders were reported to be fifty-nine dead, many of them shot while struggling in the barbed wire like flies in a spiderweb.

Frank Guidone would never forget that sight when he greeted the dawn that day.

"I looked up seaward toward the wire, and the Japanese were stuck on it," he wrote. "They hit that wire and it really busted them up. They got hooked up in the barbed wire and the tracers were just cutting them down. They were on the wire silhouetted. Tracers do the damnedest thing—it's not pretty, it's deadly."[18]

A further examination of the battlefield revealed that the enemy force was well equipped and well supplied. Their abandoned packs were heavy with food, new clothes and new shoes. The bulkiest item was rice, but there were also cans of meat and fish. Almost every pack contained rubber tubing with a chemically treated filter in the end. The contraption enabled them to drink contaminated river water when other purified water was not available.

Meanwhile, the other part of the Marine mission continued on to a successful conclusion. The three battalions (1/7, 2/7 and 3/2), after sitting out the night of October 8 in a pouring rain, crossed the river upstream the next day and marched to the sea. Only Puller's battalion on the far left ran into any significant resistance. His scouts discovered a full enemy battalion encamped in a bowl-shaped depression among the ridges. Artillery and mortar fire was called in. The shells reaped a terrible carnage and Puller's riflemen picked off many who tried to escape, virtually wiping out the Sendai Division's 700-man 3rd Battalion, 4th Regiment.

Later that day, General Vandegrift came to the Matanikau River battlefield with Edson. Seeing the pile of bloated Japanese bodies hung up in the wire and littering the ground, Vandegrift asked Edson who was responsible for this carnage.

"My Raiders, sir," Edson answered.

"They're my Raiders now," Vandegrift said.[19]

The Raiders would suffer one more blow that day when Edson's runner, Corp. Walter Burak, was killed by an enemy machine gun along the Matanikau River while carrying a message. He was the last member of the 1st Raiders to die in action on Guadalcanal.

The stoical Edson wept at the news.

Burak was more than just a runner to Edson. There was a closeness and a respect that was difficult to put into words. Burak tended to Edson's needs. He washed out some of his clothes in a helmet full of water over an open fire and performed other tasks like making his bunk or cleaning his shoes.

On the "ridge," Burak displayed his courage and value to the entire battalion. He spotted for the artillery, tended to the wounded, restrung communications wire to the command post and ran up and down the ridge through withering enemy fire, dragging heavy boxes full of grenades from foxhole to foxhole, all actions that earned him the Navy Cross.

Burak was a very religious man and spoke of joining the clergy when the war was over, according to his good friend, Fred Serral. After the ridge, Burak began to think more and more of his humanity—and perhaps his mortality. While standing in the chow line a day or two after the ridge, Serral felt someone tap him on the shoulder. It was Burak.

"Serral, why don't we sit over there to eat," he said.

"Yeah, OK, Burak," Serral answered, anxious to dig in on the usual meal of Spam on a biscuit topped with peaches.

When they reached the selected spot, Burak put his hand on Serral's shoulder and said: "Freddie, do you mind if I gave thanks for this food?"

"Sure, Walt, go ahead," Serral said, looking deeply into Burak's eyes.[20]

As a Marine it was typical to address each other by their last name. Many of the men never knew the Christian names of their fellow battalion members. When Burak used "Freddie" he appeared to be reaching out to become close to a fellow man in the middle of a jungle, and before his personal God, according to Burak's nephew, James Reynolds.

Burak wrote a letter home to his father around this time. In it, he reflected on his life and expressed his feelings toward those he was close to and cared for. Like many Raiders, he too felt he would not return home. Those feelings must have been present the day after the ridge and at the time of his mealtime prayer the following morning. This letter would be the last contact his family would ever have from him.

When Edson took over the 5th Marines, he told Burak that he would be coming with him. Burak went over to Serral's tent to give him the news. As they shook hands, few words were spoken. It was a difficult moment, almost as if Burak saw the future and knew his time would soon be up. Although Burak didn't say goodbye, Serral believed that was his intention. Serral had seen the invisible angel of death on Burak's shoulder.

"Walter Burak was clearly the best of us all," Serral said.[21]

Four years later, Edson traveled to Burak's hometown of Greensburg, Pa., to deliver a Veterans Day speech and to honor his former runner. Upon meeting Burak's father, Antoni, Edson said: "Walter was like a son to me."

Edson then eulogized Burak in his speech by saying:

"The fighting was especially heavy and the route that Walter had to follow was covered by Japanese rifle and machine gun fire. He well knew that, for we'd been over the same route just an hour before. Yet he unhesitatingly started out, and it was while performing this mission that he lost his life. His service was faithful to the end, to me, to you, and to the country—always in keeping with the highest traditions of the United States Marine Corps."[22]

22

Relief, at Last

We asked for the Doggies to come to Tulagi
But General MacArthur said, "No."
He gave as his reason:
It isn't the season.
Besides, you have no U.S.O.

Two days after the heartbreak at the Matanikau, Sgt. Frank Guidone was resting comfortably back at Able Company's bivouac and working on his long-neglected tan when a jeep drove up looking for him.

Guidone, like the other members of Able Company, was still in a state of shock over the loss of so many of his close friends and comrades just a few days earlier. Some of the survivors were bitter at what they viewed as the "needless" sacrifice of their friends. Surely, they believed, there had to have been another unit available to be called up, one in far better shape than Able Company.

Some believed that the call-up of Able Company was an act of "hubris" by Edson—or "Mad Merritt the Morgue Master" as more and more of the Raiders began calling him. It was no secret that Edson was not very happy with the performance of the 5th Marines in the two Matanikau battles. With the flamboyant Puller now on the scene, the former commander of the Raiders may have seen this latest battle as a good opportunity to show his new rival what a true fighting unit was all about. Twelve Raiders would die proving the point, just days before they were scheduled to leave the island.

The jeep ground to a halt in Able Company's bivouac area and a sergeant jumped to the ground. He asked where he could find Sergeant Guidone. After locating him, the sergeant said that Major Walt wanted to see him back at headquarters.

"I rode back to regimental headquarters and went into a tent and there was Walt at a field desk," Guidone said. "He had me sit down and, after inquiring about my health, said he wanted to have me in his Operations crew and if I agreed he would have me transferred that day to the 5th Marines."[1]

Guidone didn't need any time to think over the proposition. He answered quickly and firmly that he had no desire to remain on Guadalcanal a minute longer than he had to. No thank you, he said. He would just as soon stay with the Raiders.

Walt conducted other interviews that day and none of them proved successful. It seemed as if all the Raiders were more than anxious to get off the island.

On October 11, somebody had the bright idea to have a photo taken of the surviving officer corps of the 1st Raiders—for posterity, if for nothing else.

"I don't know who it was that arranged the picture," John Sweeney said. "Everybody knew we were getting ready to leave the island and there was a photographer back at division. Somebody went and got him and it was taken."

The picture was taken near the beach with the coconut grove in the background and shows seventeen gaunt young men who were obviously very happy at the imminent prospect of leaving Guadalcanal. The photo is perhaps more noteworthy for the twenty-three officers who were unable to be in the picture, however.

Among the missing were those who were transferred to the 5th Marines (Col. Merritt Edson, Major Lew Walt, Capt. Hank Adams and Lt. Albert Fisher); five who were killed (Maj. Ken Bailey, Maj. Robert Brown, Lt. Eugene Key, Lt. Myles Fox and Lt. Sam Miles); and fourteen who were hospitalized for either wounds or illness (Lt. Col. Sam Griffith, Maj. Lloyd Nickerson, Maj. Justice Chambers, Capt. Louis Monville, Capt. Bob Thomas, Capt. John Antonelli, Capt. William Sperling, Capt. Arthur Gewehr, Capt. Clay Boyd, Lt. Ed McLarney, Lt. Tom Mullahey, Warrant Officer Ed Mills, Marine Gunner Cecil Clark and 1st Sgt. James Childs).

The Raiders began packing the night of October 12 and most were wide awake to celebrate the arrival of the first Army troops on Guadalcanal at dawn of the next day. The transports *McCawley* and *Zeilin* unloaded almost 3,000 fresh troops of the 164th Infantry Regiment. The unit, consisting mostly of National Guard troops from the Dakotas, were part of the Americal Division.

Like the landing of the 7th Marines back on September 18, which resulted in the sinking of the USS *Wasp*, the arrival of the Army troops was preceded by a large naval battle. In what came to be called the "Battle of Cape Esperance," the American and Japanese naval forces engaged in a wild shootout around midnight of October 11 that forced both sides to cease firing for fear of hitting their own ships.

When the shooting stopped and all the smoke had cleared, the American Navy remained in the area and the ships of the Tokyo Express headed north out of harm's way.

For the first time in a long while, the U.S. Navy had met the enemy and forced them to flee. The Japanese lost a destroyer and a heavy cruiser while the United States lost a cruiser and had three others heavily damaged.

Most important, the transports bearing much-needed reinforcements were allowed to complete a safe landing.

The "doggies," as the Marines called all Army troops, endured some good-natured ribbing from the battle-hardened Marines—but they were all welcomed with open arms. They arrived loaded for battle and for trading. Many of the new troops came ashore with a large supply of chocolate bars, prime "pogey bait" for the Marines.

"By 9:00 A.M. trading was brisk on the beach," wrote Sam Griffith. "All who could find an excuse to sneak down to Lunga hurried through the shadowy coconut groves toward this unexpected bonanza. Most were equipped with Japanese rifles, sabers, pistols, flags, helmets, or officers' map cases. A samurai sword that day went for three dozen large Hershey bars, a 'meat-ball' flag—which Marines were now adept at manufacturing when supplies of originals ran low—was worth a dozen."[2]

The "doggies," under the able leadership of Col. Bryant Moore and armed with the new M-1 rifle, would fight very well in the coming weeks. They quickly earned the respect and gratitude of all the leathernecks, who paid them the supreme compliment by referring to them as the "164th Marines."

For the weary and ragged Marines, these Army troops were a morale boost well beyond the aid they represented. Commitment of the GIs seemed to indicate that the United States was finally getting serious about holding the island. Moreover, the beginning of an Army buildup portended at least the eventual evacuation of the Marines.[3]

Also coming ashore were some ground personnel of the First Marine Aircraft Wing, eighty-five Marine replacements, dozens of jeeps and trucks, ammunition and seventy days of general supplies, which included rations. Also unloaded was a supply of white wooden crosses, which were needed to mark the graves within the division cemetery, now numbering over 500.

The unloading was halted at noon because of an enemy air raid that caused severe damage to Henderson Field. Japanese planes returned in a second flight an hour and a half later. Both sorties appeared overhead without advance warning from coastwatchers, who were on the run from the Japanese on Bougainville.

Meanwhile, Admiral Turner, aboard the *McCawley*, had received word early in the afternoon that a Japanese task force, one that included the battleships *Haruna* and *Kongo,* was en route to Guadalcanal and should arrive shortly before midnight. He gave orders to speed up the unloading so that he could get the Raiders aboard and get out of the area as quickly as possible.

John Sweeney calculated that a total of nineteen officers and 426 enlisted men of the Raiders, which included two Navy medical officers and fourteen corpsmen, were loaded aboard the two transports. They represented less than half the number who began the operation back on August 7 on Tulagi. About half those going aboard the transports had to be assisted because of wounds or debilitating illnesses. Many of the "healthy" Raiders were afflicted with a latent form of malaria and wouldn't realize it until they reached their next port on New Caledonia.

As the Raiders were completing embarkation in the late afternoon, Lunga Point came under fire from enemy long-range 150mm guns from the west. It was the first

attack launched by these big guns, which were quickly
dubbed "Pistol Petes." The shells started landing on the
western end of the airport runway and then began falling
in the water near the two troop transports, causing the
excitable Turner no end of anxiety.

Finally, when one of the rounds whistled through the
McCawley's rigging, Turner had seen enough.

Striding the bridge with growing anticipation, Turner
shouted to a ship's officer on the main deck, "What's the
delay in hoisting anchor for departure?"

The officer, busy getting the last of the Raiders aboard,
turned and answered: "Admiral, we still have some of our
boats on the beach."

Turner, obviously quite agitated, cupped his hands to
his mouth and shouted for all to hear: "Fuck the boats!
Get this ship out of here!"[4]

Shortly thereafter, the *McCawley* and *Zeilin* hoisted
anchors and departed, leaving several empty Higgins
boats behind.

The Raider luck came into play one more time as the
two ships escaped unharmed before the arrival of a
Japanese battleship task force and a massive bombardment that followed. Just before midnight, the two huge
battleships, each with eight fourteen-inch guns trained on
the island, fired nearly 1,000 shells on the Marine
perimeter in a little less than two hours.

The salvos started west of the airfield and then walked
their way across the runway, through the aircraft parking
areas and coconut groves along the beach where most of
the aviation personnel were housed. Planes, ammo
dumps and gasoline storage areas erupted in flame, turning night into day. The ground trembled, shelters shook
as if they were set in jelly and metal whistled through the
air. Coconut trees were shattered and flew about like

giant toothpicks. None of the shelters had been constructed to withstand fourteen-inch shells.

Within thirty hours of the bombardment six of the
eight members of the press on the island departed, Merillat wrote, and then added: "I would have been happy to
join them."

One shell hit a ration dump, covering part of the
perimeter with a layer of Spam, providing sustenance for
the army of rats that called Guadalcanal home.

Daylight revealed that the bombardment had killed
forty-one men, including six pilots and a half dozen terrified Army troops who had just landed. Many thought
their first day on the island would be their last.

Hardly anyone was spared the terror or the experience, including General Vandegrift, who was knocked to
the ground by the concussion of a shell. Another shell
scored a direct hit on the command post of the 11th
Marines but no one was hurt.

The "Night of the Battleships," as the action came to
be called, was one of the most intense bombardments of
the entire war. More of the same continued the next
night.

The airfield was pulverized. At first light of the 14th,
General Geiger discovered he had only five operational
planes, thirty-four fewer than he had the day before.

"In twenty-four hours on October 13 and 14, fifty-
three bombs and shells hit the Henderson airstrip," said
Seabee commander Joseph P. Blundon. "During one
hour on the 14th we filled thirteen bomb craters while
our planes circled around overhead waiting to land. We
got no food during that period because our cooks were all
busy passing up the steel plank. There were not enough
shovels to go around, so some of our men used their helmets to scoop up earth and carry it to the bomb craters.

"Our worse moments were when the Jap bomb or shell failed to explode when it hit. It still tore up our mat, and it had to come out. When you see men choke down their fear and dive in after an unexploded bomb so that our planes can land safely, a lump comes in your throat and you know why America wins wars."[5]

Some of the shells were fused for delayed action, timed to explode while repair crews were busily at work. Others tore jagged pieces of steel matting from the runway and tossed them in all directions, ripping through tents and lean-tos with deadly results. The men burrowed as deeply as they could into their foxholes and covered up as shattered coconut trees crashed down upon them. Anyone caught standing up was asking for a swift death.

By then, the task force carrying off the Raiders had rounded the northwest end of Guadalcanal and was well on its way to New Caledonia, almost 1,000 miles to the southeast. Behind them, they could see some light flashes from the bombardment but couldn't hear or feel any of its effects.

Above the ships suddenly appeared a giant Kawanishi Flying Boat. The plane followed them for several hours, dropping flares over the two transports and their destroyer screen in an attempt to silhouette them for submarines in the area. The *McCawley* and *Zeilin* just kept going, as fast as they could, zigzagging every once in awhile to throw the Kawanishi pilot and any enemy submarines off course.

"It seemed like that damn plane followed us all night," John Sweeney remembered. "Some of the men hid under their bunks, as if that would have done any good."[6]

By daylight they were well away from Guadalcanal and now all they had to worry about were Japanese submarines.

• • •

Guidone remembers looking back on Guadalcanal as his ship—the *Zeilin*—was pulling out and thinking how beautiful the island looked from a distance.

"You would never believe that it was the arena for the killing and wounding of so many men," he said several years later. "I know many of us thought about those left behind. I did. I thought about the swamps, rivers and high ground that these men fought over and died for. I thought about the 12 men we lost just four days earlier. I knew nine of them personally."[7]

The men began to relax as the reality of their escape from Guadalcanal began to sink in.

"It was hard to believe we were on our way," said Guidone, who was assigned as Sergeant of the Guard aboard the *Zeilin* and given responsibility for monitoring ten Japanese prisoners in the brig.

"Our primary interests were food, showers and a change of clothes," Guidone said. Many of the Raiders had worn the same clothes for ten weeks.

"When we went through the mess lines the cooks just piled on as much as we wanted. The soda fountain on board was open most of the time for our benefit," he said.[8]

Pfc. T. D. Smith came topside the next morning after a huge breakfast to go on submarine watch. No sooner had he found a place to sit than the ship spotted a submarine.

"A bell started clanging, a whistle blew and the escort destroyers started throwing depth charges," Smith recalled. "The charges actually buckled the deck plates where we stood. We saw a submarine nose rise out of the water after a charge and later heard that they had scratched two."[9]

The Raiders were sent below to get them out of the way so the Navy could handle the situation.

There was very little air below decks as the Raiders huddled in their life jackets and helmets. The ship changed course every few minutes and some of the men who hadn't been on a ship in more than a month started to get a little paranoid and a little seasick. Some of that great food they had enjoyed was backing up in their throats. Nobody could move until they got the "all clear" horn.

"We hated this, especially if there were enemy planes around," Guidone said. "We would not have had a chance to survive if we were torpedoed or bombed. Our choice was a foxhole with a weapon."[10]

As the ships got further and further away from Guadalcanal, the men began to relax and enjoy the ride. Off came the beards and many of the men started working on a tan.

"The trip to New Caledonia gave us a chance to lighten up," Guidone said. "We were pretty much left on our own for a change. No training or exercise groups, no lectures and no drills. We were relieved. We had survived and the further away we got the better we felt."

Nobody had read a newspaper in ten weeks. They had relied totally on scuttlebutt for how they were doing in the war. The first real, official news of the events on Guadalcanal and elsewhere came from the ship's daily newsletter, which was written from radio traffic. The men read them for hours, devouring every word.

What they didn't know then, of course, was that there would be other vicious battles on Guadalcanal in the days to come, including another all-out attack on Edson's Ridge, before the rest of the 1st Marine Division would be relieved by Army troops on December 9. It would take the Army another two months of heavy fighting along the northern coastline before the island was officially declared free from organized resistance.

As the *McCawley* and *Zeilin* neared their destination, the Raiders began to look back on their experiences over the past ten weeks and gave thanks for their good fortune in escaping alive. They came to realize they owed their very lives to the efforts of thousands of other brave men. Among them:

The sailors of the U.S. Navy—especially the crews of the valiant APDs that they had trained with, that took them into battle and resupplied them when other ships were unwilling or unable to run a gauntlet through Japanese-controlled waters. These gallant APDs were the workhorses of the Navy during the critical days of the campaign. They were truly the unsung heroes of Guadalcanal. Three of the original six were at the bottom of "Iron Bottom" Sound.

The pilots and ground crews of the Cactus Air Force—Brig. Gen. Roy Geiger's patchwork, interservice group of flyers and their planes who climbed up to intercept the Japanese air assaults and gave them close air support on the ground. In the air they were always outnumbered and on the ground they took a continual pounding from Japanese ships and bombers. The neverending struggle to repair and keep the planes in the air and the almost nightly harassment by the Tokyo Express prevented the pilots and ground crews from getting any rest. In the continuing absence of Navy surface combatants, the only forces available to blunt and counter the growing troop landings were these brave pilots. They were both "sword and shield" to the Marines on the ground, men like Medal of Honor winners Marion Carl,

Jefferson LeBlanc, Joe Foss, Robert Galer and John Smith, who all became as familiar to the folks back home as matinee idols or star ballplayers.

The artillerymen of the 11th Marines—led by Col. Pedro del Valle. "Don Pedro's cannoneers" saved their bacon for two days and nights on the "ridge" and everywhere else, throwing back a determined enemy with a virtual curtain of steel that made all the difference between success or failure.

The coastwatchers—those on Guadalcanal led by the redoubtable Martin Clemens, and his brave colleagues up and down the line whose timely and accurate intelligence gave the Marines a big jump on the enemy.

Lastly, the Parachutists—who had barely survived the fierce battle on the twin islands of Gavutu-Tanambogo and then stood shoulder-to-shoulder with them on the ridge. A tip of the burlap-covered hat to these brave Marines and valued comrades all.

Late in the afternoon of October 17, after being at sea for almost four days, the island of New Caledonia came into view. Most of the men recognized it right away because they had trained there for a few weeks in July before sailing to Tulagi.

"It was a beautiful island and the weather was great," Guidone remembered. "It was the perfect place for a little R and R and the men really looked forward to it."

As the transports grew closer in the fading twilight, the men could see a large pink house on a bluff overlooking a harbor. Around it appeared to be a pretty white picket fence.

"What's that? I don't remember that," one of the Raiders asked a sailor on deck.

"You mean that pink house?" the sailor asked. "That's a whorehouse. And the picket fence? Those are swabbies waiting in line to get in."[11]

The Raiders looked at each other in disbelief. Then the smiles came. They were all thinking the same thing. After all the hell they had been through for the past ten weeks, this surely must be heaven.

EPILOGUE

When the sands of time are sifted
And glowing tales of heroes spun,
The legend of the Raiders
Will have its day in the sun!
                    RAIDER JACK L. BLAIR

The 1st Marine Raider Battalion arrived safely at New Caledonia on October 17, 1942 and moved into a tent bivouac area, which they would name Camp Bailey. It was about ten miles northeast of the capital city of Noumea. A few months later they were awarded the Presidential Unit Citation for their achievements on Tulagi and Guadalcanal.

On November 24, the Raiders departed aboard the USS *McCawley* for eight weeks of rest and recuperation in Wellington, New Zealand. Lt. Col. Sam Griffith returned from the hospital to take command on January 14, 1943.

On January 18, the Raiders departed New Zealand for Camp Bailey on New Caledonia. Over the next two months, the battalion conducted training exercises as the unit returned to full strength.

On March 15, the 1st Raiders became part of the 1st Raider Regiment under Col. Harry B. Liversedge. The 1st Raiders remained at New Caledonia, the 2nd and 4th

Raiders were stationed at Espiritu Santo and the 3rd Raiders were based at Samoa (later moved to Espiritu Santo). All units continued training for the next three months in preparation for an operation.

On June 7, the 1st Raiders departed New Caledonia aboard the USS *President Hayes* for Guadalcanal for more training. A month later, on July 4, the unit departed for action on New Georgia with the rest of the 1st Raider Regiment and two Army battalions.

On August 29, the 1st Raiders returned to Guadalcanal (total casualties on New Georgia, seventy-three killed and 131 wounded) and left a week later for New Caledonia for rest and recuperation.

Maj. George Herring assumed temporary command on September 9 as Colonel Griffith was detached and sent home. Maj. Charles Banks assumed command on October 3.

The unit departed New Caledonia on October 18 and arrived at Auckland, New Zealand on October 21 for four weeks of R and R. They departed on November 18 and returned to Camp Bailey, New Caledonia on November 21. The unit departed Camp Bailey for the last time on January 24, 1944 to establish a new camp on Guadalcanal.

On February 1, 1944, the 1st Raider Regiment was redesignated the 4th Marines, assuming the lineage of the regiment that had garrisoned Shanghai in the interwar years and fought so gallantly on Bataan and Corregidor. The old 1st Raider Battalion became the 1st Battalion, 4th Marines. Leavened with new men, the 4th Marines went on to earn additional distinctions in the assaults on Guam and Okinawa. At the close of the war, the regiment joined the occupation forces in Japan and participated in the release from POW compounds of the remaining members of the old 4th Marines.

The spirit of the Raiders lives on today in the Marine Corps' Special Operations battalions, units that stand ready on a moment's notice to deploy with amphibious-ready groups anywhere around the globe.

Many of the major figures on Guadalcanal went on to bigger and greater glory in future years.

Alexander A. Vandegrift, after seeing to the rehab of the 1st Marine Division after the Guadalcanal campaign, assumed command of the 1st Marine Amphibious Corps to oversee the initial stages of the Bougainville campaign. He received his Medal of Honor from President Roosevelt at the White House on February 5, 1943. He departed the Pacific in late 1943 to become the 18th Commandant of the Marine Corps upon the retirement of his mentor, Gen. Thomas Holcomb, on January 1, 1944. He retired in 1949 and died in 1973 at eighty-six.

Adm. Kelly Richmond Turner commanded the South Pacific's III Amphibious force well into 1943, then formed V Amphibious force to support the Central Pacific offensive. He died in 1961 at seventy-five.

Merritt A. Edson received his Medal of Honor from General Rupertus on February 3, 1943 in ceremonies in Melbourne, Australia. He went on to become chief of staff of the 2nd Marine Division at Tarawa and assistant division commander on Saipan and Tinian. Following the war, he played a prominent role in preserving the Marine Corps in the face of a congressional drive to restructure the military. He retired as a major general in 1947 and died by his own hand in 1955 at fifty-eight.

Gerald Thomas went with Vandegrift as chief of staff of the 1st Marine Amphibious Corps in 1943. He was the Director of the Division of Plans and Policies from 1944 to 1946 and was commanding general of the 1st Marine

Division in Korea in 1951. He retired as a full general in 1956 and died in 1984 at eighty-nine.

Merrill B. Twining also went with Vandegrift as assistant chief of staff of the 1st Marine Amphibious Corps in 1943. He was assistant division commander of the 1st Marine Division in Korea in 1952 and commanding general in 1955. He retired as a full general in 1959 and died in 1996 at ninety-three.

Edwin B. Wheeler participated in the New Georgia campaign, served with the 5th Marines in Korea and had two tours of duty in Vietnam, the first as commanding officer of the 3rd Marines and the second as commanding officer of the 2nd Division. He retired in 1972 as a major general and died in 1985 at sixty-seven.

Sam B. Griffith recovered from his wound and resumed command of the Raiders on January 14, 1943. He participated in the New Georgia campaign. Besides his Navy Cross earned on Guadalcanal, he was awarded the Army's Distinguished Service Cross. He retired as a brigadier general in 1956 and became a respected scholar on the People's Republic of China. He died in 1983 at seventy-six.

Pedro del Valle, the first Puerto Rican national to graduate from the U.S. Naval Academy, was promoted to brigadier general on Guadalcanal and commanded the 1st Marine Division at Okinawa. He retired as a lieutenant general and died in 1978 at eighty-four.

Lewis W. Walt fought at Cape Gloucester, Peleliu and in Korea, earning two Navy Crosses. He was commanding general of the 3rd Marine Division and III Amphibious Force in Vietnam from 1965 to 1967 and assistant commandant in 1967. He retired in 1971 and died in 1989 at seventy-six.

Justice M. Chambers earned the Medal of Honor as a

battalion commander on Iwo Jima in 1945 and was medically discharged that same year as a colonel for wounds received. He died in 1982 at seventy-four.

John Sweeney remained with the 1st Raiders at New Georgia as battalion intelligence officer, served with the 1st Marine Division in China in 1946 and was chief of staff of the 3rd Marine Division in Vietnam in 1966–1967. He retired in 1967 as a colonel and lives in Las Vegas.

Frank Guidone participated in the New Georgia campaign and was a platoon leader with the 7th Marines in Korea. He retired as a captain in 1960 and lives in Las Vegas.

Richard Tregaskis enjoyed great success with his book *Guadalcanal Diary* and a subsequent movie of the same name. In 1943 he was transferred to the Italian front and suffered a head wound. He covered the Normandy invasion and was aboard the USS *Missouri* for the signing of the surrender treaty with Japan. He spent two years in China, another in Korea and one in Vietnam in 1963. He died in 1973 at fifty-six, drowning off the coast near his Hawaiian home.

The 1st Marine Division fought on for two more months after the Raiders left, including another bloody battle on "Edson's Ridge," before they were relieved and sent to Australia for rehabilitation. General Vandegrift officially turned his command over to Army Maj. Gen. Alexander M. Patch on December 9. It would take two more months of heavy fighting before the Japanese finally conceded defeat and evacuated the island.

On February 9, 1943, General Patch sent a radio message to Admiral Halsey, telling him that the "Tokyo Express no longer has a terminus on Guadalcanal."

APPENDIX ONE

1st Raider Battalion Chain of Command—August 7, 1942

Command Group
Commanding Officer, Col. Merritt A. Edson
Executive Officer, Lt. Col. Samuel Griffith
Battalion 1 (Adjutant/Personnel), 2nd Lt. Raymond Schneider
Battalion 2 (Intelligence), Capt. Henry Adams
Battalion 3 (Operations), Maj. Robert Brown
Battalion 4 (Supply), Capt. Ira Irwin°
Battalion Medical Officer, Lt. Edward McLarney, USN
Assistant Medical Officer, Lt. Robert Skinner, USN
Communications Officer, Capt. William Stevenson
Assistant 2 (Language officer), 2nd Lt. John Erskine
Field Sgt. Maj., 1st Sgt. James Childs

Able Company
Commanding Officer, Maj. Lewis Walt
Executive Officer/Weapons Platoon Leader, 1st Lt. John Antonelli°
1st Platoon Leader, 1st Lt. Arthur Gewehr°
2nd Platoon Leader, 2nd Lt. Thomas Mullahey
3rd Platoon Leader, 1st Lt. Edward Dupras°

Baker Company
Commanding Officer, Maj. Lloyd Nickerson
Executive Officer, Capt. Louis Monville
1st Platoon Leader, 1st Lt. Eugene Key°
2nd Platoon Leader, 1st Lt. Rex Crockett°
3rd Platoon Leader, MG Cecil Clark

°Promoted one grade effective August 7.

Weapons Platoon Leader, Gunnery Sgt. Clinton Haines
Asst. Medical Officer, Lt. (jg) Samuel Miles, USN
Charlie Company
Commanding Officer, Maj. Kenneth Bailey
Executive Officer, Capt. Robert Thomas
1st Platoon Leader, 1st Lt. John Salmon°
2nd Platoon Leader, 1st Lt. Clay Boyd°
3rd Platoon Leader, 2nd Lt. Richard Sullivan
Weapons Platoon Leader, 1st Lt. Astle Ryder

Dog Company
Commanding Officer, Maj. Justice Chambers
Executive Officer/3rd Platoon Leader, Capt. William Sperling
1st Platoon Leader, 1st Lt. Robert Neufer°
2nd Platoon Leader, 1st Lt. Edwin Wheeler°
Weapons Platoon Leader, MG Elwood Gebhart

Easy Company
Company Commander, Capt. George Herring
Executive Officer, 1st Lt. Myles Fox°
1st Platoon Leader, 2nd Lt. John Goulding
2nd Platoon Leader, 2nd Lt. Albert Fisher
Mortar Platoon Leader, 1st Lt. Houston Stiff°
Demolition's Platoon Leader, 1st Lt. John Sweeney°
Asst. Demolition's Platoon Leader, 2nd Lt. James Blessing
Antitank Section Leader, Sgt. Neil Champoux

APPENDIX TWO

Highest Decorations Earned by 1st Raiders
(August 7–October 13, 1942)

Medal of Honor (2)
- Bailey, Kenneth D., Maj.°
- Edson, Merritt A., Col.

Navy Cross (37 total)
Tulagi Campaign (9)
- Ahrens, Edward H., Pfc.°
- Edson, Merritt A., Col.
- Fox, Myles C., 1st Lt.°
- Goss, Angus R., Sgt.
- Hacker, Elmer, Corp.
- Hills, Clifford C., Pfc.
- Hunt, Wilfred A., Pfc.
- Key, Eugene M., Capt.°
- Murphy, John J., Pvt.

Edson's Ridge Campaign (16)
- Arnold, Herman F., Pvt.
- Barnes, William, Pfc.
- Brown, Robert S., Maj.°
- Burak, Walter J., Corp.
- Corzine, Jimmy W., Pvt.
- Gay, Roy M., Sgt.
- Harrison, Lawrence A., Sgt.
- Holdren, Lawrence H., Sgt.

° Awarded posthumously.

Hudspeth, Daniel P., Sgt.
Kops, Stanley D., Sgt.°
Mielke, John W., Pfc.
Pettus, Francis C., Sgt.
Schneider, Robert G., Pfc.
Stevenson, William D., Capt.
Sweeney, John B., Capt.
Willox, Nicholas A., Pvt.°

Matanikau Campaign (12)

Connolly, Joseph E., Corp.°
Fedorak, Michael P., Pfc.
French, Neldon T., Corp.°
Griffith, Samuel B., Lt. Col.
Hanna, William T., Pvt.°
Heyliger, George, Pfc.°
Smith, Edward L., Jr., Pvt.°
Steinaker, Donald B., Pfc.°
Sullivan, Richard E., 1st Lt.
Thomas, Dennis F., Pfc.°
Thompson, Woodrow R., Sgt.°
Wolf, Donald W., Sgt.°

APPENDIX THREE

Navy Ships Named after 1st Raiders on Tulagi and Guadalcanal

USS *Edward H. Ahrens,* destroyer escort (DE-575)

USS *Kenneth D. Bailey,* destroyer (DD-713)

USS *Woodrow W. Barr,* high-speed transport (APD-39)

USS *Louis J. Carpellotti,* high-speed transport (APD-135)

USS *Joseph E. Connolly,* destroyer escort (DE-450)

USS *Merritt A. Edson,* destroyer (DD-946)

USS *Myles C. Fox,* destroyer (DD-829)

USS *Neldon T. French,* destroyer escort (DE-367)

USS *John J. Gilligan, Jr.,* destroyer escort (DE-508)

USS *Angus R. Goss,* destroyer escort (DE-444)

USS *Edward E. Gyatt,* destroyer (DD-712)

USS *William T. Hanna,* destroyer escort (DE-449)

USS *George Heyliger,* destroyer escort (DE-510)

USS *George A. Johnson,* destroyer escort (DE-583)

USS *Eugene M. Key,* destroyer escort (DE-348)

USS *Alexander J. Luke,* destroyer escort (DE-577)

USS *Thomas F. Nickel,* destroyer escort (DE-587)

USS *Robert I. Paine,* destroyer escort (DE-578)

USS *Donald B. Steinaker,* destroyer (DD-863)

USS *Woodrow R. Thompson,* destroyer (DD-721)

USS *Donald W. Wolf,* high-speed transport (APD-129)

Navy Medical Personnel Serving with Raiders on Tulagi

USS *Samuel S. Miles,* destroyer escort (DE-183)

NOTES

Introduction

1. William Manchester, *Goodbye Darkness*, pp. 175–176.
2. Samuel Eliot Morison, *The Struggle for Guadalcanal*, p. 4. (Morison was a professor of American history at Harvard before the war broke out.)
3. Richard B. Frank, *Guadalcanal*, p. vii.
4. Morison, op. cit., p. 117.
5. Robert Leckie, *Challenge for the Pacific*, p. viii.
6. William H. Whyte, *A Time of War*, p. 30. (Whyte achieved literary fame as the best-selling author of *The Organization Man*.)
7. Alexander A. Vandegrift, *Once a Marine*, p. 18.
8. Frank, op. cit., p. 614.
9. Joseph Alexander, *Edson's Raiders*, pp. 136–137.

Chapter 1: Background

1. Hanson Baldwin, *The Crucial Years 1939–1941*, p. 432.
2. Frank, op. cit., p. 4.
3. Leckie, op. cit., p. 3.
4. Frank, op. cit., pp. 10–11.
5. Edwin T. Layton, *And I Was There*, p. 387.
6. Carroll V. Glines, *Doolittle's Tokyo Raiders*, p. 380.
7. Samuel B. Griffith, *The Battle for Guadalcanal*, p. 9.
8. Vandegrift, op. cit., pp. 104–105.
9. Ibid, pp. 110–111.
10. Merrill B. Twining, *No Bended Knee*, pp. 29–31.
11. Leckie, *Delivered from Evil*, p. 403.
12. Alan Millett, *In Many a Strife*, p. 169.
13. Leckie, *Delivered from Evil*, p. 402.

14. Millett, op. cit., p. 184.

15. *Life Magazine,* November 16, 1942. (Other excerpts of Vandegrift's letters home that appear throughout the book came from the same magazine article.)

Chapter 2: Cactus

1. Merillat, *Guadalcanal Remembered,* p. 28.
2. Morison, op. cit., p. 4.
3. Frank, op. cit., p. 50.
4. Griffith, op. cit., p. 32.
5. Frank, op. cit., p. 54.
6. Richard Newcomb, *Savo,* p. 56.
7. Vadegrift, op. cit., p. 120.
8. John Foster, *Guadalcanal General,* p. 44.
9. Vandegrift, op. cit., p. 120.
10. Foster, op, cit., p. 45.
11. Vandegrift, op. cit., p. 120.
12. Ibid, p. 120.
13. Griffith, op. cit., pp. 30–31.
14. Merillat, op. cit., p. 39.
15. Vandegrift, op. cit., p. 122.
16. Ibid, p. 122.
17. Conversation with author.

Chapter 3: Red Mike

1. Richard Tregaskis, *Guadalcanal Diary,* p. 23.
2. Correspondence with Lee Minier's family.
3. Conversation with author.
4. Ibid.
5. Merillat, op. cit., p. 58.
6. Tegaskis, op. cit., p. 80.
7. *Saga Magazine,* "The Best Soldier I Ever Knew," February 1960.
8. Jon T. Hoffman, *Once a Legend,* p. 170.
9. Correspondence with Burak's nephew, James Reynolds.
10. Correspondence with author.
11. Hoffman, op. cit., p. 3.
12. Ibid, p. 11.
13. Ibid, p. 12.

14. Ibid, p. 20.
15. Ibid, pp. 26–27.
16. Ibid, p. 27.
17. Ibid, p. 90.
18. Ibid, p. 90.
19. Ibid, p. 120.

Chapter 4: A Wake-Up Call

1. Holland Smith and Percy Finch, *Coral and Brass,* p. 88.
2. Conversation with author.
3. Ibid.
4. Ibid.
5. Studs Terkel, *The Good War,* p. 190.
6. Layton, op. cit., p. 335.
7. Ibid, p. 337.
8. Ibid, p. 338.
9. Ibid, p. 341.
10. Ibid, p. 346.

Chapter 5: Birth of the Raiders

1. Vandegrift, op. cit., p. 100.
2. W.E.B. Griffin, *The Corps, Call to Arms,* pp. x–xi.
3. Ibid, p. xvii.
4. Russell Miller, *The Commandos,* p. 21.
5. Ibid, p. 22.
6. Ibid, p. 24.
7. Griffin, op. cit., p. xvi.
8. Ibid, pp. xvi–xvii.
9. Ibid, p. xviii.
10. Hoffman, op. cit., p. 154.
11. Conversation with author.
12. Hoffman, op. cit., p. 155.
13. Conversation with author.
14. Peatross, *Bless 'Em All,* p. 14.
15. Hoffman, op. cit., p. 157.
16. Ibid, p. 157.
17. Ibid, p. 158.
18. Vandegrift, op. cit., p. 100.
19. Conversation with author.

20. Alexander, op. cit., p. 43.
21. Ibid, p. 37.

Chapter 6: Off to Lava-Lava Land

1. Correspondence with Burak's nephew, James Reynolds.
2. Alexander, op. cit., p. 40.
3. Ibid.
4. Conversation with author.
5. Alexander, op. cit., pp. 53–54.
6. Conversation with author.
7. Alexander, op. cit., p. 58.
8. Ibid, p. 63.
9. Conversation with author.
10. Ibid.
11. Ibid.
12. Alexander, p. 68.
13. Conversation with author.
14. Ibid.
15. Ibid.
16. Twining, op. cit., pp. 40–41.
17. Alexander, op. cit., p. 75.

Chapter 7: Into the Fray

1. Poppell's diary, *Dope Sheet,* October 1956.
2. Lee, *Victory at Guadalcanal,* p. 17.
3. Alexander, op. cit., p. 80.
4. Correspondence with John Sweeney.
5. Griffith, op. cit., p. 46.
6. Correspondence with John Sweeney.
7. Ibid.
8. Alexander, op. cit., p. 80.
9. Peatross, op. cit., p. 39.
10. Sweeney unpublished papers.
11. Cassidy letter, 1956.
12. Alexander, op. cit., p. 89.
13. Sweeney's unpublished papers.
14. Ibid.
15. Alexander, op. cit., p. 93.
16. Peatross, op. cit., p. 39.

17. Tregaskis, pp. 39–40.
18. Ibid, p. 42.
19. Twining, op. cit., p. 52.
20. Foster, op. cit., p. 61.
21. Manchester, op. cit., p. 171.
22. Tregaskis, op. cit., p. 49.
23. Leckie, *Challenge for the Pacific*, p. 106.
24. Tregaskis, op. cit., pp. 55–56.
25. Whyte, op. cit., p. 29.
26. Ibid, p. 31.
27. Twining, op. cit., p. 59.

Chapter 8: Banzai
1. Conversation with author.
2. Ibid.
3. Correspondence with author.
4. Ibid.
5. Notes from Walt to Sweeney.
6. Cassidy letter to Sweeney.
7. Patrick K. O'Donnell, *Into the Rising Sun*, p. 27.
8. Alexander, op. cit., pp. 101–102.
9. *Dope Sheet*, 1957, later published as "The Night by the Ditch."
10. Griffith, op. cit., pp. 52–53.
11. Frank, op. cit., p. 81.

Chapter 9: Bugout
1. Frank, op. cit., p. 93.
2. Manchester, op. cit., p. 168.
3. Vandegrift, op. cit., pp. 129–130.
4. Foster, op. cit., p. 172.
5. Lee, op. cit., p. 34.
6. Ibid, p.34.
7. Vandegrift, op. cit., p. 130.
8. Ibid, p. 131.
9. Lee, op. cit., p. 50.
10. Ibid, p. 52.
11. Vandegrift, op. cit., p. 132.
12. Ibid, pp. 132–133.

13. Twining, op. cit., p. 69.
14. Newcomb, op. cit., p. 211.
15. Leckie, *Challenge for the Pacific,* p. 93.
16. Morison, op. cit., p. 32.
17. Griffith, op. cit., p. 62.
18. Whyte, op. cit., p. 33.
19. Griffith, op. cit., pp. 64–65.
20. Frank, op. cit., p. 121.
21. Merillat, op. cit., p. 67.
22. Morison, op. cit., p. 28.
23. Griffith, op. cit., p. 72.

Chapter 10: Time Out

1. Conversation with author.
2. Correspondence with author.
3. Griffith, op. cit., p. 74.
4. Lee, op. cit., p. 63.
5. Merillat, op. cit., p. 82.
6. Tregaskis, op. cit., p. 77.
7. Merillat, op. cit., p. 82.
8. Tregaskis, op. cit., pp. 77–78.
9. Merillat, op. cit., p. 83.
10. Tregaskis, op. cit., p. 88.
11. Ibid, p. 91.
12. Merillat, op. cit., p. 84.
13. Tregaskis, op. cit., p. 96.
14. Ibid, pp. 96–97.
15. Clemens speech, *Raider Patch,* May 1995.
16. Millett, op. cit., p. 182.
17. Griffith, op. cit., pp. 84–85.
18. Leckie, *Delivered from Evil,* p. 406.
19. Ibid, p. 406.

Chapter 11: Smitty

1. Roger Butterfield, *Al Schmid, Marine,* pp. 17–18.
2. Foster, op. cit., p. 100.
3. Ibid, p. 101.
4. Butterfield, op. cit., pp. 95–97.
5. Ibid, p. 103.

6. Ibid, p. 105.
7. Tregaskis, op. cit., p. 142.
8. *New York Times,* September 18, 1942.
9. Wheeler, *A Special Valor,* p. 61.
10. Tregaskis, op. cit., p. 147.
11. Vandegrift, op. cit., p. 142.
12. Tregaskis, op. cit., p. 148.
13. Wheeler, op. cit., p. 62.
14. Butterfield, op. cit., p. 107.
15. Ibid, p. 108.
16. Frank, op. cit., p. 156.
17. Whyte, op. cit., p. 40.
18. Griffith, op. cit., p. 88.

Chapter 12: Adding Muscle

1. Vandegrift, op. cit., p. 139.
2. Foster, op. cit., p. 97.
3. Leckie, *Challenge for the Pacific,* p. 155.
4. Vandegrift, op. cit., p. 149.
5. Hoffman, op. cit., p. 184.
6. Ibid, p. 185.
7. Conversation with author.
8. Whyte, op. cit., p. 42.
9. Ibid, pp. 42–43.
10. Millett, op. cit., p. 198.
11. Whyte, op. cit., p. 63.
12. Correspondence with author.
13. Manchester, op. cit., p. 179.
14. Vandegrift, op. cit., p. 148.
15. Tregaskis, op. cit., p. 190.
16. Conversation with author.
17. Morison, op. cit., p. 119.
18. Frank, op. cit., p. 212.
19. Ibid, p. 223.
20. Griffith, op. cit., p. 107.

Chapter 13: Tasimboko

1. Sweeney papers.
2. Alexander, op. cit., p. 122.

3. Correspondence with Burak's nephew.
4. Correspondence with Sweeney.
5. Alexander, op. cit., p. 128.
6. Frank, op. cit., p. 222.
7. Griffith, op. cit., p. 108.
8. Tregaskis, op. cit., p. 215.

Chapter 14: Storm Warnings
1. Twining, op. cit., p. 92.
2. Ibid, p. 126.
3. Ibid, p. 95.
4. Griffith, op. cit., p. 112.
5. Correspondence with author.
6. Ibid.
7. Frank, op. cit., p. 229.
8. Correspondence with author.
9. Griffith, op. cit., p. 114.
10. Vandegrift, op. cit.., p. 152.
11. Ibid, pp. 152–153.
12. Millett, op. cit., p. 191.
13. Twining, op. cit., p. 97.
14. Vandegrift, op. cit., p. 153.
15. Ibid, pp. 153–154.

Chapter 15: The Ridge, Round One
1. Alexander, op. cit., p. 145.
2. Ibid, p. 148.
3. Frank, op. cit., p. 231.
4. Ibid, p. 232
5. Ibid, p. 232.
6. Sweeney Ridge memoir.
7. Alexander, op. cit., p. 153.
8. O'Donnell, op. cit., pp. 46–47.
9. Mielke report, *Dope Sheet*, Summer 1995.
10. Ibid,

Chapter 16: Buckling Up
1. Frank, op. cit., p. 233.
2. Griffith, op. cit., p.118.

3. Correspondence with author.
4. Frank, op. cit., p. 235.
5. Twining, op. cit., pp. 101–102.
6. Alexander, op. cit., p. 169.
7. Conversation with Sweeney.
8. O'Donnell, op. cit., p. 48.
9. Sweeney Ridge memoir.

Chapter 17: The Ridge, Round Two

1. *Saturday Evening Post,* "The Battle of Bloody Hill," February 20, 1943.
2. Alexander, op. cit., p. 172.
3. O'Donnell, op. cit., p. 50.
4. *Saturday Evening Post,* op. cit.
5. Morison, op. cit., p. 128.
6. Sweeney Ridge memoir.
7. Andrew Carroll, *War Letters,* p. 207.
8. Ibid, pp. 207–208.
9. Sweeney Ridge memoir.
10. O'Donnell, op. cit., p. 50.
11. Sweeney Ridge memoir.
12. O'Donnell, op. cit., p. 51.
13. Hoffman, op. cit., p. 204.
14. Sweeney Ridge memoir.
15. Ibid.
16. Twining, op. cit., p. 100.
17. Ibid.

Chapter 18: Situation Critical

1. Alexander, op. cit., p. 185.
2. Ibid, p. 185.
3. *Saturday Evening Post,* op. cit.
4. Leckie, *Challenge for the Pacific,* pp. 180–181.
5. Frank, op. cit., p. 240.
6. Tregaskis, op. cit., pp. 228–229.
7. Frank, op. cit., p. 240–241.
8. Ibid, p. 241.
9. Correspondence with author.
10. Tregaskis, op. cit., p. 228.

11. Merillat, op. cit., pp. 139–140.
12. Tregaskis, op. cit., p. 230.
13. Thompson memoir.
14. Tregaskis, op. cit., pp. 239–240.
15. Conversation with author.
16. Griffith, op. cit., p. 120.
17. Tregaskis, op. cit., pp. 234–235.
18. Frank, op. cit., pp. 244–245.
19. Peatross, op. cit., p. 111.
20. Merillat, p. 144.
21. Conversation with Sweeney.

Chapter 19: A Brief Lull

1. Alexander, op. cit., p. 201.
2. Tregaskis, op. cit., pp. 247–248.
3. Ibid, pp. 106–107.
4. Conversation with author.
5. Frank, op. cit., p. 252.
6. Leckie, *Challenge for the Pacific,* p. 198.
7. Merillat, op. cit., p. 151.
8. Griffith, op. cit., p. 130.
9. Wheeler, op. cit., p. 81.
10. Conversation with author.
11. Ibid.

Chapter 20: New Blood

1. Merillat, op. cit., p. 150.
2. Ibid, p. 151.
3. Griffith, op. cit., p. 135.
4. Twining, op. cit., p. 112.
5. Peatross, op. cit., p. 113.
6. O'Donnell, op. cit., p. 57.
7. Griffith, op. cit., p. 136.
8. Twining, op. cit., p. 112.
9. Frank, op. cit., p. 274.
10. Merillat, op. cit., pp. 123–124.
11. Vandegrift, op. cit., p. 164.
12. Manchester, op. cit., pp. 168–169.
13. Tregaskis, op. cit., p. 252.
14. Griffith, op. cit., p. 141.

15. Vandegrift, op. cit., p. 170.
16. Ibid, pp. 171–172.

Chapter 21: One More Time

1. Guidone memoir.
2. Ibid.
3. Ibid.
4. Ibid.
5. Pettus papers.
6. Ibid.
7. Merillat, op. cit., p. 172.
8. Guidone memoir.
9. Pettus papers.
10. Ibid.
11. Guidone memoir.
12. Pettus papers.
13. Ibid.
14. O'Donnell, op. cit., p. 57.
15. Pettus papers.
16. Alexander, op. cit., p. 220.
17. Guidone memoir.
18. O'Donnell, op. cit., pp. 58–59.
19. Wheeler, op. cit., p. 92.
20. Correspondence with Burak's nephew, James Reynolds.
21. Ibid.
22. Ibid.

Chapter 22: Relief, at Last

1. Conversation with author.
2. Griffith, op. cit., pp. 151–152.
3. Wheeler, op. cit., pp. 93–94.
4. Cliff Fitzpatrick to John Sweeney.
5. Morison, op. cit., p. 77.
6. Conversation with author.
7. Correspondence with author.
8. Ibid.
9. T. D. Smith, *Dope Sheet,* October 1990.
10. Correspondence with author.
11. Conversation with John Sweeney.

SELECTED BIBLIOGRAPHY

Alexander, Joe. *Edson's Raiders*, Annapolis, MD: Naval Institute Press, 2000.

Baldwin, Hanson. *The Crucial Years 1939–1941*. New York: Harper & Row, 1976.

Blakeney, Jane. *Heroes, USMC 1861–1955*. Washington, DC: Guthrie Lithograph Co., Inc., 1957.

Blankfort, Michael. *The Big Yankee*. Boston: Little Brown & Co., 1947.

Butterfield, Roger. *Al Schmid, Marine*. New York: Farrar Rinehart, Inc., 1944.

Carroll, Andrew. *War Letters*. New York: Scribner & Sons, 2001.

Coggins, Jack. *The Campaign for Guadalcanal*. Garden City, NY: Doubleday, 1972.

Foster, John. *Guadalcanal General*. New York: William Morrow & Co., 1966.

Frank, Richard B. *Guadalcanal*. New York: Random House, 1990.

Glines, Carroll V. *Doolittle's Tokyo Raiders*. Princeton, NJ: Van Nostrand, 1964.

Griffin, W.E.B. *The Corps, Call to Arms*. New York: Berkley Publication, 1987.

Griffith, Samuel B. *The Battle for Guadalcanal*. New York: J.B. Lippincott Co., 1963.

Hammel, Eric G. *Starvation Island*. New York: Crown Publishers, 1987.

Hersey, John. *Into the Valley*. New York: Alfred A. Knopf, 1943.

Hoffman, Jon T. *Once a Legend*. Novato, CA: Presidio Press, 1994.

Layton, Edwin T. *And I Was There*. New York: William Morrow, 1985.

Leckie, Robert. *Challenge for the Pacific*. Garden City, NY: Doubleday & Co., 1965.

Leckie, Robert. *Delivered from Evil*. New York: Harper & Row, 1987.

Lee, Robert Edward. *Victory at Guadalcanal*. Novato, CA: Presidio Press, 1981.

Lord, Walter. *Lonely Vigil*. New York: Viking Press, 1977.

Manchester, William. *Goodbye Darkness*. Boston: Little, Brown & Co., 1979.

Merillat, Herbert C. *Guadalcanal Remembered*. New York: Dodd, Mead & Co., 1982.

Miller, John, Jr. *Guadalcanal: The First Offensive*. New York: BDD Co., 1949.

Miller, Russell. *The Commandos*. Alexandria, VA: Time-Life Books, 1981.

Miller, Thomas G. *The Cactus Air Force*. New York: Harper & Row, 1969.

Millett, Alan R. *In Many a Strife*. Annapolis, MD: Naval Institute Press, 1993.

Morison, Samuel Eliot. *The Struggle for Guadalcanal*. Boston: Little Brown & Co., 1969.

Newcomb, Richard F. *Savo*. New York: Holt, Rinehart & Winston, 1961.

O'Donnell, Patrick K. *Into the Rising Sun*. New York: Free Press, 2002.

Peatross, Oscar F. *Bless 'Em All*. Irvine, CA: Review Publications, 1995.

Pratt, Fletcher. *Eleven Generals*. New York: Sloane Assoc., 1949.

Smith, George W. *Carlson's Raid*. Novato, CA: Presidio Press, 2001.

Smith, Holland M., and Percy Finch. *Coral and Brass*. New York: Charles Scribner, 1948.

Terkel, Studs. *The Good War*. New York: Pantheon Books, 1984.

Tregaskis, Richard. *Guadalcanal Diary*. New York: Random House, 1943.

Twining, Merrill B. *No Bended Knee*. Novato, CA: Presidio Press, 1996.

Vandegrift, A. A., as told to R. B. Asprey. *Once a Marine*. New York: W.W. Norton & Co., 1964.

Warner, Denis, and Peggy Warner. *Disaster in the Pacific*. Annapolis, MD: Naval Institute Press, 1992.

Wheeler, Richard. *A Special Valor*. New York: Harper & Row, 1983.

Whyte, William H. *A Time of War*. New York: Fordham University Press, 2000.

Visit
❖ **Pocket Books** ❖
online at

....

www.SimonSays.com

....

Keep up on the latest new
releases from your favorite
authors, as well as author
appearances, news, chats,
special offers and more.